D0198836

UNDERSTANDING RELIGIOUS AND SPIRITUAL ASPECTS OF HUMAN SERVICE PRACTICE

Social Problems and Social Issues
Leon Ginsberg, Series Editor

Understanding Religious and Spiritual Aspects of Human Service Practice

James W. Ellor, D.Min., L.C.S.W., B.C.D., C.G.P.

F. Ellen Netting, Ph.D.

Jane M. Thibault, Ph.D.

UNIVERSITY OF SOUTH CAROLINA PRESS

© 1999 University of South Carolina

Published in Columbia, South Carolina, by the
University of South Carolina Press

Manufactured in the United States of America

03 02 01 00 99   5 4 3 2 1

Library of Congress Cataloging-in-Publication Data

Ellor, James W.
   Understanding religious and spiritual aspects of human service practice / James
W. Ellor, F. Ellen Netting, Jane M. Thibault.
      p.   cm. — (Social problems and issues)
   Includes index.
   ISBN 1-57003-262-9 (pbk.)
      1. Social service—Religious aspects.   2. Social workers—Religious life—
United States.   3. Church charities—United States.   I. Netting, F. Ellen.
II. Thibault, Jane M. (Jane Marie), 1946–   III. Title.   IV. Series: Social problems
and social issues (Columbia, S.C.)
HV530 .E62   1999
361.3'2—dc21   98-40222

This book is dedicated to our families:

To Janet, Lisa, and Maggie,
whose patience and love
is a gift that I sometimes take for granted,
but never want to be without.
J.W.E.

To Karl,
with whom I have learned
to cherish the present and whose kind and
compassionate spirit lights my future.
F.E.N.

To Ron,
a delightful combination of guiding light and
Rock of Gibraltar,
with a lively dash of humor included.
Thanks for the support and love that makes
all my work possible.
J.M.T.

CONTENTS

PREFACE

The authors of this book met at the School of Social Service Administration (SSA) at the University of Chicago in the late 1970s. Jim had already graduated from the master's program, was completing his doctorate at Chicago Theological Seminary, and was directing a project at SSA on religious congregations and how they serve the elderly. Ellen and Jane were in the doctoral program at SSA. Ellen was taking the social development (policy) track, and Jane was engaged in the social treatment (clinical) track. What we all had in common was an intense desire to understand the religious and spiritual forces that framed our work and our studies.

Our collaboration began informally. Because Jim was working with Sheldon Tobin (one of our major professors) on the grant project, Shelly saw an opportunity to get us together. Jane and Ellen had bonded out of fear in the first weeks of their studies, but they had not yet met Jim. Shelly kept telling Jane and Ellen that they needed to meet Jim because he had both a religion and social work background. He was absolutely on target, for thus began a friendship as well as a working collaboration. When Ellen decided to write her dissertation on agencies with religious affiliations, both Jim and Jane were helpful and insightful colleagues and supportive friends. Since all three of us were gerontologists, it was natural that we continue our collaboration by presenting papers and conducting workshops in the years that followed our stint in Chicago. By then Jim was still in Chicago, but Jane was in Kentucky and Ellen had gone to Arizona.

What made our collaboration stimulating was that each of us had a different perspective on religion and spirituality. Jim, being an ordained Presbyterian minister (PCUSA) as well as a social worker, held the clerical credentials so essential to understanding the institutional church. Ellen, on the other hand, was a minister's wife who had disdained that role and reacted with skepticism and irreverence in the face of expectations as to what that role implied. If anything it cast her in the role of skeptic and caused her to question the expectations that accompanied any organization of religion. Jane emerged from a Catholic background and is a member of the lay Carmelites. She instituted her own reformation by remaining a member of her Catholic parish while also joining a United Methodist church. Over the years she began conducting spirituality workshops throughout the country.

Interestingly enough, with each of us manifesting our thoughts about religion and spirituality in different ways, we are also located in three diverse settings. Jim teaches in a human service program and is parish associate at a local Presbyterian church; Ellen teaches in a school of social work; and Jane teaches in the Department of Family and Community Medicine in a medical school. Within those settings we often recognize the ways in which religious and spiritual forces influence colleagues across various fields of study and the ways that colleagues react to this influence. What is common to our experiences, however, is that no one seems to react in a nonchalant manner when religion and spirituality are discussed. Some colleagues jump on the self-transcendence bandwagon for a New Age ride; some state their commitments to local churches with which they affiliate. Others shrug their shoulders in dismay or vent anger over the inclusion of spiritual and religious content in their curriculum. Few people seem to have no opinion when it comes to religion and spirituality, and opinions can be polarizing.

Suffice it to say, that even among us there are skeptics (and Ellen has typically played that role), but we all strongly agree that it is absolutely essential to recognize and respect religious and spiritual expressions, even when there is great divergence of opinion. Given our backgrounds, which range from highly clinical to highly macro/policy, we also believe that it is essential to integrate micro and macro practice, and that religion permeates practice at whatever level one intervenes. The "new interest" among human service professionals in religion tends to be found in micropractice issues of personal spirituality. However, we believe that the impact of this topic runs across the micro to macro continua. That is why we agreed to write this book when Leon Ginsberg called us, now several years ago, after he had seen an article we had published in the *Journal of Social Work Education*.

It has taken us a long time to write this book because of relocation, job changes, floods, and a multitude of commitments along the way. On the other hand, we believe that the last untapped diversity frontier is that of religion and spirituality. For some (and probably many) reasons, human service professionals have been shy about taking on the complexities of religion and what it means. We cannot solve the problems and issues here, but we hope to raise consciousness about the ways religion and spirituality are enmeshed in our profession.

It seems to us that the need for dialogue about religion and spirituality is increasing rapidly. We will touch upon the professional uncertainty that has arisen as people across disciplines talk about spirituality. We listen to the rhetoric of religious groups engaged in the national political scene and are amazed at how diverse the voices are that proclaim religious values and approaches in this country. We see what many congregations are doing to help the homeless in their communities and are dismayed when churches are burned. Faith-based organizations represent the very fiber of their communities. We recognize that there are people in this country who are quite religious, but not Christian, and that their voices often are not heard. We have seen what can be done in the name of religion and spirituality, and we recognize the potential for tremendous good, for oppressive evil, and for everything in between. We believe that we must begin a dialogue because there are diverse views of religion and spirituality that both bind and divide our country. Human service workers cannot afford to ignore these forces.

James W. Ellor
F. Ellen Netting
Jane M. Thibault

ACKNOWLEDGMENTS

The authors wish to acknowledge the following persons for their support and assistance in writing this book: Leon Ginsberg for his encouragement throughout this project and his critique of chapter 3, particularly the section on Judaism; Naveeda Athar for her critique of chapter 3, particularly the section on Islam; Swami Bardinarda for his willingness to offer suggestions for chapter 3; Marie Bracki for her contributions to early stages of chapter 4; and Becky Jo Hollingsworth for her contributions to the draft of chapter 6. We are grateful to Joy Colbert for her ongoing help with the production of this manuscript. We would also like to thank Susan McFadden and Roy Backus for their reviews of early drafts of this book.

We owe a round of appreciation to an anonymous reviewer who gently asked us to clarify the purpose of this book. This concern helped us rethink our reasons for this project and state our intentions more clearly.

UNDERSTANDING RELIGIOUS AND SPIRITUAL ASPECTS OF HUMAN SERVICE PRACTICE

INTRODUCTION

This book is a general overview of religion and spirituality as they inform human service practice. It is intended to help students and practitioners understand the religious and spiritual context in which practice occurs. We hope to demonstrate how the integration of macro and micro issues is needed to comprehend fully the challenges of understanding religion, spirituality and human service practice at all levels. The book is intended to be read by the reflective practitioner who is interested in exploring religious/spiritual diversity. It can also serve as a supplemental text in either undergraduate or graduate level courses in which sensitivity to such diversity is a desired outcome.

Whether or not a human service worker finds meaning in an organized religious group or from personal spiritual reflection, many professionals' caseloads will include persons who do find meaning in these things. Religious and spiritual issues can influence an individual's basic coping mechanisms, orientation to life and death, and definition of self. It is simply unrealistic and insensitive to ignore religious and spiritual aspects of clients' lives. It is equally politically naive to ignore the influence of religious groups and coalitions in the United States today.

Human beings have sought connection with that which is greater than they are since before recorded time. Cave drawings, oral traditions, and early recordings of ancient peoples have reflected a search for established patterns of relationships with some force that is outside human control. In preindustrial, prescientific societies, people found what has come to be called spirituality or religion to be important both for answering the hard questions of life, and for addressing personal and community needs. For example, fertility of plants, of animals, and of women was not understood. Fertility was attributed to a source of divine power that prevented disaster and offered special favors. Humans looked for explanation and for intervention on their behalf from a source that was greater than the individual or group.

In the current epoch, many people continue to need some type of explanation of the meaning of life in a changing world. They desire resources which cannot be obtained from the human condition, a source of values consistent with the explanation of the world, and a source of meaning and transcendence. Before World War II, these needs were often met by various religious traditions

1

in which people participated. Since 1960, people in the United States have moved increasingly toward more personal expression of these needs, while others have continued to define themselves in terms of specific religious traditions. The former have often shown an increased interest in Eastern religious traditions.

Whether clients, organizations or communities are oriented to traditional religions, or to personal forms of transcendent spirituality, spiritual expression is a part of both the culture and the human experience for many persons in the United States. Spirituality is inherent in the very fabric of the diversity of human experiences in this country. Since institutional religion and personal spirituality are important to many persons, they need to be understood by the human service worker and recognized in individual treatment encounters, agency policy, and community relationships.

The difficulty inherent in discussing religion and spirituality is reflected in the tremendous diversity of beliefs and activities and the intensity of feelings accompanying them. Religious beliefs and behaviors of organized groups, as well as personal spirituality, interact with the dynamics of culture, race, gender, age and a host of other variables. Therefore, human service workers need to start with the assumption that each individual, organization, and community is unique in religious and spiritual experiences. This is not to say that there are no commonalities in experience but to recognize that no single variable predicts the fullness of the human spiritual experience. In any encounter with a client or a group of clients, the human service worker must start by listening to the client's experience for this is where an appropriate initial discussion of the perception of reality resides.

The concept of diversity as discussed in the human service literature is related to our discussion of religion. Recognizing diversity offers a perspective of the community which suggests that differences in beliefs, culture, and "norms" of behavior are to be celebrated, rather than denied. Diversity suggests acceptance of the cultural variables reflected in various client populations. Religion is an important aspect of culture and can be a significant source of culture. Yet, human service workers need to be careful not to overgeneralize the similarities of individuals within religious groups.

Particularly in a country which values individuality, religious expressions, even among persons who say they belong to the same religious tradition or group, are often different. Human service practice is not concerned with altering in any way the religious beliefs of the client. Rather, helping professionals need to understand religion and personal spirituality as important aspects of individuals, organizations and communities. Pargament (1997, 369) refers to

2

this as the "religious pluralism" approach. When approached in this way, religion and spirituality become rich resources that can be used to support clients.

Over the past sixty years, numerous observers have identified major changes in religious practices both in the United States and throughout the world. In the United States, measures of attendance at church, synagogue or temple have revealed progressively smaller percentages of adults in attendance. Further, surveys of personal practices such as prayer or meditation have also shown some decline. In 1940 the Princeton Religion Index of eight leading indicators (The Princeton Religion Research Center, 1990, 16), revealed that their sample of persons in the United States rendered an accumulative score of 73.3. This score has progressively declined to the current score of 65.4, indicating that organized, institutional religion seems to play a smaller role in American society than it did earlier. However, the need for spiritual experience seems to be increasing. A recent survey by *Newsweek* magazine reported that "now it's O.K., even chic, to use the 'S' words—soul, sacred, spiritual, sin. In a NEWSWEEK Poll, a majority of Americans (58 percent) say they feel the need to experience spiritual growth" (Kantrowitz 1994, 52–65).

Although religious or spiritual practices of persons in the United States have declined, religion continues to be important to at least half of the American people. Eighty-five percent of persons polled by the Princeton Study of Religion in the United States feel that religion is at least fairly important in their lives (The Princeton Religious Research Center 1990, 16). To whatever extent a human service worker's caseload reflects these national statistics, it is probably safe to say that many clients find religion and spiritual expression to be important.

Religious and spiritual practices are not the sole domain of the client; they are also relevant for many human service practitioners. Like their clients, human service workers are a diverse group as to their own religious or spiritual expression. Some belong to traditional or "mainstream" denominations, some are liberal, others conservative, some are committed to the practice of the various world religious traditions, some are committed solely to a personal understanding of transcendence, and others may not be religious or spiritual at all.

HISTORY OF THE RELATIONSHIP BETWEEN RELIGION AND HUMAN SERVICE PRACTICE

The historical relationship between religion and human service practice is tied to basic postulates of the separation of church and state as stated in the Bill of Rights to the United States Constitution. Choper notes that "the history of the Religion clauses, like that of most provisions of the Constitution, does not supply a detailed blueprint for resolving issues"; nevertheless, it does "divulge a broad philosophy of church-state relations" (1995, 5).

Separation of church and state has been a basic part of the fabric of this country since its inception. Many of the original settlements in the United States were composed of persons who were fleeing the oppression of the "state church." Most of the countries in Europe in the 1700s endorsed a single religious group. In France and Italy the official religion was Catholicism; in England it was the Church of England. In response to these state-run churches, Thomas Jefferson, "expressing aspects of enlightenment thinking, believed that the integrity of government could be preserved only by erecting a wall of separation between church and state. A sharp division of authority was essential, in his opinion, to insulate the democratic process from ecclesiastical depredations and excursions" (Choper 1995, 3). While much has been said about the benefits to civil government of the separation of church and state, both Roger Williams and later James Madison believed it was also important for the integrity of the church. Both perspectives can still be found in the political arena today. But there are also those who feel that government should do more to support the church.

In combination with the legal and political bases for the separation of church and state, the fields of psychology and social work have created their own version of this separation. The helping professions have drawn from the work of theorists who disagree as to the role and importance of religion. Sigmund Freud felt that "religion was only the recapitulation of the infantile, born of the need to make tolerable the helplessness of man" (1928, 28–32). Theorists such as Freud essentially treated religion as a form of psychopathology. Others, such as Alfred Adler, Carl Jung and Viktor Frankl, understood the transcendent nature of the person as a part of the human spirit. Yet these theorists did not fully incorporate a divine spirit into their possibilities for reality. The human spirit was strictly an interpersonal or self-transcendent experience.

The combination of the humanistic orientation of the counseling professions and the insistence of publicly funded agencies on maintaining the separation of church and state has contributed to the distrust of religion in the human service professions. There has not always been such a distrust. Church historian Martin Marty noted that "had we a booklet recounting the story of welfare work that dutifully proportioned its space to match the ages of recorded history, only the last page of a fifty-page book would treat of this emergence. Most of what historians know about agencies of concern, charity, and welfare until about a century ago connects them with some sort of religious impulse or auspice. At last, late in the nineteenth-century Western world, consistent patterns that we call secular came into dominance" (Marty 1980, 465). History tells us that the separation between the religious community and the human service professions predates the "new deal legislation" which brought the government of the United States reluctantly but fully into the business of social service provision.

As a result of the distrust of religion shared by the counseling professions, there is little training or even theory available outside of pastoral counseling on which to base the integration of religion and spirituality into human service practice. It is the goal of this book to begin to address this gap. Religion can be integrated into practice without implying that the human service worker needs to practice religion. Especially important, it can be integrated without imposing any particular religious or spiritual perspective onto the client, whether that client is an individual, a group, an organization, or an entire community. Rather, the spiritual and religious concerns of the client should be understood and then integrated into the intervention process. Appropriate referrals can be made when access to clergy or spiritual representatives is needed.

THE DIVERSITY ALTERNATIVE

Embedded in the basic fabric of training in all the counseling professions is the understanding that the client comes to the professional for help, not the other way around. Thus the concept of countertransference states that care is to be taken to emotionally separate the professional's issues from those of the client. This is equally true when working with religious and spiritual concerns. This book is grounded in our understanding that it is *never* appropriate to proselytize or promote the practitioner's own religious beliefs, any more than it would be appropriate to influence political or other personal beliefs. Rather, the human service worker needs to be able to understand the religious and/or spiritual concerns of clients as part of their uniqueness.

For some practitioners, this may place them in an uncomfortable value conflict between their feelings about the correctness of their own beliefs and the divergence of the client's beliefs. In many religious communities, the believer is admonished to respond to these differences by interpreting his or her religious beliefs and practices to the unbeliever. This can be referred to as proselytizing the client. Indeed, religious professionals are *expected* to play this interpretive role with members of their congregations and communities.

Human service workers, on the other hand, play an equally important role by listening to the client talk about religious beliefs and practices. It is their role to hear all of the issues and concerns of the client, which can include religious material. In listening to the client, one hears aspects of the whole person, and can help clients to identify, sort out, and claim the entire picture of themselves. Healing can be inhibited by ignoring an aspect of the person, such as the spiritual. By listening to the whole person, one can understand and facilitate growth of their entire being.

In this book we explore the impact of religion and spirituality on the behavioral, emotional, social, and transcendent aspects of the person. We articulate the effect of religious institutions on the community and on the efforts of human service workers as advocates for client needs. In this way we offer ways to integrate the spiritual and religious aspects of the person into the more established practices of mainstream human service provision.

It must be remembered that religion is neither a single entity nor a single perspective. Rather, it is a diverse, dynamic force in the lives of a significant number of people. For some it is important from a highly personal perspective. For others it is primarily a group or community experience. For some it evokes images of nature and the world around them. For others it focuses on God and God's work in the world. For yet others, it is viewed as a highly oppressive, powerful force. In this context, religion is an issue of diversity that needs to be understood from multiple perspectives.

DEFINITIONS

In this book the following definitions are used:

B.C.E./C.E.: most readers will be familiar with B.C. ("before Christ") and A.D. (an abbreviation of the Latin *anno domini,* "in the year of the Lord"). In this text we use B.C.E ("before the common era") and C.E. ("common era"). These abbreviations, while tacitly acknowledging that the Christian calendar is the one most widely used today, also acknowledge that it is not the *only* calendar.

Human service: we have used this more inclusive term to refer to persons working in all of the helping professions—social work, human services, psychiatric nursing, family and marriage therapy, recreation therapy, psychology, counseling, and others.

Religion: a social group or institution that ascribes meaning and value to individual life as well as to all of creation. This social group has received or has assumed an official "right" to tell a certain story, to promote it, and to ensure its viability and longevity with rules and principles of participant belief and behavior. A religious group has a shared history and an expectation that it will continue in the future (Thibault et al. 1991, 35). Religion also includes a particular, potentially fixed, system of beliefs. Special rites, language, and observances define this chosen practice of devotion. It is a world view, a way of revering specific people, values, politics, or philosophies. It is a creed—encompassing not just God or thoughts about the supernatural, but life itself (Sinetar 1992, 15).

Spiritual: we use David Moberg's four part definition (1984, 6), while recognizing that there are multiple ways to define this term.

1. Pertains to one's inner resources, especially one's ultimate concern.
2. Provides the basic value around which all other values are grounded.
3. The central philosophy of life—religious, nonreligious, or antireligious—which guides conduct.
4. relates to supernatural and nonmaterial dimensions of human nature.

Spirituality: An individual's unique spiritual "style"—the way he or she seeks, finds, or creates; uses; and expands personal meaning in the context of the entire universe (Thibault et al. 1991, 30).

Spiritual transformation: achievement of a new level or stage, a quality of being that would characterize development. Transformation is demonstrated by the stable expression of a new mode of functioning that is characterized by a broader locus of centrism and by greater knowledge and love (Chandler et al. 1992, 170).

Spiritual wellness: A balanced openness to or pursuit of spiritual development which may be, but is not necessarily, a conscious undertaking.

THE FLOW OF THE BOOK

This book is designed to flow from an historical to a clinical and finally to an organizational perspective. There are three parts, each with multiple chapters. Part 1 focuses on the vast historical influence religion has had and continues to have on the development of human services and the helping professions, and features a specific section on clinical connections with religion. Part 2 links three chapters that examine clinical concerns of clients, with a plea for personal and professional self-awareness issues among human service workers. Four chapters in part 3 focus respectively on community, congregation, organization, and policy issues. Each chapter will be briefly reviewed below.

Chapter 1 begins with an examination of the influence of religion on the

7

helping professions. Religion has played an important part in the development of the human service professions both as a motivating factor for individual effort and as a set of institutional efforts by denominational groups. However, the history of social welfare contains examples of religion and religious groups as being anything but concerned with human need. In this chapter, we endeavor to offer a more balanced picture.

Chapter 2 discusses the personal issues involved in religious practice. The emphasis of this chapter is on the historical development of clinical practice and how religion and spirituality have been viewed.

Chapter 3 offers a discussion of various religious practices found in this country which originate from traditional religious groups. This chapter points out the diversity of religious practices that can be found among clients in the United States. Necessarily, this chapter is only an introduction. There are many bibliographic resources for world religions from which the reader can gather additional information. This "survey" chapter is intended only as a beginning point.

Chapter 4 presents perspectives on both religious and faith development. This chapter reflects the interaction between the concepts of personal growth and religious practice.

Chapter 5 explores the beginning steps in the application of faith to clinical practice, including the fundamental issues of spiritual assessment

Chapter 6 focuses on clinical aspects of religious practice. Religion reflects personal meaning systems, coping patterns, experiences of empowerment, and other dynamics that are viewed in various contexts as relevant to human service assessment. This chapter also addresses the pathological use of religious practice. While religion can be a positive force, it can also be a negative influence.

Chapter 7 explores the issues of personal spirituality for the human service worker, as well as an approach to addressing these issues. We recognize the importance of self awareness in this chapter and encourage readers to acknowledge their own experiences which may be different from those of their colleagues and clients. Although this chapter focuses on the individual, our intent is to demonstrate how individual beliefs and perceptions are at work in both micro and macro interactions.

Chapter 8 examines modes of practice with religious groups and others in the community. Since religious groups provide services and advocate for the needs of clients, human service workers must know how to interface with such groups. This chapter discusses the role of religious groups in the community as well as ways religious groups can work more closely with social service agencies.

Chapter 9 discusses the nature and role of the religious congregation in the provision of social service. Of particular interest is developing research that focuses on congregations as voluntary associations. Chapter 10 discusses the nature of religiously affiliated agencies. Throughout social welfare history, some social service agencies have been affiliated with religious groups. Because they are part of the social service delivery system, their various ideologies must be considered and acknowledged by human services workers.

Chapter 11 outlines the issues that are important to the public policy debate. The basis for many agency decisions is found in the separation between church and state. This chapter explores these questions and frames the larger societal context in which religious and spiritual issues interface with secular forces.

REFERENCES

Allport, G. W., 1950. *The individual and his religion.* New York: Macmillan. As cited in Malony, H. 1995. *The psychology of religion for ministry.* New York: Paulist Press.

Chandler, C., J. Holder, and C. Kolander 1992. Counseling for spiritual wellness: theory and practice. *Journal of Counseling and Development* 71 (November–December): 168–75.

Choper, J. H. 1995. *Securing religious liberty: principles for judicial interpretation of the religion clauses.* Chicago: University of Chicago Press.

Freud, S. 1928. *The future of an illusion.* London: W. D. Robson-Scott.

Kantrowitz, B., et al. 1994. In search of the sacred. *Newsweek,* 28 November, 52–65.

Marty, M. E. 1980. Social service: godly and godless. *Social Service Review* 54 (4): 463–81.

Moberg, D. O. 1971. Spiritual well-being: background and issues. In D. O. Moberg, 1984 "Subjective measures of spiritual well-being," *Review of Religious Research,* 25 (4): 4.

Pargament, K. I. 1997. *The psychology of religion and coping.* New York: Guilford Press. 369.

Princeton Religion Research Center. 1990. *Religion in America 1990.* Princeton, N.J.: Princeton Religion Research Center.

Sinetar, M. 1992. *A way without words.* New York: Paulist Press.

Thibault, J. M., J. W. Ellor, and F. E. Netting 1991. "A conceptual framework for assessing the spiritual functioning and fulfillment of older adults in long term care settings." *Journal of Religious Gerontology,* 7 (4): 29–46.

PART I

HISTORICAL INFLUENCES OF RELIGION ON HUMAN SERVICES

Before the twentieth century, religion and human service practice were important companions, each working with the other. Historically, there were times when religious groups were clearly misguided. At other times, religious groups played positive roles. This section articulates the basis of religious integration through understanding the diverse role of religion in the lives of clients.

The chapters that address clinical issues end with case studies, designed to offer opportunities for reflection on the material presented. For the sake of continuity, all the case studies will be geographically located in a fictitious community called "Home Town, U.S.A." Home Town is anyone's community. It is in the mountains and in the desert; it is on the ocean shore and in the Middle West; it is urban, suburban, and rural; but it is a community. The basic features of Home Town will be spelled out below and then modified to fit into each case study. The features are intended to be generic in order to form a backdrop for specific elements of the chapter cases.

HOME TOWN, U.S.A.

Home Town is a community at the crossroads. It is composed of persons from a wide scope of socioeconomic, racial, and ethnic backgrounds as well as a variety of religious preferences. Two-thirds of Home Town is Caucasian while one-third is composed of persons of color. This community has a historical section where older adults have aged in place, and another section where the housing is more modest and the incomes of the residents are smaller. In these two sections there are numerous multiple family housing units, some subsidized by public funds. The community also has several new housing developments composed primarily of single family homes and town houses; some of these units are quite expensive.

Home Town has an older section where the original "downtown" shops and residents reside. A large new shopping mall is located on the outskirts of the town. Some of the neighborhoods are better integrated in terms of socioeconomic status and race than others. The infrastructure of the community is reasonably good in terms of police and fire departments and of utilities. However, the social service structure in the community is consistent with the current picture of both private and public funding for social service needs. There are some coordinating groups available to support agency responses.

Home Town has a large number of religious buildings. It has Unitarian, Metropolitan, and a variety of Protestant churches; several Roman and Eastern Orthodox Catholic churches, as well as temples and synagogues for the Orthodox, Conservative, and Reform Jewish residents. Home Town also has Hindu and Buddhist temples, as well as a mosque for Islamic residents. Within Home Town it is also known that there are meetings of persons from non-"church" oriented traditions, such as the Bahá'i tradition. A clergy council attempts to coordinate social and service activities of the various religious groups. However, it is difficult for the council's leaders to get together without a specific crisis to address.

Home Town has identified meeting the needs of children, adolescents, adults, and senior citizens as critical to the future of this community. Programs are in place to address substance abuse, family violence, child welfare, health care, and recreational needs of the citizens. It is often noted that if the community could just come together and agree on the needs, they would be addressed. However, the lack of agreement and frustration with systems external to the control of Home Town residents make it difficult to launch any real effort to eliminate the problems identified by the residents.

Home Town is anyone's town. As one reads the cases one can transpose them to a familiar community in order to make them relevant to one's needs.

Chapter 1

THE INFLUENCE OF RELIGIOUS GROUPS ON THE HISTORICAL DEVELOPMENT OF THE HELPING PROFESSIONS

It is generally accepted that the concept of human services emerged, at least partially, from a religious base. However, among helping professionals there is ambivalence about how these roots are perceived. For example, in the 1995 *Encyclopedia of Social Work,* no sections are devoted exclusively to religion or to spirituality. Yet references to religion and spirituality are found under categories labeled "Church Social Work" (Garland 1995), and "Sectarian Agencies" (Ortiz 1995). Fowler's seven stages of faith development are cited under "Human Development" (Beckett 1995, 1393). The full diversity of religious groups, organizations and ideologies are just not addressed to any great extent. In the *Social Work Dictionary* (Barker 1995), spiritual counseling and spirituality are defined, with a special reference to the transpersonal (363). In a way, these references reflect how the helping professions have dealt with religion and spirituality over the years. The terms are included, but a full explication is not provided. There are references, but the categories have not been fully developed. We have observed a sort of "approach-avoidance" when it comes to religion, spirituality and professionalism.

Although there is disagreement over whether and how religion and spirituality should be incorporated into contemporary practice, it is recognized that the helping professions in the United States were influenced by a long history of religious traditions. "Beginning in the second half of the nineteenth century, ethical precepts of charity reaching back to the ancient Hebrews and ethical precepts of philanthropy dating to the Athenian Greeks were gradually merged and transformed into the modern, organized institutional base of social service" (Lohmann 1992, 215). The professions that developed to deliver these services did not entirely replace "voluntary acts of charity nor [cause] amateur organized charities to disappear" (Lohmann 1992, 216). In fact, the social welfare system that emerged was and continues to be a mixed assortment of public and private organizations and groups, as well as to encompass a diversity of viewpoints and perspectives.

Given this long tradition in which religion and service intermingled, one might assume that there is a rich scholarly research tradition that focuses on these relationships. Yet "religious organizations are usually part of the definition but rarely part of the analysis of the nonprofit sector" (Cormode 1994, 171). The 1990s, however, have witnessed a renewed interest in theory development and research that sheds light on how religious and spiritual influences interface with secular initiatives in the United States. For example, in 1995–1996 the Program on Non-Profit Organizations (PONPO) and the Departments of Religious Studies and Sociology at Yale University initiated a series of workshops designed to reshape "our conceptual lenses" regarding religion and society.

This chapter focuses on the historical influences that have made religion and spirituality forces in human development. Specifically, we examine the religious roots throughout the world that helped shape human service organizations, programs, and partnerships throughout the United States. We begin with a very early historical perspective, and quickly focus our discussion on the evolution of the helping professions in American society.

EARLY HISTORICAL PERSPECTIVES

The evolution of social welfare represents the interplay of belief systems and the desire to survive. Archeological evidence dating to approximately 25,000 B.C.E. reveals nomadic gathering and hunting societies in which communal tribes focused on survival needs: food, shelter, and safety. Food *was* the economic system, and deities were petitioned for assistance. Deities were primarily female because women were viewed as sacred, most likely because they could bear life (Day 1989, 65).

A transformation in the economy occurred after the Ice Ages when women began to farm the land and men began to breed and raise animals. With people able for the first time to live in one place year round, it became possible to conceive of owning land and to gain from the products raised on it. Religion also changed. The relationship between intercourse and pregnancy was realized, dropping women from their sacred status. "Gender oppression began with women's double loss of economic input and sacred status until eventually women too became the property of male landowners" (Day 1989, 66). Male deities became more powerful and were called upon to support aggression against others for the accumulation of wealth and land.

Once it became possible to remain in one geographical location, between 6000 and 3000 B.C.E. permanent settlements emerged throughout the world, from the Mediterranean to the valley of the Nile in Egypt to the rivers of China. Changes in social structure accompanied settlement, as the need emerged for workers to control flooding, to irrigate fields, and to plant crops. Each civilization had some system for social welfare. The Egyptian belief that the poor could curse oppressors into eternity and the need for a healthy work force resulted in the development of poor laws to assist those in need. Between 3000 to 1200 B.C.E. Sumerians in Mesopotamia created shrines for widows, orphans and the poor which were overseen by the goddess Nanshe. Eventually, the shrines began to lend with interest, causing persons without resources to become prisoners or slaves after defaulting (Day 1989, 68).

As conquest and war developed among nations, people who believed in gods alien to the religion of a particular nation were viewed as out groups and patriarchal religions prevailed. "Semitic barbarians formed a confederation called the Twelve Tribes of Israel. Inspired by a male war god and teaching a new monotheism, they ravaged Assyria and much of the Middle East for three centuries. More deadly than their enemies because they believed that worshipers of other gods should be killed, the Israelites often slew every living creature and burned every field in the kingdoms they conquered. . . . These Holy Wars aimed at spreading monotheism and the Israelite god" (Day 1989, 70).

ROOTS OF MODERN WELFARE SYSTEMS EMANATING FROM THE MIDDLE EAST

Jewish and Christian traditions have dominated the processes which have shaped values and guided social welfare policy in the United States. Throughout Middle Eastern and, subsequently, Western history, definitions of the "deserving poor" and "philanthropy" have been influenced by a combination of religious and governmental philosophies and practices. Often religion and government were either synonymous or very closely related. A brief examination of the impact of religion on the historical development of social welfare largely reflects the dominance of Christian and Jewish thought.

Israel

Hebrew Scriptures (Christians often refer to this body of writings as the "Old Testament") document the emergence of human service prescriptions as the Israelite society developed. Mandates to care for orphans, widows, and the poor were paralleled by oppression of women and persons who were not part of the faith tradition. "Aid became a necessary addition to a stratified society, to maintain allegiance and a work force. Warlords and priests became the elite upper classes" (Day 1989, 71).

Later Judaic teachings sought to redress the aggressive nature of early Israelite behavior. Morris sets the beginnings of Western charity in approximately 800 B.C.E., when an ethical responsibility to do good works emerged in the Hebrew tradition (Morris 1986). An institutional and universal approach to welfare became hallmarks of the Judaic welfare system. The Chamber of Whispers was a place set aside in the synagogue in which people would leave resources for those who needed them, donors and recipients remaining anonymous. The principle of tithing was embraced as a way to redistribute resources, with one-tenth of one's harvest being given to the Lord to support the faith as well as the poor. Corners of each field were left unharvested so that the poor could gather grain (Lohmann 1992, 217).

Greece and Rome

Around the height of ancient Judaism in the Middle East, other civilizations such as Greece and Rome developed. The concepts of democracy and philanthropy emerged in the Greek city-states. An individualistic freedom was limited to persons who were not owned by others. Philanthropy, which originally meant benevolence of gods toward humankind, evolved to mean an obligation to serve others. This obligation was viewed as a way to gain honor in a society that had a definite stratification between the deserving and undeserving poor. Greek society cared for the poor by providing grain during food shortages and offering some custodial care. There were orphanages and pensions for children who had lost their fathers to war. Although these services were in place, the welfare system was harsh. "Plato urged euthanasia for the disabled or aged. Slavery, concubinage, and enforced colonization were also considered welfare, despite the fact that the concept of philanthropy originated in Greece, the spirit of philanthropy never existed there" (Day 1989, 79–80).

Just as kinship and membership in the synagogue precipitated the giving of welfare in Judaism and a system of honor required Greek citizens to give, in Roman society welfare developed as a form of political patronage. Men and boys received doles that were intended to buy votes. Women could not vote, so there was little reason to provide doles to them. In later years there were efforts by wealthy citizens to provide food to the needy and to hold public feasts, but these were private efforts (Day 1989, 80–81).

"At the turn of the millennium, Greek, Roman, Jewish, Egyptian and Eastern societies converged and blended, and Rome moved fully into Empire to become ruler of the Western world. . . . Unbelievable poverty existed" (Day 1989, 81). Roman religion was very patriarchal and denied women the right to hold office. The Cult of Isis did respond to women, slaves, and others who had been excluded from the dominant religion of the time. As the Roman Republic matured, limits were set on the subjugation of women (Day 1989, 81).

Emergence of Christianity

Born into this time, Jesus of Nazareth was viewed as a revolutionary in part because he opposed both class and gender oppression. Drawing from the ethical tradition emphasized in Judaism, Christianity reflected much of these teachings. During the Middle Ages and to the time of the Elizabethan Poor Law and Statute of Charitable Uses in 1601, Christian welfare was part of the institutional church. As early as C.E. 150 each church established a fund to aid the poor. In C.E. 369 the first documented hospital was developed in a bishop's house and grew into a set of pavilions in which different diseases were treated (Lohmann 1992, 217).

If the history of religious influence on the development of the helping professions was a linear chronicle of how people of various civilizations learned from one another and matured in their attitudes toward the poor, this would be an easy book to write. Paradoxically, the history of how religion, politics, and economics intertwine is instructive in different ways. There were times in various societies when religious people were kind and caring because they truly believed that the poor were deserving. There were often distinctions made between which of the poor were deserving and which were not. Often harsh laws prevailed because of who was in power and the economic conditions of the day. The juxtaposition of cruelty and caring has remained throughout the centuries, as has the mixture of concern for the poor and the suspicion that the help provided will be misused in some way.

This was evident in Christianity when St. John Chrysostom promoted open generosity and unconstrained compassion for those in need, as compared with St. Ambrose, St. Augustine of Hippo, and others who indicated that the poor needed counsel so that they would spend their funds correctly, and that some monitoring of these funds should be established (Morris 1986).

Islam

Lohmann points out that "a similar profile emerges in Islamic zakat, which involves personal ethical obligations much like those incumbent upon

17

Jews and Christians. . . . Aiding those in need is the personal obligation of every Muslim" (1992, 218). Lohmann goes on to explain, however, that the zakat is different from Western charitable systems in that it is essentially a religious tax. "We might also note that the Judeo-Christian-Islamic ethical tradition of charity is distinctive but not entirely unique among the world's major religions. . . . Within Buddhism, there is an equally distinctive emergence of charitable norms and practices" (Lohmann 1992, 218).

MIDDLE AGES IN EUROPE

The Roman Catholic Church in feudal times was tied to the economic structure of the host land. During the Dark Ages, the Church had its own army. Muslims, Jews, and non-Catholic Christians were persecuted. Church leaders had a great deal of power, but it is recorded that only the lower levels of the Church remained committed to serving the poor. At that time economic and social need was still generally considered to be a result of societal forces, rather than personal failure. By the sixth century, religious communities called monastic orders had developed and the monastic movement resulted in many charitable practices that converged over the following centuries. Orders of women focused on services to the poor and pioneered in the care of the aged.

Church and societal reform marked the sixteenth and seventeenth centuries that became known as the Reformation. Whereas poverty and compassion had traditionally held somewhat of a mystical aura, attitudes changed. John Calvin, the Swiss Protestant reformer, preached that the poor were seen as special friends of God to which the rich should commit resources. Good works were highly esteemed and a test of one's faith.

One of the key issues in the Protestant Reformation was the focus on the Bible as the authoritative source of knowledge about God and personal salvation. The concept of the sale of indulgences which was being practiced in this time period by the Roman Catholic Church came under sharp criticism by the reformers. Indulgences were one method offered by the Roman Church for clarifying the individual's relationship with God and assuring salvation in the life to come. Protestant reformers such as John Calvin and Martin Luther took the position that an all knowing God, to be all knowing, must already know who will obtain salvation and who will not.

This discussion, for John Calvin, was a part of a greater discussion that examined how God takes care of people. This concept was labeled "the doctrine of predestination." The question posed for humanity, however, was that while God knows who is going to be saved, how do the common people obtain this same knowledge? While not the official policy of the Roman Church, the concept of the average person was that by purchasing an indulgence for any real or potential sin, one was purchasing salvation. But if indulgences were no longer an option, then how did the average person know if he or she was saved? Calvin offered several different ways of knowing when one is saved, one of which reflected the fact that the poor had offered the rich an opportunity to demonstrate their election through hard work (Zietz 1970).

Calvin is also credited by Max Weber with solidifying the concept of the Protestant work ethic. Believing that people were preordained to salvation or destruction, outward signs of giving charity were viewed as inward signs of grace. John Knox, who introduced Calvinism into England and Scotland, gradually altered Calvin's teachings and it was believed that there were indeed outward signs of spiritual grace. "From the ideas of Luther and Calvin came the concepts of the importance of the individual, the primacy of work, and the freedom from religious control of much of secular life" (Zietz 1970, 10).

After Henry VIII of England was excommunicated from the Roman Catholic Church, the state moved to suppress the monasteries, seize their wealth, reform welfare. Lands formerly owned by religious orders passed into hands outside the Church. Henry VIII, like Luther, believed that giving should be voluntary but he quickly realized that someone had to take responsibility for the poor. Without the motivation to give based on the connection of good works with salvation, it was necessary for the English Parliament to enact laws for the poor. The Church of England served as the conduit for the collection of alms, as mandated by the Parliament.

In the course of the Reformation, the greatest evils became laziness and idleness and they were to be dealt with harshly. Societal forces were not to blame, but personal reform was needed in order to get the poor to conform to the work ethic. "The Protestant ethic became the keynote of Western society's policies in social welfare. Its psychological impact was phenomenal, for it fostered alienation from family and community, justified social stratification by income, became the model for self-concept, and made work the definition of spirituality. Poverty became moral degeneracy, and fault became centered in the self rather than in the structures of society" (Day 1989, 109).

With the rise of industrialization, numerous laws were passed to deal with the increasing number of poor. Strict restrictions were placed on begging and the Statute of Laborers in 1349 was designed to keep able bodied jobless persons in one location so that they would be required to work for whoever needed them. Giving alms to the able bodied was outlawed. But it was the Elizabethan or the 1601 English Poor Law that most influenced the development of social welfare in England and the United States. Reflecting the publicizing of social welfare, the 1601 Poor Law required that each parish in the kingdom have an overseer of the poor. Indoor relief was provided for those who needed shelter and was in the form of almshouses for the disabled, mentally ill, old, blind, and others who were deemed needy. The English Poor Law distinguished between the deserving and undeserving poor, and essentially worked to control the labor force (Karger and Stoesz 1990). In the Act of Settlement of 1662, each parish was responsible for those persons who lived within the community. The intent was to return persons to their place of legal residence and to reduce vagabondage by the unemployed.

When the North American Continent was settled, colonists brought much of the structure established in England for the provision of services to the poor. It was expected that private citizens would care for their own, but in situations where this was not possible, limited public assistance was available. Puritan and Anglican ministers raised small amounts of money for widows, orphans, the aged, and the disabled (Chambers 1985).

PROVISION OF SERVICES IN THE UNITED STATES

It is impossible to cover adequately the development of services for various population groups in the United States in one short chapter. There are many books and articles that recount historical developments in detail. Suffice it to say that the many influences alluded to above have remained a part of what is often a contradictory system of social welfare. It is possible to find almost every viewpoint represented among the diverse citizenry of the United States. Whereas one group may believe strongly in a libertarian philosophy of a no or limited government, others may believe strongly in the provision of services through public dollars and agencies. Others may feel strongly about religious influences in service provision, both for and against. And in the range of attitudes toward the poor, there are vestiges of all the themes mentioned above, from perceptions that the poor are totally to blame for not having what they need, to those who think that the poor are not responsible for their plight in a society gone awry. One thing that all these groups have in common is that there are strong traditions for all of their viewpoints and opinions that have emerged from an interplay of economic, political, and religious influences over centuries. It is our contention that people are not always aware of these strong traditions that influence their thinking.

RELIGION IN COLONIAL AMERICA

The development of services in the Colonies followed parallel courses in the public and private sectors. Just as local public coffers were made available for indigent relief, so did private charities arise. Yet, the colonists did not spend time fretting over whether organizations that provided services were public or private, for profit or not for profit, religious or secular. There were other pressing issues such as survival to consider (O'Neill 1989). It is estimated that only one percent of the population of the colonists received assistance from outside sources (Karger and Stoesz 1990, 33). "The church was not a subdivision of the state or vice versa, but the two were so closely connected as to be sometimes almost indistinguishable. Both church and state were intertwined with business, as is evident in the charters and activities of such joint stock settlement corporations as the Virginia Company, the Massachusetts Bay Company, and the Dutch East Indies Company" (O'Neill 1989, 24).

Diversity among religious groups was an important theme in the new world. British colonies were much more denominationally diverse than the Spanish or French colonies were. Anglicans, Baptists, Quakers, German Pietists, Dutch Calvinists, French Huguenots, Catholics, and Puritans were all represented. Among Puritans, there were wide ranges of attitudes and beliefs (O'Neill 1989). Bailyn describes the society as "boiling with 'dissident' beliefs and sectors. The 'dissidents,' the 'radicals,' in seventeenth century New England—separatists, Anabaptists, Quakers, extreme millenarians, spiritists, antinomians, Socinians, Gortonists, and miscellaneous seekers [were all types of Puritans]" (Bailyn 1986, 48–49).

PROLIFERATION OF PRIVATE CHARITIES

During Colonial times as well as after the Revolutionary War, the United States depended upon local relief and private charity. There was essentially no national oversight of public services. During the early 1800s the process of caring for the poor changed. Rather than depending on outdoor relief (the equivalent to home- and community-based services today), there was a much greater reliance upon indoor relief (institutions). In the New England states, workhouses funded by local government were viewed as places for the poor to go because it was widely believed that poverty was linked to moral weakness, a value held by Puritan believers (Karger and Stoesz 1990).

It was in the 1800s that private charities proliferated in the United States, particularly in the larger cities of the Northeast. Increasing numbers of immigrants and the development of urban centers served as driving forces to meet growing human service needs. Religion has been referred to as the "Godmother of the Nonprofit Sector" and as having given birth to the institutions of health care, education, social service, international assistance, advocacy, and mutual assistance (O'Neill 1989, 20) in the United States. The vast majority of private education was religiously affiliated, and most hospitals can trace their origins to religious sources. Organizations such as Big Brothers and Big Sisters and the YMCA acknowledge religious roots. In the 1870s the United Way was founded in Denver under the leadership of two ministers, a priest, and a rabbi (O'Neill 1989).

Private benevolent societies grew as social problems increased. Inadequate public health, safety, and education were evident as inner city slums developed. Traditional informal systems of assistance could not keep pace with these emerging needs. The Second Great Awakening of Protestant evangelism (1800—1830) inspired the saving of souls. It was hoped that persons who had fallen from grace would become responsible citizens, get off the relief rolls, and out of the poorhouses. The benevolent societies attempted to address the here and now, as well as the future salvation of the poor and downtrodden. Sunday schools were established for the urban poor and religious tracts were widely distributed. City missions focused on concrete needs, and some societies targeted special population groups—widows with young children, abandoned children, and persons who were developmentally and physically disabled. The names of these organizations captured their missions, ranging from The Society for Poor Widows with Small Children to Home for Little Wanderers (Chambers 1985). These societies often manifested the ideas and practices of Protestant groups that had refused to conform to the dictates of the Church of England. These faith traditions were described as more personal and emotional than the more formalized traditions inherent in the Anglican Church. Charity was perceived to be an awakening of the spirit (Leiby 1987).

Simultaneous with the development of societies by these evangelical sects, the Episcopal (Anglican) Church, which appealed to the more affluent, and other more formalized congregations of Congregationalists and Presbyterians in New England, the Dutch Reformed Church in New York and New Jersey, and the Quakers around Philadelphia engaged in fund raising events for charity. Balls, benefits, and bazaars were held to support human service efforts. Members of these more established churches were as likely to give to public charity causes as they were to voluntary sector groups and societies (Leiby 1987).

As Protestant societies developed and grew, Catholic churches most often serving Irish and German parishes, instituted their own sectarian organizations. Like their Protestant counterparts, Catholic parishes developed specialized services for the needy. The Sisters of Charity, Sisters of the Poor, Sisters of Mercy, and others focused on persons who were in unfortunate circumstances. Catholic adoption agencies specialized in placing children in good Catholic families (Chambers 1985). Groups of Lutherans from Germany and Scandinavia, Jews from Russia, and congregations of Greeks, Russians, Armenians, and Turks supported their own groups of immigrants who had recently come to the United States. Generally, these religious groups were strongly sectarian, holding together their communities in terms of ethnic integrity as well as religious convictions (Leiby 1987).

The 1800s in the United States was a time of growing complexity in human service delivery. Public assistance through local auspices provided relief, and religiously inspired societies attempted to fill in where public relief did not reach. Chambers (1985) tells us that historians have no way of assessing just how influential each of these organizations were, apart from recognizing that the beginnings were very mixed and complex. Without a systematic approach, an abandoned child was as likely to end up in a public institution as to be assigned to a religious orphanage. Laws were vague and there were not clear lines of authority and responsibility. By the 1860s, thousands of benevolent societies were "founded, financed, and managed by prospering middle class and professional men. Society executives tended to be drawn from ministerial ranks or from persons trained for the cloth. Much of the volunteer work . . . was taken over by lady volunteers" (Chambers 1985, 10). Interestingly, women were often assigned to run programs that focused on women and children because it was believed that they could lead those "who had strayed from the path of virtue back to the way of righteousness" (Chambers 1985, 11).

THE PROFESSIONALIZATION OF HELPING

After the Civil War and into the last part of the 1800s, there was great frustration over the lack of coordination and chaotic conditions imposed by having so many societies and institutions attempting to serve people's needs. Coordination and organization was eagerly sought by persons interested in a more scientific approach to charity. The first Charity Organization Society (COS) emerged in 1877 in Buffalo, New York. Member agencies agreed to coordinate their efforts and COSs emerged in cities across the country. Centralized files were generated and paid workers were sent into homes to investigate need (Chambers 1985).

In the 1890s the settlement house movement began as well. The first American settlement was Neighborhood Guild in New York, established in 1886. By 1911 there were almost 400 settlement houses throughout the United States. Many of the settlements were begun by religious leaders, but there were secular influences as well. Settlements were designed to serve the immigrants in urban areas, helping them to adjust to the new world and focusing heavily upon educational activities and neighborly services.

The Progressive Era and Professionalism

The COS and settlement house movements are generally credited with the beginning of professional social work. The roots of these movements are grounded in the concepts of charities and corrections, both of which have religious connotations, as used during the late 1800s. "Charity" was viewed as serving humankind so as to serve God, whereas "correction" referred to reform and conversion, the notion of inner change. "Arising from these notions of charity and correction was a religious ideal of a community, suggested by Hebrew prophecy and by Jesus' parable of the Kingdom of God" (Leiby 1987, 763).

It was during the Progressive Era (1900–1930) that the term "social welfare" came into vogue. The terms *philanthropist* and *charity worker* moved over to become "social worker." These more secular terms probably signified a movement toward the recognition of more and more nonsectarian agencies and publicly sponsored welfare. In this era many of the helping professions emerged. Public health workers began to clean up the streets and work toward sanitary and humane conditions in people's homes as well as places of work. Social workers began to search for a professional identity at a time when the professions were seen as ministry, medicine, and law—occupations composed primarily of men. The professions of engineering, agriculture, dentistry, pharmacy, nursing, teaching, business, library science, public administration, and others emerged during this time (Leiby 1987). The Progressive Era represented the professionalization of those fields of study that would move the United States into the twentieth century.

There was discussion of what competencies each of these professions would bring to the world. Specifically, among helping professions there were questions about how social work differed from what nurses, physicians, or teachers did. The market for social workers became those very agencies that had emerged during the 1800s and the method was called casework. Social workers were also hired to work in public agencies, schools, hospitals, prisons, institutions for the mentally ill and mentally retarded, and other similar settings (Leiby 1987).

As the helping professionals rounded their way into the 20th century, the influence of religion began to wane in light of the secularization of human services. Loewenberg indicates that "while the seeds of the break between the religious and the secular delivery systems were already planted in the fifteenth and sixteenth centuries, the actual break was gradual and was not completed until the latter part of the nineteenth century" (1988, 18). Loewenberg attributes these changes to the increased division of labor, the rise of positivism and the competition for resources.

Professional Roles

With the division of labor came a redefinition of the role of clergy. Whereas clergy had been the leaders of the premodern world, in the twentieth century their role narrowed to that of specialist in religious matters. Institutions in which the church had previously taken full responsibility were spun off to other domains. For example, education became the realm of public schools, and social services were delivered by nonsectarian agencies (Loewenberg 1988, 18). Social workers and psychotherapists began to perform tasks previously within the province of religious professionals. Specht and Courtney elaborate, "In earlier times, churches were great institutions located in impressive edifices with elaborate services and other ceremonial activities presided over by the clergy. More important, the church brought the community together and told people how to live and love, what was right and wrong, and how properly to raise a family. . . . The established churches are now used primarily as social gathering places on Sundays and holidays, and psychotherapists have become secular priests and psychotherapy the modern day church of individual repair" (1994, 13) Scientism is the belief that knowledge found through science and this will lead to problem solving within all realms. This belief emerged in the 1800s and the COS movement was based on this belief system. The helping professions embraced this approach to the world in a fervent manner, "even while the churches, at least the more traditional and conservative ones, remained among the few social institutions that attempted to resist the trend" (Loewenberg 1988, 19).

Given the competition for limited resources, secular agencies began to compete with religious affiliates. These agencies competed for qualified personnel as well as for funding. Persons like Jane Addams made choices between becoming a religious missionary or becoming a social worker (Marty 1980, 475).

And last, Loewenberg suggests that statism had its influence on the break between the religious and the secular. As the nation-state developed, a natural extension was to move toward state and federal types of relief. During the 1900s, as the social welfare state developed, many helping professionals moved into public agencies and pursued opportunities that were nonsectarian. If one were a linear thinker, the progression toward a secular state would parallel the professionalization of the helping fields, and religion would move to a distant past. Interestingly enough, what has occurred is a debate in the literature and among professions about where religion fits into the postmodern world. The ragged course of history during the twentieth century has made for a fascinating journey that is difficult to sort out and even more complex than one might have anticipated.

In the early part of the 1900s, the helping professions defined their curricula and attempted to carve their niches in the societal fabric. However, the questions about overlap among professional roles and domains have not disappeared. In fact, they have continued unabated and are currently inflammatory. Social work, psychology, and ministry particularly are struggling with potentially overlapping professional roles.

PROFESSIONAL UNCERTAINTY

Martin Luther held that all persons had vocations or "callings" to which they should aspire and which came from God. Calvin referred to the "secret call" that was God's indication a person should go into the ministry. In more recent years, the term "calling" has appeared in the literature in discussing the nature of professions, both secular and religious (Bellah, Madsen, Sullivan, Swidler, and Tipton 1985; Gustafson 1982; Sullivan 1995).

Gustafson (1982) discusses professions as callings, characterized by three criteria. First, professionals learn to apply an extensive body of knowledge to real world situations. A professional therefore has to think about the relevance of the knowledge to the actual situation because there are no hard and fast rules. Discretion is essential. Second, professions are institutionalized and controlled so that the practice of one's profession is held to standards. With this institutionalization comes a sense of identity with the "professional community." Third, professions are service oriented, intended to address individual and community needs. It is this latter characteristic of a profession that leads Gustafson to label professions as callings. "Not only subjective motives are involved; some vision of better lives for individuals, for groups, and even for the commonweal of the human community are part of a 'calling'" (1982, 511).

In *Habits of the Heart,* Bellah and his colleagues examine the concepts of job, career, vocation, and calling. A calling is viewed as linking the individual with the collective so that one can contribute to the common good. "A calling links a person to the larger community, a whole in which the calling of each is a contribution to the good of all" (Bellah et al. 1985, 66). These writers go on to say that as the world has become more complicated and roles more specialized, it has also become harder to see how one's work is connected with the larger whole.

Sullivan (1995) builds on previous work as he examines the development of professionalism in American society. Professionalism is viewed as having great potential if professionals remember that their purpose for being is to serve the client. However, much skepticism has developed in recent years and no profession has remained untarnished. Professionalism has taken on a life of its own, often losing sight of social responsibility. It has become a source of identity unto itself, and such overlapping roles and relationships have evolved that "in an increasingly competitive cultural environment, religious professionals are often hard to distinguish from therapists, guidance counselors, and other human services personnel" (14).

Whereas Specht and Courtney (1994) offer perspectives on how the profession of social work must question its identity, Gustafson, Bellah et al., and Sullivan offer a glimpse of what may be the core of professional uncertainty. If professionals are those who use judgment in complex situations that affect individuals and communities, then they bear tremendous responsibility. If professionals across fields view persons within the context of their communities and draw from extensive interdisciplinary knowledge bases, then it is virtually impossible for one profession to totally distinguish itself from another. There is bound to be overlap; otherwise, professionals would not be seeing the whole person. Holistic practice is embraced by social workers, clergy, nurses, physicians, and others as a matter of course today. Whether motivated by secular, religious, spiritual, economic, social, psychological, and/or other reasons to perform professional work, professionals struggle with who they are in relation to many constituencies.

SPIRITUALITY AND RELIGION

Part of the search for meaning, both personal and professional, is seen in an emerging literature that links professional practice with spirituality. This literature will be discussed in later chapters. As professional roles evolved in the 1900s, there were many influences in psychological theory embraced by helping professionals. So where is religion in the human services? What has transpired in the helping professions?

Religion as it was previously conceived will likely never be the same. Religion as an organized, institutional arrangement is certainly a viable and lasting entity in the United States. However, it encompasses more and more sects and represents a tremendous and growing diversity—points to which we will return in the next chapter. In the meantime, the relationship of religion and helping professionals today appears to be largely one of approach/avoidance behavior.

Religion as part of human services has a long, ongoing, and incredibly complex history. There are religious affiliates to this day that espouse certain values that represent a long and lasting faith tradition. These affiliations will be explored in a later chapter. These formalized vehicles of service delivery are typically related to more established religious groups that have sponsored human services for many years. At times they look very secular in their approaches and they rarely serve only "their own," but the influences are there, even if in subtle ways.

The helping professions are another story entirely. Social workers, psychologists, clergy, and others appear to be at a crossroads of indecision about who they are and what they will be. Over the last century, each group embraced what they believed to be the competencies that gave them their reason for being. Studies are being published that examine how religious each of these professional groups are (see for example: Sheridan and Bullis 1992; Sheridan, Bullis, Adcock, Berlin, and Miller 1992). Even clergy appear to be uncertain about just how religious they should be and they certainly feel the encroachment of other professions in the realm of spirituality.

The word *spirituality* itself is sometimes used to avoid the word *religion*. "In aspiring to work with the transpersonal or spiritual dimension, it is crucial that client system and social worker come to a common understanding or shared meaning about the term spiritual. . . . Not contained by the theological walls of any specific ideological system, spirituality is not considered as equivalent with religion, religiosity, or theology" (Cowley 1994, 33). Spirituality then is something that the atheist can embrace, just as the devoutly religious person. Not to offend those who feel uncomfortable with the term religious, spirituality then offers the opportunity to develop one's self beyond traditional religious parameters.

Among the helping professions, it seems to be "politically correct" and liberal to recognize spirituality as a given and to chastise our colleagues if they do not see the importance of personal self-transcendence. On the other hand, it appears "politically incorrect" to be religious; moreover, religion has increasingly become equated with fundamentalist and politically conservative. Separating faith from self and trivializing religious devotion in the public arena are the subjects of *The Culture of Disbelief* (Carter 1993) and will be discussed in more detail later.

CONCLUSION

Understanding the influence of religion on the development of social services in the United States requires a knowledge of the history of humankind. Within the last century, as helping professions emerged to battle the ills of society and became increasingly organized, a move toward secularization also occurred. Referred to as "secular priests," these professionals have assumed many of the roles traditionally performed by clergy. In an attempt to reclaim their leadership role, clergy have embraced many of the approaches and strategies that secular helpers have adopted. As the twenty-first century approaches, many secular helpers have turned to spirituality and self-transcendence to find meaning for themselves and their clients. Whatever it is called—religion, theology, spirituality, meaning, self-transcendence—both secular and religious priests are referred to as professionals, and both are seeking something beyond the self. Their clients are also engaged in this exploration.

This book is devoted to exploring the great diversity among seekers, both professionals and clients. We believe that the exploration of religious and spiritual diversity is necessary to understanding contemporary practice in the human services within the United States.

REFERENCES

Bailyn, B. 1986. *The Peopling of British North America: An introduction.* New York: Knopf.

Barker, R. O. 1995. *The Social Work Dictionary.* Washington, D.C.: National Association of Social Workers.

Beckett, J. O. 1995. Human development. In R. L. Edwards and J. G. Hopps, eds. *Encyclopedia of Social Work.* 19th ed. Washington, D.C.: National Association of Social Workers, 1385–1404.

Bellah, R. N., R. Madsen, W. M. Sullivan, A. Swidler, and S. M. Tipton. 1985. *Habits of the heart: Individualism and commitment in American life.* New York: Harper and Row.

Carter, S. L. 1993. *The culture of disbelief.* New York: Basic Books.

Chambers, C. A. 1985. The historical role of the voluntary sector in human service delivery in urban America. In *Social planning and human service delivery in the voluntary sector,* ed. Gary A. Tobin, 3–28. Westport, Conn.: Greenwood Press.

Cormode, D. S. 1994. Review essay: Religion and the nonprofit sector. *Nonprofit and Voluntary Sector Quarterly* 23 (2): 171–82.

Cowley, A. S. 1993. Transpersonal social work: A theory for the 1990s. *Social Work* 38 (5): 527–34.

———. 1994. Transpersonal psychology and social work education. *Journal of Social Work Education* 30 (1): 32–41.

Day, P. J. 1989. *A new history of social welfare.* Englewood Cliffs, N.J.: Prentice-Hall.

Garland, D. R. 1995. Church social work. In R. L. Edwards and J. G. Hopps, eds. *Encyclopedia of Social Work.* 19th ed. Washington, D.C.: National Association of Social Workers, 475–83.

Gustafson, J. M. 1982. Professions as "callings." *Social Service Review* 56 (4): 501–15.

Karger, H. J., and D. Stoesz. 1990. *American social welfare policy: A structural approach.* White Plains, N.Y.: Longman.

Leiby, J. 1987. History of social welfare. In *Encyclopedia of social work,* ed. Anne Minahan, 755–88. 18th ed. Silver Spring, Md.: National Association of Social Workers.

Loewenberg, F. M. 1988. *Religion and social work practice in contemporary American society.* New York: Columbia University Press.

Lohmann, R. 1992. *The commons: New perspectives on nonprofit organizations and voluntary action.* San Francisco: Jossey-Bass.

Marty, M. E. 1980. Social service: Godly and godless. *Social Service Review,* 54 (4): 463–81.

Morris, R. 1986. *Rethinking social welfare: Why care for the stranger?* White Plains, N.Y.: Longman.

O'Neill, M. 1989. *The third America: The emergence of the nonprofit sector in the United States.* San Francisco: Jossey-Bass.

Ortiz, L. 1995. Sectarian agencies. In R. L. Edwards and J. G. Hopps, eds. *Encyclopedia of Social Work.* 19th ed. Washington, D.C.: National Association of Social Workers, 2109–116.

Sheridan, M. J., and R. K. Bullis. 1992. Practitioners' views of religion and spirituality: A qualitative study. *Spirituality and Social Work Journal* 2 (2): 2–10.

Sheridan, M. J., R. K. Bullis, C. R. Adcock, S. D. Berlin, and P. C. Miller. 1992. Practitioners' personal and professional attitudes and behaviors toward religion and spirituality: Issues for education and practice. *Journal of Social Work Education* 28 (2): 190–203.

Specht, H., and M. Courtney. 1994. *Unfaithful angels: How social work has abandoned its mission.* New York: Free Press.

Sullivan, W. M. 1995. *Work and integrity: The crisis and promise of professionalism in America.* New York: Harper Business.

Zietz, D., and R. Smith, R. 1970. American social welfare institutions. New York: John Wiley and Sons.

Chapter 2

THE INFLUENCE OF RELIGION ON THE HISTORICAL DEVELOPMENT OF CLINICAL PRACTICE

In other parts of the book, we examine how religion and spirituality have influenced the development of the helping professions and the establishment of community faith traditions within the United States. In this chapter we take direct clinical practice and examine how religion has influenced the ways human service providers work with individuals and families.

THE CODEVELOPMENT OF RELIGIOUS AND PSYCHOLOGICAL VIEWS OF HUMAN NATURE

The basic "nature" of the person and the individual's behavior and development through the lifespan has been a focus of thought and study for philosophers, theologians, and therapeutic practitioners (physicians, priests, shamans, psychologists, social workers, etc.) from earliest times. Ideas concerning normal and abnormal growth and development and the treatment of pathological states extend far back into history. As early as the Stone Age, according to drawings on the walls of caves, humans were treating mental disorders demonstrated by socially aberrant behavior by cutting openings called trephines into the skull. These openings were presumably made to permit the escape of evil spirits which were believed to be the cause of physical pain and dysfunctional behavior in the person.

In the scriptures of the Hebrews, which form the basis of the subsequent Christian and Islamic sacred scriptures, there are two very different accounts of the creation and developmental stages of the human being. These accounts have resulted in at least two major divergent understandings of the nature of humanity and the developmental tasks of the lifespan. In the first account of creation, Genesis 1–2:3, God takes seven days to create the heavens, the earth, and humankind. In this account, both male and female are given identification with God, i.e., made in his image, as a gift freely given, without constraints and without having to earn or develop into identity with the divine.

In the second creation account, Genesis 2:4–3:24, God creates Adam from the earth, then Eve from Adam's rib. The two are given dominion over the Garden, except for one constraint—they are not to eat of the tree of the knowledge of good and evil because that will bring them death. The serpent talks to Eve, suggesting that if she eats the fruit she will not die but have an understanding of good and evil, just as God does. (This is apparently the ultimate knowledge). In this way she would take identification with God by force, rather than receiving it as a gift inherent in created human nature. Eve, desiring this wisdom, wanting this attribute of God, takes the fruit and gives it to her husband as well. Immediately after eating the forbidden fruit, they understand themselves as bad—they see that they are naked. They are ashamed to face God and are full of fear. In his anger, God curses the serpent and dooms the man and woman, who have been disobedient, to a future of interpersonal misunderstanding, physical pain, power/dominance contests between the sexes, struggle to subsist, and ultimately, personal death. In addition, God banishes them from the Garden so that they will not be able to seize and eat of the tree of life, which would restore them to eternal life. From now on, man and woman are set free to find their difficult way back to identification with God by their own daily struggle for basic survival.

In summary, the first account mentions no sin, and humans are freely given their identification with God. They never lose their basic goodness or their relationship with one another, with creation, and with God. In the second account, they lose this identification, and their lives are to be spent trying to regain goodness, including intimate and just relationships with one another, with creation, and with God. These two accounts of creation of human beings reflect the two emergent views of human development—the pathology oriented and the transcendent oriented understanding of the nature of the person.

From the second account it is concluded that the temptation and fall of humankind and the consequent banishment from Paradise resulted in the need for redemption or "salvation," to bring human beings back to goodness and identification with God. They did not have the power to do it by themselves. This fall from original grace, called "original sin," became a powerful negative image of basic human nature. Humankind, instead of being inherently good became basically bad. In addition, women were believed to be even more evil than men because, in this account, it was Eve who succumbed to the power of the evil serpent and was then responsible for tempting Adam to sin.

In subsequent writings of the Hebrews and in early writings of the Chinese, Egyptians, and Greeks, mental disorders (considered an outward sign of the inherent "badness" of humans and demonstrated by behavior deviant from the rules and order of the society in which the afflicted person lived), were attributed to demons that had taken possession of the person. Similarly, good and bad spirits were the explanation for such natural phenomena as bad weather and all forms of physical illness.

Views of Aberrant Behavior

The understanding of the nature of the human being was highly dependent on the person's place in the specific culture of the time. Thus, aberrant behaviors were not static, but were related to the needs and expectations of the specific society. Because the definition of "healthy" or "unhealthy" was so culturally determined, assessment of whether a person was "possessed" by good or evil spirits was based on symptoms. If one spoke in religious terms, then it was assumed that the person was possessed by a good spirit, and he or she was treated with awe. However, most persons were assumed to be possessed by "evil spirits, particularly when the individual became excited and overactive and engaged in behavior contrary to religious teachings. Among the ancient Hebrews, such possessions were thought to represent the wrath and punishment of God" (Coleman 1976, 5).

One common treatment for possession by evil spirits was exorcism, the purpose of which was to coax or force the demon or demons out of the afflicted person. Techniques of exorcism included prayer, incantations, loud noises, and symbolic drinks, such as a combination of herbs, animal parts, and excrement. When the demon was particularly resistant, exorcists attempted to make the body an uncomfortable place to inhabit; the person might be flogged, starved, pin pricked, or tortured in a variety of other ways.

Initially, the responsibility for dealing with these powerful forces of evil belonged to community shamans. Later, in Greece and Egypt, the task was given to the priests, whose social role was actually a combination of priest, physician, psychologist, and magician. While the therapeutic activity was primarily exorcism, by 860 B.C.E. in the temples of Asclepius in Greece, which were healing sites for physical disease, the priests attempted to treat mental disorders more humanely. They combined the prayers of exorcism with behavioral interventions such as exercise, recreational activities (including theater and music), and an attitude of kindness in place of cruelty and punishment.

Around 500 B.C.E., the Greek philosopher Heraclitus, in his contemplation

33

of human existence, noted the significance of movement and change and their relationship to the growth of the person over time. He "felt that the multiple changes of human life and the universe moved progressively through strife between opposing forces and felt that this tension was 'the father of all and the king of all.'" (Oates 1957, 141–42) Heraclitus used the word *logos* for the order underlying this process of continuous change and growth. "Everything changes, but the way in which everything changes remains constant. This is the logos. Here [is found] an early intuition of the fact of lawful process in human experience" (Oates 1957, 141–42).

By around 400 B.C.E. the role of evil spirits and demons in the development of behavioral dysfunction was being questioned by therapeutic practitioners. This was the Golden Age of Greece. Whereas priest-physicians had customarily inherited their roles as healers in the temples, the rule was eased to include individuals who began to study healing processes and techniques. Thus, "schools" of early medicine arose. The Greek physician, Hippocrates, the "father of modern medicine," was one of these "schooled" practitioners. After careful observation of physically and mentally ill persons, he announced: "For my own part, I do not believe that the human body is ever befouled by a God" (Lewis 1941, 37). He believed that both physical and mental disorders were natural phenomena requiring natural treatments.

Hippocrates reasserted Pythagoras' earlier view that the brain was the organ responsible for intellectual activity and that mental disorders were due to physiological diseases of the brain. In addition, Hippocrates noted the effects of heredity on a predisposition to certain mental conditions and claimed that physical damage to the head and brain could cause behavioral changes. Based on his thorough clinical observations, he categorized all of the mental aberrations of the time into three conditions—mania, melancholia, and phrenitis. He also anticipated modern psychotherapies by his emphasis on the importance of dreams to the understanding of the personality of the patient.

Another citizen of golden age Greece, the philosopher Plato, noted the importance of the influence of the culture and the society on individuals' behavior and beliefs. He also taught that mental disorders were due to a combination of organic disease, moral disorder, and divine intervention. Near the end of the first century B.C.E., Aretaeus proposed that mental disorders had nothing to do with divine intervention but were extensions of the continuum of normal human behavior. He was the first to suggest that mania and melancholia were two aspects of the same disease.

With the collapse of the Greek and Roman civilizations and the onset of intellectual darkness in the Middle Ages, the only culture that maintained a physiological approach to the etiology and treatment of mental and physical illness was in Arabia. The first mental hospital was built in Baghdad in 792 C.E. The leading proponent of the organic approach in Arabian medicine was Avicenna (circa 980–1037 C.E.), given the title "prince of physicians." Throughout the rest of Europe the Middle Ages themselves represented a regression to animism, demonism, and antirational magic. "Human beings now became the battleground of demons and spirits who waged eternal war for the possession of their souls. Mental disorders were apparently quite frequent throughout the Middle Ages, and toward the end of the period, when medieval institutions began to collapse, their incidence seems to have increased" (Coleman 1976, 31).

In the latter half of the Middle Ages, the phenomenon of mass mental disorders of unknown origin became widespread. Frenzied bodily movements affected large groups of people simultaneously. Convulsions, wild body movements, dancing, jumping, and screaming occurred. This phenomenon was initially termed tarantism but later came to be known as St. Vitus' Dance. Responsibility for treatment of such disorders and of all people with mental disease returned to the clergy. Monasteries became havens for the disturbed, who were treated initially with compassion and with medicinal concoctions made from herbs grown in monastery gardens. As time progressed, more "spiritual" remedies were incorporated, including laying on of hands, prayer, sprinkling with holy water, and the touching of relics. Later, the understanding of mental disorders came to link them with possession by Satan the devil who led Eve astray and who was thought to continue to be victorious over the fate of human beings.

"During the latter part of the fifteenth century, it became the accepted theological belief that demoniacal possessions were of two general types: (a) possession in which the victim was unwillingly seized by the devil as a punishment by God for past sins, and (b) possession in which the individual was actually in league with the devil" (Coleman 1976, 33–34).

Eradication of "Witchcraft"

Exorcisms were developed based on the concept that Satan's downfall was caused by his inflated pride. Therefore, treating a possessed person meant striking a fatal blow that would not only insult the devil, but literally hurt his pride. Calling the devil horrible and obscene names was combined with excessive cursing; there were thought to cure the person.

The people beset by psychological maladies who were "diagnosed" as being in league with the devil were labeled as "witches." Because of the scriptural command "Thou shalt not suffer a witch to live" (Exodus 22:18), righteous religious people felt it was their duty to rid society of this ill, primarily by exorcism and, when that did not work, by torture and, most often, burning alive.

On December 7, 1484, Pope Innocent VIII made public his papal bull entitled *Summis, Desiderantes, Affectibus*, which authorized clergy to find and eradicate witches. Thus began, in the sixteenth and seventeenth centuries, the darkest era in the conceptualization of human nature and mental disorders. Before this era ended thousands of people in Europe and in the American colonies had been tortured and killed. In the Middle Ages, a person literally risked their life if they criticized or questioned the theology of demonology. "The basic ideas of mental disorder as representing punishment by God or deliberate association with the devil continued to dominate popular thought until well into the nineteenth century" (Coleman 1976, 36).

Possibly the most famous American example was the Salem witch trials in seventeenth-century Massachusetts. Modern scientific evidence (Morgan and King 1966) suggests that a particular mold grew only on the corn that was raised in the southern half of the village. This mold had hallucinatory properties. Studies of the witch trials suggested that those persons accused of being witches all lived on the south side of town. Thus it would seem plausible that a hallucinogenic mold, not an alliance with the devil was the source of the visions seen by the victims of the trials. In this case, religious principles were substituted for phenomena that were not understood by the science of that time.

Reconceptualizations: The Medical Model

The conceptualization of human nature as being tied so closely with sin, evil, and the negative side of the spiritual domain began to change toward the end of the Middle Ages, with the emergence of a number of more enlightened individuals. Paracelsus (1490–1541) declared that the dancing mania was an organic disease of the body and should be treated medically, not theologically, as a form of possession. This early scientist formulated other ideas—that the instinctive nature of the human is in conflict with the spiritual nature; that there are psychic etiologies of mental illness; and that the use of hypnotism ("bodily magnetism") could be used as a therapeutic modality.

The physician John Weyer published what amounted to an exposé of witchcraft in 1563. Weyer, who had been greatly disturbed by the torture and methods of killing of those accused of pacts with the devil, wrote that the majority of people who had been tortured or burned had actually been victims of mental or physical disorders, not spiritual misdeeds. In 1584 Reginald Scot published a book entitled *Discovery of Witchcraft,* in which he asserted that evil spirits and demons were in no way the cause of the mental disorders that were so quickly labeled "witchcraft." King James I of England later had the book burned. In France, St. Vincent de Paul risked his life by declaring publicly that "mental disease is no different to bodily disease and Christianity demands of the humane and powerful to protect, and the skillful to relieve the one as well as the other" (Coleman 1976, 37).

Gradually, reason began to triumph over spiritism, and the eighteenth century brought an age of humanitarian reform. Public institutions were developed for care of the mentally ill. A therapeutic approach called "moral treatment" was prevalent in the early part of this period. This mode of treatment was based on the belief that the mentally ill were actually normal people who could be cured through the application of a healthy environment and interpersonal help with their problems. Now those stricken with insanity were viewed as normal persons who had been harmed by severe emotional or social stress. These stresses "were called the moral causes of insanity, and moral treatment aimed at relieving the patient by friendly association, discussion of his difficulties, and the daily pursuit of purposeful activity, in other words, social therapy, individual therapy, and occupational therapy" (Rees 1957, 306–307). Moral therapy appears to have been effective, with documented "cure" rates of 70 to 80 percent ("cure" meaning that the patients were functional enough to be discharged from the asylum and return to normal life).

In the last part of the nineteenth century, interest in this form of intervention waned, primarily because of moral therapy's insistence that the insane are basically "normal." Rather, the accepted theory of the new era was that the insane are mentally "ill." Instead of having a behavioral or social problem which could be alleviated through psycho-social means, the mentally ill were redefined as being medically sick and physical medicine became the preferred mode of intervention; it was deemed more "scientific" than the prevailing social or psychological therapies. However, hospital records indicate that cure or discharge rates declined when the medical model became the dominant intervention. Increasing numbers of asylums for the insane were built and essentially became long term living sites, with little real attempts at therapy. Such was the situation until the 1960s when community mental health became the prevalent mode of treatment.

THE DAWN OF CONTEMPORARY MENTAL HEALTH METHODS

The truly scientific understanding, assessment, and treatment of the mentally ill were slow to emerge. By the mid-1800s virtually no advances had been made in the classification of mental disorders and the age old belief in evil as the cause of such aberration was still prevalent. In 1840 a Dr. Heinroth of Germany was asserting that insanity was caused by sin and could only be cured by repentance and living a pious life.

Perhaps the strongest advocates for the systematic study and treatment of insanity and the humane care of the mentally ill in the United States were Benjamin Rush (1745–1813) and Dorothea Dix (1802–1887). Rush, a Pennsylvania physician, was deeply influenced by the work of Pinel in France and Tuke in England, both of whom unchained the mentally ill in asylums, cleaned their filthy living spaces, and advocated kindness and gentle care. Rush, now considered the founder of American psychiatry, encouraged humane care, taught the first medical school class in psychiatry, and in 1812 published a psychiatry text entitled *Medical Inquiries and Observations upon the Diseases of the Mind*. But even his theories of the etiology of mental disorders were influenced by a belief in astrology.

Dorothea Dix was a schoolteacher in New England who was forced to retire due to recurrent tuberculosis. She became involved in teaching Sunday school classes to female prisoners in jails and through this contact became aware of the inhumane and often brutal treatment afforded inmates in prisons, asylums, and poorhouses. She reported her observations to Congress in 1848 and devoted the next forty years of her life to advocating for and raising the consciousness of the public about the plight of the mentally ill and the inadequacy of their care.

By the beginning of the twentieth century, the German psychiatrist Emil Kraepelin (1856–1926) was advancing the understanding of psychopathology through his systematic classification of mental disorders, which he asserted were caused by organic brain pathology. Kraepelin's emphasis on the classification of patterns of symptoms led to an era called the "descriptive period" in the study of brain pathology. The investigation and discovery of a treatment for general paresis, a brain pathology caused by syphilis, was the most dramatic success of the research of this time. Because of it, nearly all researchers and practitioners in the area of mental diseases were led to believe that all mental disorders were caused by organic pathology in the brain and nervous system. The medical model took deep roots.

However, as investigation continued it soon became apparent that for most psychopathology, no organic etiology could be found. Many researchers redoubled their efforts to find physical abnormalities. There were some who began to think that there might be psychological causes for mental illness. This was a radical view because the psychological study of the person was in its infancy—a mere twenty years old in 1900. The question was asked, "How do psychological factors actually cause mental illness?"

With that question emerged an entirely new era, that of the "psychosocial therapeutic viewpoint." The prevalent models, which have evolved up to the present time include the (1) dynamic, (2) behavioral, (3) experiential/humanistic/existential, and (4) transpersonal approaches to psychological understanding and treatment. According to Cowley, the transpersonal approach "is the only theory that focuses on the spiritual dimension and legitimatizes the development of higher states of consciousness as being exceptionally healthy or as representing the epitome of human potential." She states that the other three approaches are grounded in a preoccupation with pathology; "other theories do not recognize higher levels of consciousness and thus their exclusive use may inhibit the optimal development of the spiritual dimension" (Cowley 1993, 527). Cowley also believes that the transpersonal approach to therapy provides more promise for treating the social ills of the end of the millennium particularly violence, addiction, and spiritual malaise.

Just what is this "spiritual malaise" for which a therapy is needed? Is it not adequately attended to by formal religion, and in fact, is it not the rightful domain of religion and outside of the realm of clinical therapeutic intervention? Why should human service providers concern themselves with the spiritual factor—was it not relinquished when demons and spirits were debunked as causes of mental illness?

THE INCLUSION OF SPIRITUAL VARIABLES IN ASSESSING AND TREATING CLIENTS

In his article "The Repression of the Sublime," clinical psychologist Frank Haronian discusses the seemingly innate human urge to strive for meaning and reality beyond the everyday self and its mundane experiences. He states that "it is out of a sense of boredom and dissatisfaction with the gratification of the senses that we begin to look for higher meanings in our life" (Haronian 1974, 52). Haronian's definition of activity directed toward the "sublime" includes the following:

1. all of a human being's impulses, urges, and drives to be something greater than he or she is;
2. orientation toward the true, good, and beautiful in life;
3. an impulse toward community, brotherliness, and caring, based on the belief that ultimately we all share the same destiny;

4. the finding of one's deepest satisfaction in some form of service to others;
5. the urge to trust life, give freely of oneself, and go beyond interest in one's own concerns;
6. the need to ask and answer for oneself the basic, existential questions—Who am I? Why am I here? Where am I going?
7. the desire to dedicate oneself to a purpose that seems more significant than one's transient existence and powers.

Haronian further states: "When we sense the sublime as the feeling of communion with and dedication to something that is greater than us, then we are experiencing this basic spiritual impulse. It may be religious, agnostic, or atheistic; it does not require a belief in God, but it is consonant with such a belief" (1974, 52–53). He asserts that it is the role of the direct practitioner to aid the client in becoming more in tune with what are normal spiritual impulses and to free one's mind from any ill conceived theology that may have been acquired in childhood. Equally challenging for the clinician is to assist the client in converting spiritual energy into reflection and mindfulness that result in action that goes beyond passionate thinking.

Haronian claims that the urge toward the sublime is common to all, but that it is often repressed or denied. Evasion of opportunities for personal growth due to fear of abandoning the familiar for the unknown, excessive fear of death, loss of a sense of community with others through emphasis on independence and personal autonomy, overvaluing the material goods of life, and excessive demands for security are all symptoms of this repression of the sublime in one's life.

In recent years there has been evidence of a renewed interest in the area of the sublime in popular American culture. News magazines contain articles dealing with God, angels, prayer, and near death experiences. The immense popularity of the book *The Celestine Prophecy* and its subsequent workbook by James Redfield and Carol Adrienne is another indication that the urge toward the sublime is gaining social acceptability. There are more opportunities to express this urge than ever before: books, tapes, retreats, workshops, etc.

Many researchers in the area of spirituality are coming to believe that the spiritual/religious/sublime urge is an innate aspect of the human being. From the need to worship the sun and rain and other elements of nature to the development of humanlike gods and goddesses, men and women have intuited some element of life that transcends themselves. They have been enormously attracted to this transcendence; they have attempted to describe and define it and institutionalize it in numerous ways. They have attempted to interact in some way with the transcendent out of a desire to grow closer, to gain knowledge, even to become an integral part of that reality in some way.

As has been stated, from very early human history, institutional religions defined and organized the way this urge for the sublime was to be experienced and acted upon by the individual and by groups of people. Both philosophical and religious views of human nature developed concurrently with the development of the ability to reflect on human experience.

Despite the second version of the creation of humankind in Genesis, with the emphasis through the centuries on the fall and sinfulness of men and women, there has been retained in the Judaic and most Christian traditions a belief—though at times a very faint belief—that human beings really are created in the image of God. The mission of Jesus, as the early Christians came to understand and interpret it, was to redeem or "save" fallen humankind, the New Testament is full of his belief in the goodness of people and his promises of a "more abundant life" available to all those who seek it. This new kind of life is based on loving God and neighbor and self—and doing so radically, beyond the bounds of conventional society. Acceptance of the "stranger" as "neighbor"—equal to and like oneself—was basic to Jesus' teachings.

As Christianity developed through the first centuries, the early Eastern Christian tradition espoused the goodness of the person far more than did Western Christianity, particularly in the mystical theology of Origen and Gregory of Nyssa. The Greeks believed that the image of the divine in the person had been damaged but not destroyed, and that the life task of male and female was to restore this image to its fullness. This process was called "deification" or "divinization" (Ruffing 1993, 47).

Roman Catholic mystics from the Middle Ages to the present have often described detailed developmental stages of psychospiritual growth toward union with God when prayer and meditation are used as the primary modes of introspection and therapeutic self-analysis. Among the greatest of these mystics, the Carmelite nun Teresa of Jesus of Avila (1515–1582), was called by William James "the expert of experts in describing such conditions." Explaining her own psychospiritual development from "sinfulness" to identification with the image of God, which she termed "spiritual marriage," Teresa provides a detailed description of the psychological stages of spiritual growth in her work *The Interior Castle.* She was a genius at introspection and presents herself in an almost Freudian stream of consciousness in narrating her spiritual autobiography.

The founder of the Jesuit order, Ignatius of Loyola (1491–1556), developed an intricate method for analysis of the self and a thirty day "treatment" program to enhance the person's relationship with God. Of his *Spiritual Exercises,* which are carried out by the person with the help of a spiritual counselor over an intense period, Ignatius claimed: "(1) that one can actually seek and find God's specific will for oneself; and (2) that God will communicate Himself to the devout soul and deal directly with the creature, and the creature directly with his Creator and Lord" (Egan 1993, 523).

The idea of oneness with the divine, fruition, of becoming whole and then transcending that "whole" self continues to exert influence to this day. In this century developmental psychologists such as Erik Erikson, M. Scott Peck, and Robert Loevinger have espoused the concepts of developmental tasks that need to be accomplished to come to full stature as a "whole" human being. Analytic psychiatrist Carl Jung spoke of "individuation" as the fullness of males and females, and humanistic psychologist Maslow asserted that the highest human needs were for self-actualization and, ultimately, self-transcendence. Existentialist Assagioli developed a parallel system based on the need for psychospiritual development, which he called "psychosynthesis." According to Keen, "Psychosynthesis insists that the needs for meaning, for higher values, for a spiritual life, are as real as biological or social needs" (1974, 98).

In *Psychosynthesis,* Assagioli lists the contributors to the psychological understanding of the potentially transcendent human being. Beginning with the initial analytical work of Freud, Adler, and Jung, he proceeds to cite the following movements: psychosomatic medicine, the psychology of religion, the investigation of the superconscious, psychical research or parapsychology, Eastern psychology, "creative understanding," the holistic approach and the psychology of the personality, interindividual and social psychology and psychiatry and the anthropological study of humankind, and "active techniques" for the treatment and development of the personality (Assagioli 1975, 14–15).

The work in transpersonal psychology of Wilber, Engler, and Brown has emerged as a strong force within the past fifteen years. These researchers have devoted themselves to the study of consciousness and its modes of transformation to the highest known levels of awareness and transcendence.

CONCLUSION

Normative views of the human have emerged within this century which include very strong attempts to incorporate the spiritual within the definition of the human being, as well as, in the description of human development, in the treatment of psychospiritual pathology, and in counseling toward the highest potentials for human growth. The historical influences of religious and spiritual thought are evident in human service direct practice.

REFERENCES

Assagioli, R. 1965. *Psychosynthesis.* New York: Viking.

Coleman, J. 1976. *Abnormal psychology and modern life.* Glenview, Ill.: Scott, Foresman.

Cowley, A. S. 1993. Transpersonal social work: A theory for the 1990's. *Social Work* 38 (5): 527–34.

Egan, H. D. 1993. Ignatian spirituality. In *The new dictionary of Catholic spirituality,* ed. Michael Downey, 521–29. Collegeville, Minn.: Liturgical Press.

Haronian, F. 1974. The repression of the sublime. *Synthesis* 1 (1): 51–62.

Kavanaugh, K., and O. Rodriguez, trans. 1976. *The collected works of Saint Teresa of Avila.* Washington, D.C.: ICS Publications.

Keen, S. 1974. The golden mean of Robert Assagioli. *Psychology Today* 8 (10): 97–107.

Lewis, N. D. C. 1941. *A short history of psychiatric achievement.* New York: Norton.

Loevinger, J. 1976. *Ego development.* San Francisco: Jossey-Bass.

Morgan, C. T., and R. A. King. 1966. *Introduction to psychology.* New York: McGraw-Hill.

New Revised Standard Version Bible.1989. New York: Oxford University Press.

Oates, W. 1957. *The religious dimensions of personality.* New York: Association Press.

Redfield, J., and C. Adrienne. 1995. *The celestine prophecy: An experiential guide.* New York: Warner Books.

Rees, T. P. 1957. Back to moral treatment and community care. *Journal of Mental Science* 103: 303–13.

Ruffing, J. K. 1993. Theological anthropology. In *The new dictionary of Catholic spirituality,* ed. Michael Downey, 47–50. Collegeville, Minn.: Liturgical Press.

Thibault, J., J. Ellor, and E. Netting. 1991. A conceptual framework for assessing the spiritual functioning and fulfillment of older adults in long-term care settings. *Journal of Religious Gerontology* 7 (4): 29–46.

Wilber, K., J. Engler, and D. Brown. 1986. *Transformations of consciousness: Conventional and contemplative perspectives on development.* Boston: New Science Library.

Chapter 3

UNDERSTANDING THE DIVERSITY OF RELIGIOUS GROUPS IN THE UNITED STATES

For many clients seen by helping professionals in the United States, religious faith is a significant part of daily life. Anthropologists have pointed out that for thousands of years, religious beliefs offered explanations for the unknown. Furthermore, religions are the earliest forms of cultural systems which offer rules for living in groups or communities. Today, religion may offer clients answers to questions raised when one doesn't understand "why bad things happen to good people." Religion may be a significant source of meaning and a critical source of hope for persons who find other emotional and service resources limited. A recent survey by the Princeton Religious Research Center indicated that 61 percent of persons surveyed said that religion can answer "all or most of today's problems." (Gallup 1990, 58).

Individuals experience religion and spirituality as a reflection of several factors, including culture, patterns established early in life, and current life experiences. The interaction of these factors make religion and spirituality a unique human experience.

The United States is a country where religious diversity is the critical element in understanding the spiritual experience. Wiggins notes, "Not only will human beings and societies continue to reckon with the reality of historic religions, but they will also have to contend with them, in their remarkable diversity of practices and beliefs, much closer to home than ever before" (1996, 1). Martin Marty and others have suggested that with cultural diversity has come religious diversity as well as a movement toward personal piety that has been particularly evident since World War II.

Our discussion starts and ends with an admonishment to listen to the client. In this chapter we can offer some useful generalizations about various religious preferences. However, it is critical to understand the religious and

44

spiritual beliefs of the client from the client's perspective, whether the client is an individual, a family, an organization, or an entire community. The first distinction that needs to be made is between "formal religious organizations" and the "personal experience of religion or spirituality." Organized religions offer statements of faith which are recited by a congregation as a declaration of mutual belief. However, if one asks ten persons in a congregation what that statement means to them, one may hear ten slightly different responses. Given the nature of spiritual diversity it is not possible to predict the elements of religion or spirituality that are more likely to be important to the individual client. The personal experiences of religion are colored by numerous variables including personality and life experience, culture, and even the presence of individual or family pathologies. One must remember also that on the other side of this discussion is the power of religion to leave the person feeling rejected. This is particularly powerful when it reflects issues of lifestyle or disagreement with religiously defined moral preference.

We begin with a brief examination of world religions. The purpose of this section is to offer a starting point for dialogue about these traditions. It does not replace the need to talk directly with informed persons from these religious traditions who can more fully explain the important elements of their beliefs and practices. We will then focus on the nature of religious diversity in the United States. We attempt to set a stage for understanding that religious diversity exists among world traditions as well as within each faith community.

EXAMINING WORLD RELIGIOUS TRADITIONS

Working with individual clients or groups of clients should always begin by listening to that individual or group's understanding of what their faith tradition means to them. It can be useful to know something about the religious tradition with which the individual or group associates as a supplement to the perspective of the client. One way to do this larger investigation is to seek an expert from that tradition who can assist the service provider. For example, local clergy (ministers, priests, or rabbis), shaman, or philosophers can be helpful interpreters.

In this section we offer a brief outline of some of the important features of the various religious traditions commonly found in the United States. However, this selection is based on the statistical presence of various groups. This dialogue is intended to offer a model for the types of information needed to work with someone from a religious tradition that is not fully understood by the human service worker. We are painfully aware that we are unable to address every aspect of religious practice. Particularly missing are data on the rich variety of New Age traditions. Further, the human service worker should examine the voices of persons of color as well as feminist theologies. The following religious groups will be discussed briefly: Christianity (Catholicism, Protestantism, Orthodox Christianity), Judaism, Islam, Hinduism, and Buddhism. Each of these groups offers a rich history as well as theological, philosophical, and ethical traditions. However, in this brief format, we have only tried to develop a guide to understanding the practice of the various faith traditions. Readers interested in greater depth should obtain additional materials. (See: Berry 1971, Bullis 1996, Canada 1986, Canada 1988, Canada and Phaobtong 1992, Hopfe 1994, McDowell and Stewart 1992, Neusner 1994, Rowan 1993). In selecting these materials, be aware that one has to go to persons from the tradition one is trying to study in order to hear the voices of those persons who are from that tradition. Most texts found in bookstores in the United States which discuss the world religious traditions are written by Christian authors and thus the information is filtered through the lenses of persons who are outside of that tradition.

According to the Christian author Hopfe (1994) traditional study of world religions identifies three useful groups. "Religions Originating in the Middle East, Religions Originating in India, and Religions Originating in China and Japan." (See Figure 1) In order to focus our discussion, we will discuss elements of two of these groups, religions of the Middle East and those originating in India. These have been selected due to the numbers of persons who believe in these traditions found in the United States.

When investigating a religious tradition, some of the important questions to ask reflect the specific concerns of the client. In a more general context, however, it is important to know some simple facts about the faith tradition in order to be sensitive to the client's spiritual needs. These would include topics like, name of the founder (if any), name of the holy books, some key beliefs and practices, the major sects or schools of thought within the tradition, some history of the tradition, and especially the holidays commonly celebrated. Names of the founder, holy books, and even the name for God(s) are important since the client may reference them. To have some idea what they refer to will aid in understanding the context of the client's discussion. Key beliefs are important as beliefs frame many questions about life, particularly in terms of suffering and death. The schools of thought may matter if the person is from a tradition which is common in the United States, but the sect or school isn't. In this case the individual may still feel displaced in this country even if there are others from their basic faith tradition. Some history of the tradition will also

The World Religions Organized in Traditional Perspective

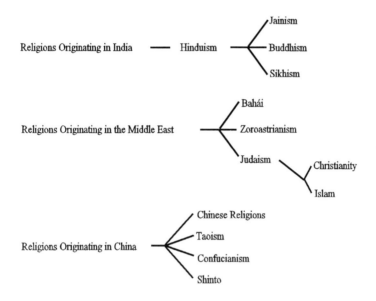

Figure 1

help to acclimate the human service worker to the concerns of the client. Finally, the holidays of importance will impact everything from specific concerns raised to scheduling. The material that follows reflects these data.

Judaism

Judaism is one of the four oldest and most significant religions in the United States and has its origins in the Middle East. From the fertile foundations of Judaism have come several of the major world traditions, including Christianity and Islam. Both of these newer faith traditions continue many of the practices and beliefs of their Jewish ancestors.

Founder. There is not a single founder of the Jewish tradition. Rather, Judaism traces its beginnings to the biblical holy men or patriarchs. Starting with Abraham, a number of patriarchs helped to shape the beliefs and consciousness of the community found today in modern Judaism.

47

Scripture. The Jewish scriptures were originally written and are often read today in Hebrew. This is largely the same text that is called the "Old Testament" by Christians. The first five books are referred to as the Torah and hold special significance as they reflect the covenant God made with the Jewish people as well as the laws, which include the Ten Commandments. The other books and rabbinical writings add historical as well as ethical and theological significance. Also important, though not considered to be scripture, are the historical writings of key rabbis in the Rabbinic Literature, such as the Talmud.

Key Beliefs. The Jewish community was distinct from its neighbors in ancient times because they worshiped one God, who created all things and was therefore God of all things. This God reflected qualities of judgement as well as mercy. This God made a covenant, a type of mutual contract, with the Jews promising to care and protect them. During the time of the prophets, after the era of the great Kings of Israel, a Messiah was promised. He would be a leader anointed by God. Jews continue to wait for this Messiah.

Practices. Jewish congregations worship in synagogues or temples. Saturday, the seventh day of the week, as commanded in the Ten Commandments is known as the Sabbath, the day of rest and worship. Services of worship are commonly held on Friday evening and Saturday. Because each day begins with sundown, the Sabbath begins at sundown on Friday and ends at sundown on Saturday. Worship consists of the reading of scripture, chanting or singing, and prayer. Worship may be conducted in part or in whole in Hebrew.

Schools and Sects. Historically, Judaism has developed into three major branches. While today some other branches also exist, the three largest groups are Orthodox, Reform, and Conservative. Orthodox Judaism is the most "conservative." Orthodox Jews observe the laws of clean and unclean foods and purification known as "keeping kosher." Conservative Judaism is the most recent of the three branches and offers a middle ground between Orthodox and Reform Judaism. Reform Judaism is strong in the United States. It is understood by many to be the more "liberal" branch. Reform Jews follow the "spirit" of the Jewish traditions, but modify some of the traditional laws of conduct and ritual. In many cases this can include relinquishment of the dietary restrictions.

History. Judaism reflects the rich history of the Middle East. Significant to the history of Judaism is the coalition of diverse Semitic tribes and the movement of many Israelites both into and then out of Egypt. Led by Moses, the Hebrew people left Egypt (in a departure referred to as the Exodus) to find the place which Hebrew scripture called the promised land. Along the way, Hebrew scripture records that God gave to Moses the Ten Commandments which continue to be the basis for some civil and religious laws in the United States.

About 1000 B.C.E. major Kings, David and Solomon, brought the various subgroups of the Jewish community together into a single kingdom. After the reign of David's son Solomon, the kingdom was divided into two, one in the north, Israel, and one in the south, Judah. Both kingdoms eventually fell to neighboring kingdoms. When Judah fell to the Babylonians, Jews were taken as slaves. At that time Solomon's temple at Jerusalem was destroyed. When the slaves were freed, they returned to rebuild the temple. Around 100 B.C.E. this region was again conquered, this time by the Romans. As the result of a revolt in 70 C.E., the temple was again destroyed, and the Jewish people were again dispersed over the known world. The modern state of Israel was founded in 1948.

Judaism has survived in many parts of the world. Although some Jews have always lived in the Middle East, many others migrated to Europe, especially Spain, France, Germany, Poland, and Western Russia. In many cases, such as in Germany, Jews were invited in to the country and then in subsequent generations persecuted for being Jewish. The story of the Jewish community historically reflects tremendous persecution at the hands of Christians and other religious groups.

Holidays. While there are many important holidays celebrated in the Jewish faith, four of the most commonly celebrated are Passover, Chanukah, Rosh Hashanah, and Yom Kippur.

Passover commemorates the Exodus. Rosh Hashanah is the Jewish New Year. According to tradition, "the completely wicked are inscribed in the Book of Death on Rosh Hashanah, the completely virtuous in the Book of Life, while for the in-betweens judgement is suspended until Yom Kippur" (Bowker 1997, 824). Yom Kippur is the Day of Atonement, a time of prayer and remembrance. It is the most important day in the Jewish calendar. Chanukah is a feast of dedication in which "Jews celebrate one of the few holidays not associated with the Exodus. In 165 B.C.E., Judas Maccabaeus retook the Temple from the Syrian Greeks and rededicated it. Only one small container of oil was available for lighting the temple. It should have lasted only one day. Miraculously, however, the oil lasted for eight days" (Hopfe 1994, 299). In purely religious terms Chanukah is a minor holiday, and in some nations Jews do not celebrate it.

Clergy. The clergy in Judaism are called rabbis. The rabbi is a specially educated individual who offers leadership and insight into Scripture and the laws, as well as care and support for members of the Jewish community.

Christianity

Sociologists divide the various Christian traditions in the United States up into subgroups in numerous ways. Some categorize them by theology, others by historical traditions, still others by practices. We will discuss three subgroups: Protestant, Roman Catholic, and Orthodox. The largest group is the Protestants, with an estimated 134,900,000 members in the United States; Roman Catholics number 86,500,000, and Orthodox Christians 5,800,000 (Wright 1996, 383).

Founder. Christianity traces its origin to Jesus. Many Middle Eastern religions consider Jesus an important prophet, but to Christians he is the son of God. The Julian and Gregorian calendars were designed to begin with the traditional year of Jesus' birth. Scholars now believe he actually lived from the year 3 B.C.E. to 30 C.E. He was born, lived, and died in the Middle East. He was raised in a traditional Jewish family, and according to Christian Scripture, he is the Messiah awaited by the Jewish people for thousands of years.

Scripture. The central book for Christians is the Bible. It contains two sections, one that reflects the Jewish heritage called Hebrew Scripture or the Old Testament, most of which was originally written in Hebrew. The writings that resulted from the life of Jesus Christ and his disciples are called the Greek Scriptures or New Testament, most of which was originally written in either Greek or Aramaic. Christians understand that both the principles of Hebrew Scripture and those of the Greek Scriptures are relevant to living according to their faith tradition. Thus, for example, both the Ten Commandments and the words of Christ and his disciples are important. It should be understood, however, that the amount of use of both texts or even the Bible itself will vary from person to person and denomination to denomination.

Key Beliefs. Traditionally, Christians believe that there is one God, revealed in three persons, God the Father (the creator), God the Son (Jesus Christ, the redeemer), and the Holy Spirit (the sanctifier). Through his virgin birth, death on the cross, and resurrection from the dead, Christ is understood to be the Son of God and to have restored sinful humanity to a "right" relationship with God, abolishing the finality of human death.

Practices. Practices vary widely from one denominational group to the next. Most observe the ritual of baptism, administered to children, young adults, or to newly converted members as a sign of admission into the Christian community. The Eucharist, or Communion, which commemorates the last Passover supper of Jesus Christ and involves consumption of bread and wine in remembrance of him, is also an important ritual.

Most Christians belong to a congregation which gathers in a church.

Churches are generally members of a denomination. The practices of an individual congregation will vary from one to the next, based both on cultural and local preferences and those of the denomination. Worship, for example, is generally on either Sunday morning or Saturday evening, though it is sometimes on Friday evening.

Schools and Sects.   Historically, two principal divisions occurred among Christians. Christianity grew to prominence within the Roman Empire. As that empire broke up, the religion underwent the first of the two splits. In 1054 C.E. the Eastern, or Orthodox, church and the Western, or Roman, church separated (Rausch and Voss 1993, 167). There are several different explanations of this separation. In the United States, the Eastern Church comprises such groups as the Russian Orthodox, the Greek Orthodox, and the Eastern Orthodox.

The second great split, which involved the Western church, came in the sixteenth and seventeenth centuries. Beginning with the actions of the reformer Martin Luther and others, it led to many new denominations of Protestant ("protesting") Christians. Numerous other groups broke away from the Roman Church both before and after this time. Although the Roman Catholic Church is estimated to be the largest Christian group worldwide, the many Protestant denominations collectively outnumber Catholics. All three traditions have been involved in extensive missionary efforts through the years bringing persons of many cultures and ethnic backgrounds together.

History.   The first Christians were Middle Eastern Jews whose lives were influenced by Jesus. Jesus called upon twelve men as his original disciples. After Jesus was put to death, they and their followers spread the faith to the various parts of the Middle East. Some went north into present day Turkey and Greece, others went west into Egypt and North Africa. Each missionary group had a slightly different emphasis or interpretation of the events of Jesus' life and death. From the beginning, much effort was expended to bring these groups together and maintain a single message. However, over time Christianity has formally and informally split into many different denominations, representing various ways of interpreting the teaching of Jesus.

Holidays.   The critical holidays for the various Christian groups are reflected in the everyday calendars of citizens of the United States. The most important are Christmas, celebrating the birth of Jesus, and Easter, commemorating his resurrection after death. Many other holidays and memorial dates are important to specific groups of Christians. Not all Christians celebrate these holidays on the same date. For example, Christmas is celebrated on December 25 in the Roman Catholic and most Protestant churches, but on January 7 by some Orthodox denominations. Seventh Day Adventists and Jehovah's Witnesses, respectively, recognize Saturday and Friday, not Sunday, as the Sabbath.

Clergy. The clergy—ministers or priests—in most Christian churches are key to both the work of the congregation as well as to the visibility of their congregations within the larger community. Although clergy may not be able to provide services needed by clients of human service workers, they generally know about community resources, and they are often gatekeepers for their congregations' activities.

Islam

Islam is the second Middle Eastern tradition whose foundation can be traced to Judaism. Founded after Christianity, it was seen as a corrective for both Judaism and Christianity. Muslims in the United States are a diverse group reflecting both the wealth of the religious tradition and the many cultures whose members embrace it.

Founder. Islam was founded by Muhammad, whom believers regard as a prophet of God. Muhammad was born about 570 C.E. in Mecca and died in 632 C.E. in Medina. Both cities are in present day Saudi Arabia.

Scripture. Holy Scripture in Islam is the Koran. This book, originally written in Arabic, is considered to be the word of God, given to Muhammad by the angel Gabriel. Even when English words are applied to the text, they are understood to be transliterated, not translated. To a Muslim, this is understood to mean that the original text and its meaning is always preserved. Like many holy texts, Muslims treat the Koran with reverence. It is never touched casually. To read the Koran, one must first insure that the reader has cleansed his or her hands and is spiritually ready to read this holy book.

Key Beliefs. The teachings of Muhammad are based on both Judaism and Christianity. Muhammad preached that there is only one God, who is called Allah. Muslims recognize the history of the ancient Jews and the prophets of Hebrew Scripture; they also recognize and honor the prophets and understand Jesus to be a prophet of God also. However, the teachings of Muhammad in the Koran constitute a distinct new revelation; Muhammad is regarded as the last and perfect prophet.

Practices. The main religious duties of Muslims, referred to as the Five Pillars of Islam, can be summarized as follows:

1. To profess faith in a statement that may be translated, "There is only one God, and Muhammad is his prophet."
2. To pray five times each day, facing in the direction of Mecca. Visitors

to Islamic countries will hear criers in tall minarets to tell the people when to pray.

3. To give alms for the support of the faith and the poor.
4. To observe a solemn fast during Ramadan, the ninth month in the Islamic calendar.
5. To make, at least once in a lifetime, a pilgrimage to either Mecca (for Sunni Muslims) or Karbala, in northern Iraq (for Shi'ite Muslims).

Muslims follow many of the Jewish dietary laws, including abstinence from pork. The principal weekly worship is conducted at noon on Fridays. The Muslim house of worship is known as a mosque.

Schools and Sects. Although most Muslims agree on basic principles, there are several subgroups. In the United States the two major subgroups, the Sunni and the Shi'ite. The Sunni are more numerous worldwide, constituting about 85 percent of all Muslims. The Shi'ite tradition is a smaller group which has split from the Sunni tradition over the succession of authority from Muhammad.

Islam, like Christianity, in the Untied States reflects other schisms between groups of adherents. Some of these are based more on religious principles, others seem to be more involved in culture. It is impossible in this format to mention all of the possible groups. One group, however, which is particularly visible in the media is the Nation of Islam. About a third of the Muslims in the United States are found in the African American community. In the first half of the twentieth century, a number of African Americans converted to Islam and established their own religious movements. The Nation of Islam, founded by Elijah Muhammad, is the most prominent of these groups. According to Esposito: "Elijah Muhammad's message of black separatism, with its denunciation of 'white devils,' created suspicion and fear among many white Americans, as well as Muslim immigrants, all of whom regarded it as a radical organization. After the death of Elijah Muhammad in 1975, his son, Warith D. Muhammad, succeeded him. Warith D. Muhammad subsequently rejected the separatist teachings of his father and brought many of his other teachings into line more closely with Islamic belief and practice. By 1985, he had integrated his organization into the worldwide Muslim community" (1994, 255). Some controversy continues regarding this organization because of Louis Farrakhan and some of his views, which do not seem to always be embraced by other groups within the Muslim tradition.

History. Islam had its origin in the Arabian desert during a time when Byzantine Christianity and Judaism were geographic neighbors and recurrently the source of government for the major cities. Just before the rise of this new religious tradition, Christianity was in conflict with itself. The people of Arabia were also familiar with the Jewish tradition. It is not clear as to the origins of the various tribes, but it is speculated that some of them may have been forced out of Judea when the Romans put down rebellion in the land in 70 C.E. and again in 135 C.E. (Esposito 1994, 364). These influences seem to have come together along with other local traditions to form the fertile ground upon which the new revelation given to Muhammad could be planted.

Holidays. The month in the Muslim calendar that is the most important is Ramadan. During this month, Muslims are committed to fasting and prayer. A pilgrimage, is called the Hajj. (Members of the Sunni community make their journey to Mecca, members of the Shi'ite community make their pilgrimage to Karbala in Iraq.) It is generally performed during the last month of the Islamic calendar, Zil-Hajj. In the Muslim calendar there are two annual feasts, the Feast of Fast-breaking which ends the month of Ramadan celebrating the return to a normal routine, and the Feast of Sacrifice which "commemorates the time when Abraham was commanded by God to sacrifice his son, Ishmael." (Hopfe 1994, 391) Two other events are celebrated, the New Year, which comes during the month of Muharram as the beginning of the Muslim calendar, and the Birthday of the prophet Muhammad, which is celebrated on the twelfth day of the third month of the Muslim calendar. The birthdays of other Muslim saints are also remembered by different groups within the Muslim community.

Clergy. Answering the question, "what should a good Muslim be doing?" became the job of the Islamic scholars who devoted their lives to study, debate, and spelling out as fully as possible God's law. (Eposito 1994, 246) These individuals are the teachers and guardians of the faith.

Hinduism

Hinduism is one of, if not *the* oldest of the major world religions. Hinduism is bound culturally and historically to India. Many Hindus live outside of India, including a large group in the United States. Hinduism is the third largest of the world traditions behind Christianity, and Islam.

Founder. There is not a single founder of this tradition. As one of the oldest religions, its origins have been obscured by time. Some aspects and artifacts can be dated before 3000 b.c.e. Hinduism has been through many different stages and changes during 5000 years of practice. Hinduism is the founding source of two other major religious traditions, Buddhism, and

Sikhism. Hopfe (1994) notes, "The word Hindu comes from the Sanskrit name for the river Indus, Sindhu" (76).

Scripture. The Hindu traditions span both culture and time. Thus, it also reflects many different sacred writings. As one might expect, a religion that is as old and rich as Hinduism has a large number of holy or sacred books. These books are divided into two groups, the Sruti or "what is heard" and the Smriti or what the seers saw or heard (McDowell and Stewart 1992, 288). Within these groups there are the books of the law, as well as the stories and legends which offer substance to the beliefs of modern Hindus. These include the Vedas, the Ramayana and the Mahabharata, the Bhagavadgita, and the Upanishads. These texts include hymns, prayers, rituals, and philosophy. All were first written in Sanskrit, which is the ancient language still taught by devoted followers.

Key Beliefs. Hinduism recognizes many different gods. Brahma, the creator, Vishnu, who preserves the world, and Siva, the god of destruction are among the most important. Hindus have a deep respect for all living things. This includes insects and animals. The most holy animal is the cow. Hindus do not kill cattle for their meat.

When the Hindu believer dies, it is said that the soul sheds its body. The believer understands that his or her soul lives on and appears in a new body. This is called reincarnation. If the soul has performed good things in this life, he or she may reappear as a person of higher standing. The soul who does not may reappear as a lower life form. In this country, one of the most commonly known practices is that of Hatha Yoga. In this practice, the student learns body and emotionally based exercises. In western countries this practice is often separated from the original religious heritage and taught as a form of holistic health.

Practice. The practice of the Hindu tradition is mostly understood in the context of the family. There is no regular worship or meeting place. Individual shrines are developed in private homes and some significant shrines have been built in places of significance all over the world.

Hindu temples are buildings that have been dedicated to a particular god or group of gods. Priests at the temple are caretakers for all that the temple stands for. Periodically, a temple will celebrate a holy day in honor of the god of the temple. On that day, many of the faithful will come to worship and participate in the event. The traditional practice of observing the caste or division of the people into four major groups plus one that are the outcasts was outlawed by the British in 1950, but is still practiced in many areas of India.

Schools and Sects. Ancient religions like Hinduism cannot be understood by taking a snapshot of the tradition at a single time and then making assumptions. Rather, such religions need to be understood as having evolved. Hindus understand life as an endless cycle of birth, life, death, and rebirth. Sometimes referred to as reincarnation, Hinduism understands that life is governed by the continuing behaviors of the individual. The word "karma means action" and refers to the actions that contribute to what the person is becoming (Larson 1994, 187). In the Hindu tradition the actions that one experiences in this life do not just contribute to the quality of this life, but to the hierarchy of living forms. Larson refers to Karma as a "law of cause and effect" in the universe (1994, 177).

The Hindu tradition offers a strong connection between the person and knowledge, and the person and the environment. Living things are sacred, even the smallest life forms. The knowledge of the faith is critical for understanding all of the various aspects of life. Hopfe notes, "therefore, humankind's basic problem is not wickedness, but ignorance" (1994, 105).

Larson suggests that there are "five basic types of Hinduism in America: Secular Hinduism, Nonsectarian Hinduism, Bhakti or Devotional Hinduism, Reformist-Nationalist Neo-Hinduism, and Guru-Internationalist-Missionizing Neo-Hinduism" (1994, 196). The Hindu concept of God reflects this same diversity; however, it is difficult to explain to persons from outside the faith. One reads of the various gods and goddesses of Hinduism and assumes there to be more than one, yet for the modern Hindu, there is "one, all-pervasive Supreme Being." (Larson 1994, 197)

In practice Hinduism has many different sects and subgroups. When working with clients of this faith tradition, the human service worker will need to inquire of the individual how he or she understands his or her faith and tradition.

History. Larson notes, "altogether it is useful to identify six such fundamental periods for the development of Hinduism: the Indus Valley Period (circa 3000–1500 B.C.E.), the Brahmanical Period (circa 1500—600 B.C.E.), the Buddhist and Shramana Period (circa 600 B.C.E.—300 C.E.), the Classical Hindu Period (circa 300—1200, C.E.), the Muslim Period (circa 1200–1757 C.E.), and the Modern Period (circa 1757—Present)" (1994, 180). Different authors disagree as to both the names and time frames of these periods, but all agree that periods similar to the above are critical to understanding both the evolution of Hinduism and its diversity.

Holidays. Hindus celebrate three major holy days. The first is *Holi* celebrated in February/March, and for the purpose of welcoming the onset of spring. It is dedicated to the God Krishna. During this time many of the caste and taboo restrictions are set aside. *Divali* welcomes the New Year. Celebrated in November, this festival of lights is associated with the goddesses Kali and Lakshmi. It is believed that "Lakshmi visits every house that is lit with a lamp and brings to it prosperity and good fortune" (Hopfe 1994, 112). Dasehra occurs in October and honors Durga, a consort of Siva. "Presents are exchanged. There are dances and processions in honor of the Goddess." (Hopfe 1994, 112)

Clergy. In the sense that Christians or Jews would understand clergy, the Hindu religion does not support such a role. The various temples have priests who care for the temple and scholars who offer the great philosophies of this tradition, but since there are no congregations as understood in Christianity, Judaism, and Islam there are also no clergy.

Buddhism

Buddhism is a religious tradition whose roots were developed in the environment of Hinduism and is over two thousand years old. While Buddhism originated in India, most of its followers are currently found in the east, particularly East Asia. Buddhism has come to the United States with its Asian immigrants and has had an impact on American society. From the martial arts to the values for nature as seen in some of our gardening practices, many persons in the United States would be surprised at how much influence Buddhism has had.

Founder. Scholars suggest Buddhism began with a man named Siddhartha Gautama who lived about five hundred years before Christ in what is now southern India. According to the sacred writings of the Buddhist tradition, Siddhartha Gautama was born into a royal family. As a prince of great wealth, he could have lived the enjoyable life style of his family. At the age of 29 he received a series of visions which persuaded him to leave his home in search of enlightenment and the reason for human suffering. He wandered for many years until one day he was sitting under a bo tree in a village and he was granted enlightenment. His followers soon referred to him as the "Enlightened One," or Buddha. Siddhartha Gautama, the Buddha, spent the rest of his life in northern India sharing his understanding of life. He is believed to have lived approximately 80 years.

Scripture. Several holy writings are important in this religious tradition. Central for most Buddhists is the Tripitika, which means "Three Baskets." This is a collection of sayings and rules for the conduct of life written down by the followers of Buddha.

Key Beliefs. One key element of Buddhism is a shared belief with Hinduism in reincarnation. Like Hinduism, when Buddhists die, they return as persons of greater comfort and wealth. Unlike Hinduism, Buddhism teaches that there is an end to this cycle of birth, death, and rebirth. Buddha taught that the individual could seek a state of detachment from worldly concerns called nirvāna. Achieving the state of nirvāna would bring true contentment and an end to the cycle for the soul.

Practices. Collective rituals play only a small part in Buddhism. While prayer and visiting sacred temples are an important practice, by comparison with Christian and Jewish traditions, most of the practice of Buddhism occurs at home. Emphasis is on the inner life. From the earliest records of this tradition, it is clear that orders of monks were developed to live apart from the world in a simple life of meditation. Some persons come into the temple for training and leave as lay persons, others stay and join the order for life.

Schools and Sects. There are major divisions of Buddhism, the Theravada and Mahayana schools. Theravada is prominent in Sri Lanka, Burma, Thailand, and Cambodia. Mahayana is more common in Tibet, China, and Japan and emphasizes the importance of each person's becoming more like Buddha through compassion and actions, along with meditation. Tibetan Buddhism developed "its own character" (Bowker 1997, 975). Many of the elements of Tibetan Buddhism were grounded in the distinct character of the Buddhist tradition in India and to some extent in China. The strength of the monastic movement, which at one time included 25 percent of the male population of the country and the emphasis on the oral teacher disciple transmission are key features in this tradition (Bowker 1997, 975).

The sectarian landscape of Buddhism, like that of Christianity and most other religions, reflects both the thought of persons continuing to consider the truths of the faith as well as the historic political and geographical conflicts. For example near the end of the eighth century C.E., the overland route between China and India was blocked at the western end by Muslim armies, preventing the dialogue which had kept these two great continents together in understanding their beliefs (Bowker 1997, 174). Thus, Chinese schools developed that had somewhat different interpretations of fundamental belief. Different groups also sprang up in Korea and Japan as the result of the various adaptations of culture and geography. Many of the differences are reflective of emphasis rather than major differences in fundamental belief.

History. By comparison with the Middle Eastern religions, (Judaism, Christianity, and Islam), Buddhism is a nontheistic approach to life. Theologically, Buddhism is not oriented to a personal God, rather it is oriented to the meaning of life as experienced in the context of the natural world. After the awakening, Siddhartha, or the Buddha, engaged in a quest for enlightenment. He started out by seeking enlightenment, or understanding, through philosophy and then through asceticism or self-discipline. However, "apparently, the turning point in Gautama's quest came one day when he was walking near a stream. Because he had been terribly weakened by his ordeals, he fainted and fell into the stream. The cold water revived him; when he was able to contemplate his situation, he realized that although he had done everything that could be expected of an ascetic, he still had not found satisfaction" (Hopfe 1994, 40). After realizing that questing through physical discipline for enlightenment did not seem to have worked, he turned to meditation. "In his meditation, the Buddha had satisfaction" (Hopfe 1994, 40). Gautama turned from asceticism to meditation, and by this means, while sitting under a tree in a village, he suddenly attained enlightenment. He "had a vision of the endless cycle of birth and death that is the lot of humankind. It was revealed to him that people were bound to this cycle because of *tanha* ('desire,' 'thirst,' 'craving') which causes deep human suffering. It is desire that causes karma and thus fetters people. The Buddha had desired enlightenment and had sought it through asceticism and knowledge, but it had eluded him. When he had ceased to desire, he found enlightenment" (Hopfe 1994, 141).

The Buddhist understanding of appropriate living is reflected in the "three stages of perfection, virtue (Sila), a deepening inner awareness (Samadhi), and saving wisdom (Panna)." The famous "Eightfold Path" is divided into these three concepts: "right speech, right action, and right livelihoods which are associated with the class of virtue. Right effort, right mindfulness, and right concentration are in the class of concentration. Right views and right purposes are in the class of wisdom" (Berry 1971, 151). Buddhism's understanding of the human condition is referred to as the Four Noble Truths. These truths refer to the truth of pain suffered by human beings and point to the relief of that pain as coming from the noble Eightfold Path of living. Although only a monk or nun can fully follow the Eightfold Path, it serves as an ideal for all Buddhists.

The diversity of those persons who practice Buddhism is reflected in the individualism of the message of enlightenment as well as in the cultures and experience of this religious tradition in the various countries in which it is practiced. Buddhism has temples and images of the Buddha for purposes of meditation, but Buddhists do not center their week around attendance of a worship service or listening to a learned person. In many ways, for the Buddhist, every minute is a pilgrimage into spiritual enlightenment for the person who is willing to experience it.

Holidays. The Buddhist celebrates four important holy days. The New Year, which is in April, is celebrated with three days of preparation for the expectation for time to come. Buddha's birthday, celebrated on April 8 in China and Japan and on the last full moon in May in Southeast Asia, is a joyful event and a time to renew or wash statues of the Buddha in the temples. During July in Japan and August in China, "Buddhists believe that purgatory is opened and the souls of the dead are allowed to wander about the world. Out of compassion, families leave gifts of food for these wandering spirits" (Hopfe 1994, 159). Finally, "in November, at the end of the rainy season, Theravada Buddhists celebrate the sending forth of the first Buddhist missionaries" (Hopfe 1994, 159).

Clergy. After Gautama achieved enlightenment, his ascetic friends observed the change in him and accepted his teaching. They became his first followers, or *Sangha* (similar to a monastic order in Catholicism). These persons, often referred to as priests, perform some of the functions of clergy, in terms of interpretation of sacred scripture and models of persons following their belief, as understood in Christianity or Judaism. However, due to the individual emphasis of Buddhism, they are not "leaders of a flock" or congregation as in a church or synagogue.

MAJOR RELIGIOUS GROUPS IN THE UNITED STATES

The first religions in the United States were those of the Native Americans. Each tribal community tended to have its own religious traditions. While these traditions had elements in common, the original diversity of religious beliefs in this country reflect the diversity of the first inhabitants. When Europeans arrived, they also brought with them their own religious beliefs and practices. Persons from Spanish, French, Polish, Portuguese, and Italian speaking countries tended to bring Roman Catholicism, the English brought both the Church of England as well as other Protestant groups, the Scandinavian and Germanic groups brought the Lutheran denominations. Jews also came to this country from several different European countries. The practice of African religions were restricted, as the Europeans brought most Africans to this country as slaves, but they brought African religious influences. As each immigrating group has come to this country, along with other elements of their culture, religious traditions emerged. Thus the demography of religion in this country reflects the practices of those who were here, or who have come here.

TABLE 1
Religious Adherence in the United States (1990)

Group	Percentage
Roman Catholic	26.2
Other Christian	60.3
Jewish	1.8
Islamic	0.3
All other non-Christian groups	0.9
Agnostic	0.7
No Religion	7.5
Refused response to survey	2.3

Source: Adopted from Kosmin 1990, 3–4

Religious Demographics

Table 1 gives the percentages of self-reported adherence to major religions in the United States. Surveys of this kind generally underreport members of Native American groups, as well as other major religions of the world.
However, it does confirm a generalization that this country is made up of persons who adhere largely to some form of Christianity, 86 percent (Kosmin
1991, 3–4). Studies have also shown that the fastest growing groups are from
the other world religions. The percentages found in Table 1 may also fail to reflect the religious demography of any specific community. For example, in the
city of Chicago, Illinois it is estimated that over 60 percent of adults identify
with the Roman Catholic Church. The percentage of Catholics is not as large
in many other parts of the country.

Religious Elements

While more than half of all persons in the United States belong to the
group identified as Protestant/Christian, there are eight different elements or
categories in religion that merit discussion. The material in this section is intended to be a brief description and is not intended to replace a complete investigation into any one of these rich religious traditions. We recommend
further reading in this area as well as the possibility of a consultant who can
be contacted for dialogue if aspects of a client's religious experience are not
understood by a human service provider. (See: Hopfe 1994, McDowell and
Stewart 1992, Neusner 1994).

In considering any of the religious traditions discussed in this chapter, it becomes obvious that denominations and religious groups are no more static than the people who comprise their memberships. Depending on the age of the client, he or she may not be able to worship in the church or synagogue that utilizes the same name as the one he or she attended as a child. This is due to the various mergers and changes, particularly in the Protestant and Roman Catholic traditions. Possibly the best known change in a denomination is found in the Roman Catholic Church. This happened as the result of a meeting of the Second Vatican Council, often referred to as Vatican II, in the 1960s. As the result of this event, the worship and practice experiences of the members have been significantly changed.

In Protestant Christian denominations, there have been numerous mergers. For example, two different groups of Lutherans came together to form the current Evangelical Lutheran Church in America, and two Presbyterian denominations formed the largest Presbyterian Church in the United States of America (PCUSA). These changes were radical at the level of the denominational structures, but in many ways they were not as radical in terms of practice as was Vatican II for the Roman Catholics. Possibly the more significant impact was in terms of ethnic and national identities which accompanied the denominational identities rather than the ritual experience itself. Changes in hymnals and prayer books are also significant changes that have had an impact on the religious experience. The significance to clients at the individual, organizational and community levels, particularly when working with older clients who are long time members of faith traditions, should be acknowledged.

Basic Elements of a Religion

In his classic text on comparative religions Hopfe (1994) notes that there are eight common features found in all religions:

1. *animism,* a belief that the world is filled with souls or spirits;
2. *divination,* the supposed ability of some persons to foresee the future;
3. *magic,* the notion that the performance of some ritual action will produce a desired result;
4. *myth,* a story that might be historically inaccurate but has philosophical meaning;
5. *ritual,* the specifically religious acts or practices of a faith tradition; however, the word also implies something similar to Erikson's use of it in describing children who perform repetitious activities. These activities are meaningful, either in the origin of the act or in the repetition of the act.

6. *sacrifice,* originally referring to the killing of an animal (or even a human being) to propitiate a god, but now used for other acts intended to bridge the gap between human beings and deities;
7. *taboo,* used by Freud and others to denote the avoidance of something for religious or spiritual reasons;
8. *totem,* also used by Freud and indicating a spiritual or religious kinship within a group (for example, in many Native American tribal communities, groups claimed kinship based on animal totems—"snake people," "owl people," and so on).

Hopfe (1994) argues that from these common elements of the basic religions, various practices and beliefs have evolved. It should be noted that if clients believe in a personal spirituality, but not a formal religion, then a more personal definition of these elements and others may need to be explored.

Another thread of commonality reflects religion's relationship to culture. Various religious traditions reflect the many cultures in which they are and have been practiced. In the case of African Americans and Hispanic Americans, the majority of the denominations often fail to acknowledge the contributions of these groups until they experience worship in another country where this influence has not been felt. Particularly in Protestant traditions, the voices of women are having a new impact that will be added to the traditional voices of women in the church.

One of the ironies of religious diversity in the United States is that while this country started out as a place for various religious groups to be able to practice their faith traditions, each group had its own strong, often excessive opinions as to the "right way" to practice their religion. The Pilgrims rejected individuals who did not follow the rules of the elders, and the various European groups rejected the religious beliefs of the Native Americans.

In many European countries from which the founders of the United States Constitution came, there were "state religions." State religions were specific religious traditions which were mandated by the monarchy or rulers of the country. Other religious groups were often only marginally tolerated. Jews, for example, suffered significant persecution in both Spain and Germany on different occasions. Many of the Protestant reform groups which are the forerunners of the Lutheran, Presbyterian, and Baptist denominations as they exist in this country date back to a time when there was a persecution of their founders by the Roman Catholic hierarchy in their countries of origin. More recently, in this country, various religious groups have persecuted others by excluding them from living in specific areas or joining specific clubs. Clearly, the United

States is a country where freedom of religion is espoused, but in which politicians and citizens are often intolerant of religious preferences that differ from their own. This is a country where many different religious groups are allowed to practice their faith by law, but may still be persecuted by their fellow citizens.

In today's political climate, the assumption is made that the United States is a "Christian" country. When statistics on denominational preference are collected, the majority of respondents do indeed affiliate with Christianity. To assume, however, that one faith tradition should superimpose specific values on the entire country generally offends as many Christians as it does persons from other religious traditions. It also fails to reflect the needs and concerns of persons from other religious traditions who have played important roles in the development of this country. If we shift the focus to the needs of individual clients, even such simple assumptions as the dates of holidays can create difficulty. For example, in the Eastern Orthodox tradition, Christmas is not celebrated on December 25, as the Orthodox traditions follow a different calendar. Because this tradition is different, some persons will make the assumption that they are wrong to celebrate at a slightly different time. This assumption fails to reflect both the diverse needs of individuals as well as the realities of church history. This example may be more dramatically seen by persons from other world traditions. For example, since the Gulf War with Iraq, Muslims in the United States have seen renewed persecution both as individuals and as a group.

Diversity in religious practice suggests that the human service worker needs to be careful to listen to the spiritual needs and concerns of the individual. Each person expresses his or her faith differently. Even though persons on questionnaires can pick a specific religious tradition, they often do not believe everything that is taught in that tradition. Thus, even if the human service worker feels he or she knows something about a particular religious group, he or she may not fully comprehend the faith journey of that individual. Honoring diversity means listening to clients, hearing what they are saying about the impact of their faith and religious tradition, and avoiding generalizations that might not be useful and, in fact, might be harmful.

Often the life story of persons from "non majority" religious groups include dialogue about the pain of being different. Ironically, one can hear this discussion from Christians as well as persons from other world traditions. In one community in a large midwest metropolitan area, the older adults talk about their community when they were growing up. The Catholics were not allowed to travel east of a particular road and Jews were not allowed to live north of another one. Similarly, a Jew in the Northeast recounts the fact that there are still separate Christian and Jewish country clubs in her city. Incredibly traumatic are many Native American experiences. Native American religious practices were assaulted by both the United States Army and missionaries from various Christian groups. For these persons, their native religious practices are not easily recovered, particularly in cultures where they were not preserved in written documents.

One final area of concern surfaces when studying the world religious traditions. All of the world traditions have developed calendars. In the United States and in many of the countries of the world for purposes of communication, the Christian or Gregorian calendar is the dominant approach to time. This calendar was originally developed by Emperor Julian of Rome based on the solar year of 365 days. It was determined during the time of Pope Gregory XIII in 1582 that some adjustment needed to be made, and thus every four years a leap year was added (Bowker 1997, 187). Much older calendars were developed by the Hindu, Chinese, and Jewish traditions. Calendars can also be found among communities in Africa and among Native Americans. These calendars are no less valid, only different. Thus, in writing this book, we have used the terms Common Era and Before the Common Era. The calendar of the common era coincides with the Christian calendar, which begins with the Birth of Christ, but, it is best that our terminologies acknowledge that the use of the calendar is a political compromise, not the only way of thinking about time.

HOW RELIGIOUS BELIEFS AND PRACTICES INFLUENCE HUMAN SERVICE WORK

No matter what denomination or religion (or even the lack of a belief system) is important to the client or a group of clients, religion and personal spirituality impact the person or group's perceptions of the world, the way he or she thinks about reality, and the behaviors or activities of faith. The spiritual aspect of a person has *cognitive, affective,* and *behavioral* dimensions.

Fundamental to all world religions is a belief in something. In the United States, 94 percent of the respondents to one survey said that they believe in God, and 70 percent that they believe in a life after death (Gallup 1990, 21, 25). These beliefs and others that accompany them are part of the cognitive and intellectual impact of religion in the life of the individual. These beliefs, however, are more than intellectual ideas. They also make a difference to the individual at the level of their feelings or affect. Religion may offer support by influencing the way one copes with difficult times in their lives.

Religious Beliefs

Three areas of religious beliefs will be briefly examined. These include life after death, prayer, and sin.

Beliefs about an afterlife may make a difference for persons as they experience the death of someone they care about or face their own death. These beliefs are different across the world traditions. In some there is no afterlife, in others it is movement to another form of existence, for still others it is to a place called heaven. While the place or concept is different, the importance of these beliefs in providing comfort cannot be underestimated.

The name of God may be different and the way a prayer is framed may be different, but the notion that there is something greater than us, and that this greater power may assist the individual or group may be similar. For many, God provides a sense that there is some power that can make sense of things that are not understood in this life. For others, God offers a source of support and assistance. For still others, God is the ultimate source of explanation. These often come together to help the individual address anxiety and fear of the unknown. After times of tragedy, one often hears that "if it weren't for God, I don't know how I would have gotten through." God may be understood to be a sustainer in times of crisis.

Many religions assert that God judges humanity, both individually and as a group. For some this judgment takes the form of deciding whether the person moves on to nirvāna or comes back in a new incarnation, in others it may be whether the person's soul ends up in heaven or hell. Not all of the decisions are this significant. In many societies, God shows judgment by giving good weather, or responding in some other ways to human requests. This may become important to persons who feel powerless as they can be comforted that judgment will come from a higher source.

Religious Practices and Behaviors

The behaviors that relate to religion are particularly relevant for helping professionals. For counselors who utilize behavior modification or cognitive behavioral methods, acknowledging the behavioral dimensions of religion may be a first step toward understanding a person's feelings. All religions entail behaviors that are intended to be congruent with the basic tenets of the faith. Most of the world traditions have specific rituals in which members participate. Indeed, to demonstrate one's faithfulness, one does the rituals. The importance of ritual to the individual may become a problem in the human service context when there is some reason that the person is unable to practice the ritual. For example, how does an elderly Jew or Muslim keep the dietary laws of the faith when physically unable to shop at stores that sell the things the laws require? Something as simple as a marshmallow is normally made with a gelatin extracted from the inedible parts of pigs; marshmallows to be allowed in the diet of either a strictly observant Jew or Muslim must be made with a special gelatin derived from cattle, and are obviously not found in every neighborhood store.

Some persons who are unable to follow the prescribed ritual, due to logistical or health problems, substitute behaviors. This is referred to as the "functional equivalence" of religious practice. Functional equivalence is useful when the substitutions are appropriate; it is a problem when they are not. For example, a nurse's aide who attempts to provide Communion for his or her patient when no priest is available presents problems within the Roman Catholic tradition.

BRIDGES BETWEEN PSYCHOLOGY AND THEOLOGY

Human service practitioners are professionally educated in the human services, but they may have only limited training in their personal religion. In order to bring the religious and spiritual concerns together with counseling and human service practice, the bridges found in psychology and theology can be helpful. Building bridges between the social science based professions and that of religion requires translation of terms, concepts and ideas to show where they are similar as well as different. Four areas for bridging are available to the counseling practitioner. At the basis of both social sciences and faith approaches at the first level is some type of theory of explanation, or statement of faith, that offers values, meaning, and a perspective on life. The second level in social science terms reflect coping or the reaction to the theory of explanation. The individual interprets the world using his or her own theory of explanation. At specific times when they interpret life, such as during stress or when "bad things" happen, they turn to their theory of explanation as a basis for intellectual coping.

Last, theory influences the person. Each individual interprets his or her experience of the world through "feelings," "beliefs," and "behaviors." As can be seen in Figure 2, as each person experiences relationship with that which is greater than self is, as well as other human beings, he or she filters all of this through cognitive understandings of this experience. In religious practice this is often understood as the knowledge of the faith. This reflects the facts, both historical and interpretive, as they affect the believer. The believer will also respond to his or her beliefs through practices and actions of his or her faith tra-

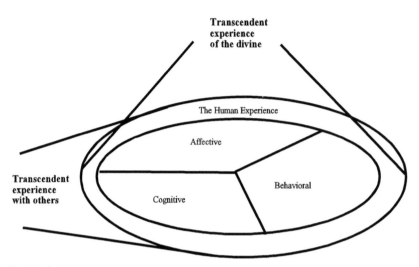

Figure 2

dition. Finally at the level of faith, the individual will have feelings and emotional responses to the experience of faith. In these interpretations, the process of the experience of that which is greater than oneself, is handled in a similar fashion to one's experience of other persons, friends, loved ones, even enemies.

Thus, human experience is the first bridge between spiritual and social science concepts. Social agencies and religious institutions both deal in basic human experience. Translation between the assumptions made by professionals from the various disciplines requires a willingness to listen and a desire to collaborate on behalf of the people one cares about.

One obstacle to building bridges between religion and the social sciences is the assumption that the theory of explanation (hermeneutic) for spiritual concern is radically different from that of the social sciences. The social sciences offer observable behavior and theories that can be verified by quantitative research. Clergy and persons speaking for spiritual concerns are concerned with the relationship with a supreme being which requires faith as evidence of transcendent concern. To understand the nature of the relationship with God in terms of observable, objective measures would seem to be an impossible task.

This task *is* impossible if it requires the person doing the assessment to "know the mind of God." One can know God through Scripture and through

68

the works of God, but these tend not to satisfy the social science understanding of method or authority. In the social sciences, the consistent use of prescribed methods of observation is what makes the outcomes of study "reliable" and authoritative. Across religious denominations and faith traditions, there is less agreement as to the method of approaching and interpreting a relationship with God. In order to facilitate bridging the human service practice and spiritual concerns, three assumptions need to be present:

1. If the practitioner starts from the social sciences, it is appropriate to begin from the human experience of the divine. Theologians posit two ways to approach an understanding of God—by listening to what God says and by starting from what one understands of God. Transcendent relationships can exist between two persons or between a person and God. If one attempts to start this interpretation from the mind of God, since human beings can not fully know all of what God thinks, and the social science offers very little support to help us do it, the task of interpreting the human experience of the spiritual is difficult at best. However, if one follows the lead of theologians like Paul Tillich, who start from the experience of the person in relationship with God, the task is possible. What this theological issue now has that allows it to be interpreted by the social sciences is the transcendent human experience.

2. Respect the beliefs of all faith traditions. A human being might experience a transcendent relationship with God, but to understand this relationship fully implies understanding how God experiences it as well—which is not possible. Thus, the transcendent aspect of faith and belief can only be respected, not assessed. What one can assess is the person's experience of faith. Whether or not one agrees with the theology stated, one needs to honor the experience. This may feel reductionistic to some as it implies that one is listening to the faith of the client, without necessarily interpreting it for assessment.

3. Address only human experience. Information to be addressed in the human service context need not reflect every philosophical aspect of the "ultimate" only those which are reflected in the experience of the person. If one restricts one's understanding of the human experience to aspects of faith, belief, and the understanding of the transcendent relationship with God, the challenge of recording and interpreting it to human service practice is a real possibility.

Studies of the psychology of religion point to four areas in which people employ the experience of their beliefs in their lives: *coping, modeling, meaning,* and *service support.*

Coping: For many persons, one important aspect of faith and belief is that of finding comfort in times of suffering and sorrow. Knowing that God is present during times of trial is very important to the human experience. Here the social science concept of coping is pertinent, because religion and personal spirituality can offer the basis for important coping mechanisms.

Modeling: Religious writings include many accounts of saints and other persons who offer rich role models because of their courage, generosity, and other positive qualities.

Meaning: The search for meaning is important to many clients, particularly older adults. Religious practice and personal spirituality offer a way of interpreting the meaning of life which may resolve many anxieties about both life and death.

Support: Many religious congregations offer resources in the form of pastoral services, community support, and even direct social services to members.

CONCLUSION

This chapter is intended to offer a brief sketch of the various world traditions which may be encountered in human service practice. It is not intended to replace direct dialogue with these traditions. Rather, we have offered examples of the types of diversity among religious perspectives based on world traditions. If it offers a place to begin to ask appropriate questions, then it has been successful. Missing from this discussion is dialogue on Native American, African, and feminist spirituality which has begun to be studied in the context of comparative religion. These voices need to be heard in their context from the speaker or client. As noted, listening to the client's understanding of personal faith tradition is critical to understanding the nature of the person and the meaning of the chosen religious or faith position. Consultants in the various religious traditions found in the practitioner's community can help interpret the faith tradition, but only the client can fully interpret its meaning for him-or herself. When the client is an entire group, organization or community it is important to recognize that there will be differences within faith traditions and possibly different interpretations of what religion means.

70

REFERENCES

Berry, T. 1971. *Religions of India.* New York: Bruce.

Bowker, J., ed. 1997. *The Oxford dictionary of world religions.* Oxford: Oxford University Press.

Bullis, R. K. 1996. *Spirituality in social work practice.* Washington, D.C.: Taylor and Francis.

Canda, E. 1988. Spirituality, religious diversity, and social work practice. *Social Casework* 69 (4): 238–47.

Canda, E., and T. Phaobtong. 1992. Buddhism as a support system for Southeastern Asian refugees. *Social Work* 37 (1): 61–67.

Esposito, J. L. 1994. Islam in the world and in America. In *World religions in America: An introduction,* ed. J Neusner, 243–58. Louisville: Westminster/John Knox Press.

Gallup, G. H. 1990. *Religion in America: Approaching the year 2000. . . .* Princeton, N.J.: Princeton Religion Research Center.

Hopfe, L. M. 1994. *Religions of the world.* 6th ed. New York: Macmillan College Publishing.

Kosmin, B. A. 1991. *The national survey of religious identification,* 1989–1990 (Research Report) New York: Graduate School and University Center of the City University of New York.

Larson, G. J. 1994. Hinduism in India and in America. In *World religions in America: An introduction,* ed. J. Neusner, 177–202. Louisville: Westminster/John Knox Press.

McDowell, J., and D. Stewart. 1992. *Handbook of today's religions.* San Bernardino, Calif.: Here's Life.

Neusner, J., ed. 1994. *World religions in America: An introduction.* Louisville: Westminster/John Knox Press.

Rausch, D. A., and C. H. Voss. 1993. *World religions: Our quest for meaning.* Valley Forge: Trinity Press International.

Rowan, J. 1993. *The Transpersonal: Psychotherapy and counseling.* New York: Routledge.

Wiggins, J. B. 1996. *In praise of religious diversity.* New York: Routledge.

Wright, John W., ed. 1996. *The universal almanac* 1997. Kansas City, Mo.: Andrews and McMell.

PART II

CLINICAL APPLICATIONS AND SELF-AWARENESS

Chapter 4

RELIGIOUS DIVERSITY AND
FAITH DEVELOPMENT

Part I provided perspectives on how religious experience has been subject to various interpretations throughout the history of humankind. This chapter brings into focus theories of human development, particularly as they influence the way in which we understand the development of faith. We will focus on how human service practitioners can better understand their clients in the context of diverse religious experiences and beliefs.

An important distinction when discussing the diversity of religious experiences is found at the intersection of psychology and religion. At these crossroads what is called religious development converges with what is known about human development. Psychologists George Galloway (1909), William James (1902), and others brought psychology into this dialogue. Over time, many theories and theoreticians have emerged. Probably, the most commonly used theory of human development is that of Erik Erikson.

The work of James Fowler (1981) has offered a new perspective on this discussion. Fowler's Faith Development theory offers a fresh approach to the question, "How do we understand the intersection between human development as understood by psychology and the process of becoming a person of faith?" Another way of asking this question is, "At what age does an individual understand such issues as morality and other transpersonal concerns?" The history of developmental psychology started with questions about moral development. In the current practice of human services, these older studies by Galloway and James become relevant in terms of such questions as, "At what age do children understand death and the concept of an afterlife as described by their faith tradition?" In order to understand these concepts we need to examine some of the theoretical insights into faith development.

Much of the literature on faith development reflects the Jewish and Christian goals of becoming closer to God and growing in faith. Other religious groups, however, have different goals. For example, in the Hindu tradition, the human predicament is that human beings "remain in bondage, going through millions of births and rebirths, until the individual has learned to withdraw his or her mind from all sense objects" (Bharati 1973, 167); thus, the spiritual goal is to break the cycle of attachment. Although Fowler and his colleagues (Fowler, Nipkow, and Schweitzer 1991) have begun to expand their work beyond the Judeo-Christian experience, the applicability of this concept is most compatible with the Jewish and Christian experiences.

Common definitions of both *faith* and *faith development* reflect primarily Judeo-Christian, Muslim thinking. Hellwig writes that "the term 'faith' ranges in meaning from a general religious attitude on the one hand to personal acceptance of a specific set of beliefs on the other hand." (1990, 3) She goes on to note that the term *faith* has its origin in Hebrew scriptures. Faith seems to reflect belief, an understanding that God is trustworthy and reliable. The term *faith development* reflects the observation that these beliefs change over the life of the individual. Fowler and the other theorists who offer more concise definitions develop these assumptions more concretely as a part of the theological and psychological theories utilized in their work. These definitions may be helpful to the human service worker but must be understood in the context of their religious, theological, and psychological traditions.

HUMAN DEVELOPMENT: ERIKSON'S CONTRIBUTIONS

Development implies growth. An obvious example is a child's physical development. A child is born, grows in the ability to learn, talk, socialize with others, and understand their environment. Psychological development also offers important insight. Erikson's work has dominated the literature available to religious educators and human service workers in the United States over the past thirty years.

Erikson's theory depicts development across the human lifespan, which he divides into eight stages. The life cycle is the most celebrated concept within Erikson's thought. First introduced in his text, *Childhood and Society,* this concept permeates all of his subsequent work. Erikson was one of the first to articulate a theory of development that encompassed the entire life cycle; his students referred to it as his *"womb to tomb"* concept (Fowler, Nipkow, and Schweitzer 1991). The two structural aspects of the life cycle are (1) the psychosocial crisis and (2) the basic strength. The concept of a psychosocial crisis "is used here in a developmental sense to connote not a threat of a catastrophe, but a turning point, a crucial period of increased vulnerability and heightened potential, and therefore, the ontogenetic source of generational strength and maladjustment" (Erikson 1968, 96). Erikson expresses this concept of a crisis in his use of a matrix that illustrates two concepts held in tension with each other. Erikson borrows two words from epidemiology, *dystonic* ("pulled apart") and *syntonic* ("brought together"), to describe the polarities of the crisis that must be addressed at each life stage. Erikson then discusses the vital strength that emerges from successful resolution of each psychosocial crisis, such as hope, will, etc.

The life cycle is held together by a concept that Erikson calls *epigenesis.* He defines this term according to its components: "*epi* can mean 'above' in space as well as 'before' in time, and in connection with *genesis* can well represent the space—time nature of all development" (Erikson, Erikson, and Kivnick 1986, 38). In essence, epigenesis means that all of the developmental aspects of a person are available to that person all of the time, throughout life. Erikson particularly used this concept as he discussed the eighth and final stage. In his books, *The Life Cycle Completed 1982* and *Vital Involvement in Old Age,* Erikson begins his discussion with the eighth stage, effectively exploring the life cycle in reverse. This tactic allows him to explore his concept with the fullness of all eight stages from the beginning, rather than describing one stage at a time. This concept is particularly useful in working with older adults as it pulls the helping professional away from simply the here and now and puts the person's entire life into perspective. On this point, Erikson is trying to draw a tension between what is an artificial concept of stages with the more fluid nature of human existence. Developmental stages offer a fuller view of the emotional needs and concerns of living. Yet few people live life like a person walking from car to car in a moving train. Particularly when we look back at our lives, the stages do not stand out. Thus, by starting at the end, the tension between what is helpful about stages and the artificial transitions can be mediated.

HUMAN AND RELIGIOUS DEVELOPMENT: A CONNECTION?

Erikson's work addresses the question, "At what age is a child able to comprehend the various messages of a faith tradition?" Different religious and psychological traditions continue to answer this question differently. Each has been developed to reflect the learning capacities of the child.

Pervading Erikson's depiction of the life cycle is an understanding of its relation to the various aspects of religious life. For Erikson, religion is not merely attendance in a church, synagogue, or temple, or prayer before each meal and at bed time. Rather, religion went beyond behavioral activities to provide developmental threads that are woven throughout life. While Erikson did not speak extensively about religion in religious language, he believed that all of human development and even our reality as persons cannot be understood as exclusively rational. "In observing and describing development, Erikson is forced to conclude that there is something *More"* (Wright 1982, 148).

Three basic concepts help to build an understanding of Erikson's reflection on religion: *playfulness, transcendence,* and *trust.*

Playfulness may seem out of place in this discussion, but Erikson sees it as a part of the developmental life cycle and links it to ritual. Some of the first expressions of caring for others (transcendence) are found in the play of the child. Based on the theory of epigenesis, all of the elements of the self are present at all stages; therefore, playfulness needs to be a part of the ongoing development of the adult. Erikson understands that religion is not just a left brain activity, full of intellect and wisdom. Rather, it is reflective of the joys of creation, the power of human experience, and the importance of the transcendent encounter between the "I" and the "other."

Transcendence is experienced by the child at an early age. At the mother's breast, children experience the reality of another person who cares about them. At play with siblings and friends, children work out patterns of behavior that allow them to interact successfully with others. All through life the human being experiences the importance of the transcendent relationship with the world. It is in this way that the emerging "I" is molded into the person we see as a mature adult and later as an older adult. Persons from the religious community assert that experience of the transcendent comes from more than interpersonal contact; More importantly, it comes from one's relationship with the divine. Erikson stops short of reference to the divine, but interpreters of his work have suggested its applicability to religion.

The third ingredient in Erikson's thinking to which he refers as having religious qualities, is *trust.* Like transcendence, trust is built early in the life of the individual. One learns to trust in interaction with parents, then with siblings and friends, and finally with the larger society. As one develops trust, one is fully able to interact with the world. In trust the child incorporates into the self part of the world while sharing part of the self with the world. For Erikson, this is a critical form of religious experience, for it lies at the foundation of faith.

THE IMPORTANCE OF RITUAL IN DEVELOPMENT

Building on these elements, Erikson contributes to the understanding of ritual. In his study of children, he noticed that there were activities that were both repetitive and meaningful. When the infant is hungry, he or she is fed. From toileting to eating to playing with siblings, the child is subjected to rituals, often formulated originally by adults. In each of these rituals the elements of play, transcendence, and trust are embedded and continue to be developed. If we take this understanding of ritual throughout the life cycle into work with clients, we need to remember that rituals and their meaning are not exclusively built into the elements of traditional religious practice. Rather, ritual expresses feelings, the need for trust and the power of transcendence. The need not wait for the test of time or the edict of a central authority figure to be valued by the individual. Ritual is an expression of the whole fabric of the person. Parents model ritual and its importance to the child. As adults, people continue to participate in rituals that have been a part of their lives since childhood. For many persons, the rituals that were developed centuries earlier and that were practiced in some form by many generations of families, are now a part of one's life which are passed on to children. In this way, ritual is more than just an activity for today; it is a rich source of linkage to the past and the future.

As a foundation for interpreting ritual across the life cycle, the work of Erikson offers some intriguing evidence of one's humanity as one seeks the depths of spirituality. Although he did not attempt to apply his work directly to the traditional religions, his work has been drawn upon, particularly by persons who wish to explore new ways to celebrate life in the latter portion of the life cycle that has not received much attention from traditional practitioners.

The concept of *ethos* is introduced in several places in Erikson's work. In *Childhood and Society* (1950, 258) he refers to an economic and a technological ethos. In *Identity, Youth and Crisis* (1968, 120) he adds an ethos of action. In each case he is referring to an *ideal* activity supported by the community. In developing this concept, he refers back to the constructive element of identity as it is influenced by cultural organizations. Other holistic philosophers simply call this the "social" or "self-transcendent dimension." For Erikson the connection between ethos and religion is found in the relationship with the social, and in some cases, the moral aspect of the person. The use of ethos, whether in terms of the social—cultural aspects of the person, or in terms of the self-transcendent can be understood as a mechanism for influence on ego development, much like the family.

Erikson's work is often applied to religion by persons in the religious sector as a way of understanding human development. However, it is clear that this was not Erikson's own priority. Missing from the dialogue about the use of Erikson's work is a widely accepted, full articulation of the exchange between Erikson's concepts and any particular theological understanding of the development of faith. This is to say that the work of Erikson has never been successfully brought together with the work of a major theologian in a format that is widely accepted by the religious community in the United States.

BEYOND ERIKSON: MODELS OF RELIGIOUS DEVELOPMENT

Gleason

John Gleason's work represents one attempt to determine the types of spirituality used by different persons. Gleason (1990) suggests that spirituality exists on a continuum between literalism and symbolism. His continuum is explained as a four-world model.

World A: This state of being is reminiscent of what Paul Tillich, in his *Dynamics of Faith* (1957), referred to as *natural literalism*. Persons in World A exhibit blind faith in a dominant external authority. Any effort to persuade them of other realities is simply not understood. The World A individual does respond to rituals as symbols and practices repetitious, familiar routine as a part of his or her religion. Fundamentalism is grounded in this style.

World B: The World B person also relies on an external authority to receive answers and to reduce doubts and fears. However, for this person, some doubt, fear, and even anger remain. Doubt may be pushed to the limits of the conscious mind. However, it resides there requiring constant reinforcement from the external authority as to the authenticity of the religious practice. This is what Tillich would refer to as *repressed literalism*.

World C: The world C person experiences a stronger inner authority than external authority. World C is referred to in Tillich's terms as *broken myth*. This individual can relate to worlds A and B with empathy, but understands that when he or she relates to the divine, it is different than it was in worlds A and B. Doubt is something that is easier for this person to experience and express. This person is able to understand the literal emphasis of worlds A and B, but translates it into symbols. For example, the story of Adam and Eve offer a symbol of creation and the snake the symbol of evil. These need not be literal studies to be useful in understanding creation and evil. The World C person is able relate to others without fear of losing his or her own orientation.

World D: The World D person is exploring the fringes of religion and spirituality. It can be a lonely experience. Such persons are generally considered theological geniuses or mentally ill. Historically, they have been loved by some and feared by others. Gleason notes that he has never met such a person, but conceives of their potential. Martin Luther and the Bahaullah (from the Bahai tradition) are examples of World D's spiritual explorers.

Gleason stresses that his four "worlds" do not represent progressive or linear stages of spirituality, but rather different and diverse understandings of it. He also notes that a mystic can live in any one of the four worlds. This concept is useful from a theoretical perspective: although conceptually there is a linear continuum between symbolic and literal understandings of spirituality, the four worlds are not in a linear relationship.

Gleason's model also illustrates the difficulty of quantifying or measuring the differences among varieties of spiritual experiences; in fact, the model lacks any measurable constructive elements. However, it provides fertile ground for a beginning philosophical understanding of diverse orientations to faith development and for realizing the complications in trying to quantify and measure such diverse perspectives.

Fowler

Since 1980 the works of James Fowler have offered fertile ground for investigating the ways in which people, particularly those from Christian traditions, develop in faith. Fowler's work is based on bringing together the developmental psychology of Jean Piaget (as presented by L. Kohlberg with the theological work of Reinhold Niebuhr and Paul Tillich). Fowler views human development from the perspective of Kohlberg's learning theory. However, unlike human growth and development models, Fowler tries not to place a value judgment on any of his stages. Fowler notes, "In no way will we be suggesting that a person characterized by one of the less developed stages is any less a person than one described by a more developed stage. Our concern, rather, will be to try to grasp the potentials and limits for the human covenant partnership with God and neighbor which are characteristic of each of the stages" (Fowler 1987, 57). Furnish adds, "Although often and erroneously used as a synonym for 'religious development,' faith development in Fowler's terms goes far beyond the acquisition of religious concepts. Faith, for Fowler, is the *way* a person finds meaning in life, not the set of religious concepts which may be articulated." (1990, 58)

Two key assumptions undergird Fowler's work. First, following Piaget, Fowler assumes that "knowledge is constructed in the interaction between the genetically given cognitive propensities of the individual, and the data derived from the environment and logically ordered along hierarchical and invariant stages. This constructivist view has been adopted by Lawrence Kohlberg and his associates in their differentiation between cognitive *structures* and *content* issues such as religion and faith" (Mosely 1993, 147). Thus, human beings can be understood as developing cognitive structures that reflect a hierarchical order. These structures can, however, be influenced by environmental factors such as religion and faith.

Both Piaget and Fowler struggle with the question of why different people behave differently. Human development theory has been dominated by assumed genetically and hierarchically based approaches that are heavily dependent on linear thinking, it is difficult to break out of these dominant frames and rethink the diversity of development. Thus, the influence of the environment, which in this case includes culture, family, and religious beliefs is critical to understanding the diversity of the human experience, including faith development.

Mosely points out a second key assumption in Fowler's work, "the divine human relationship is a significant dimension of human experience." (1993,148) Fowler's work offers a rich basis for bringing together theology and psychology. Fowler views faith as a universal aspect of the human experience; it is related, but not limited to religion and religious experience. Faith has three dimensions. First, it "is a dynamic pattern of personal trust in and loyalty to a *center* or *centers of value.*" Put another way, "we attach our affections to those persons, institutions, causes, or things that promise to give worth and meaning to our lives." Second, "faith is trust in and loyalty to *images and realities of power.*" Finite and vulnerable, one looks to that which can sustain oneself through all life's turbulence, a source of power that is greater than that which makes one feel vulnerable. Third, "faith is trust in and loyalty to a *shared master story or core story.*" All of the world religious traditions reflect stories of faith through the events and actions of central persons and gods. These individual stories come together to form *the* faith story that offers comfort, hope, and meaning to the believer (Fowler, Nipkow, and Schweitzer 1991, 22–23).

Fowler and his colleagues (1991, 24–25) describe seven stages of faith, summarized as follows:

Primal faith (infancy): The infant exhibits a prelingual level of trust toward parents and others. This trust balances the anxiety felt during the separations involved in infant development.

Intuitive projective faith (early childhood): At this stage the child is stimulated by the stories and symbols that present in his or her world. However, the child is not yet controlled by an internal use of logic. These images represent "both the protective and threatening powers surrounding one's life."

Mythic literal faith (childhood and beyond): The individual develops the use of logic, which brings organization and order to the world. This organization serves to create an awareness of causality and enables the child to be able to begin to see things the way someone else sees them.

Synthetic conventional faith (adolescence and beyond): The adolescent develops the ability to integrate the perspectives of others into his or her self-image. "A personal and largely unreflective synthesis of beliefs and values evolves to support identity and to unite one in emotional solidarity with others."

Individuative reflective faith (young adulthood and beyond): Building upon and going beyond the ability to relate the views of others to his or her self-image, the individual can now see past his or her own feelings and emotions to be able to see the greater picture of community and society, can recognize authority, and can assume responsibility for making choices that develop ideology and lifestyle.

Conjunctive faith (midlife and beyond): In this stage, a person is able to comprehend the polarities of life as well as the gray areas in between. "Symbol and story, metaphor and myth (from one's traditions and others') are newly appreciated (second, or willed naïveté) as vehicles for expressing truth."

Universalizing faith (midlife and beyond): "Beyond the paradox and polarities, persons in this stage are grounded in a oneness with the power of being. Their visions and commitments free them for a passionate yet detached spending of the self in love, devoted to overcoming division, oppression, and violence, and in effective anticipatory response to a breaking commonwealth of love and justice."

Fowler describes each stage as "an integrated system of operations (structures) of thought and valuing which makes for an equilibrated constitutive knowing of a person's relevant environment" (1986, 31). Each of the seven stages in turn has seven structural aspects: form of logic, role taking, form of moral judgment, bounds of social awareness, loci of authority, form of world coherence, and symbolic functioning. Human development through the stages depends on the combination of these internal (genetic) and external (environmental) factors. Fowler warns that the stages of faith are not to be understood as goals of development which people should be rushed through. Rather, they offer a rich identification of the multifaceted nature of the person, in light of his or her environment, in his or her journey within the faith experience.

CONCLUSION

Many authors of faith development literature are quick to separate discussions of literal faith from symbolic faith and human development. However, Fowler and Gleason suggest that literal and symbolic faith are simply different perceptions of spirituality and faith. The answer to the question as to what age a child understands a spiritual issue like death and an afterlife is generally answered by developmental psychology. Clinically helpful is the awareness that an adult may have heard about an afterlife in religious education as a child, then suffered the loss of a sibling, parent, or grandparent and formed an idea of death/afterlife that was developmentally consistent. However, now as an adult, this understanding needs to be revisited and brought into consistency with their current understanding of self and faith.

Other applications of the faith development concept for human service professionals include its use in diagnosis and in terms of understanding faith in the life of the client. The concept of faith development offers insight into the answer to the question, "How does the client perceive his or her faith?" and "How does he or she use this faith?" The individual who perceives faith literally may respond in the same way to other aspects of his or her life. Similarly the person who sees faith symbolically may see other things symbolically as well.

CASE FOR REFLECTION

Henry has lived in Home Town most of his life. As a child he attended a conservative Protestant church several times a week with his family. He describes his childhood as a happy one during which he believed that God was always present in his life and would actively protect him from adversity. When he was sixteen, he was in an automobile accident. His girl friend was severely injured. Henry, his family and his entire congregation prayed for her, but she died. Henry notes that this was the first time that God let him down.

After graduating from high school, Henry went into the army. On his second tour in Vietnam, he was wounded in a firefight. He remembers praying for his life and those of his friends. The next thing he remembered, he was in a hospital, his left leg having been amputated. He later learned that his unit had been wiped out. He had been left for dead. After this experience, and upon leaving military service, Henry went looking for his faith. God had let him down.

Henry then went to college. During college he found a group that identified with a Protestant sect/denomination which is highly philosophical. He found that the answer to his problem of why God abandoned him is that God is not able to change everything. In fact, people are, and people can make a lot of mistakes and do hurtful things. Henry married Jane who was a member of his church and they raised their family in their religious tradition.

Henry has presented at the Home Town Mental Health Clinic with a profound depression. He says that he is "being eaten from within." The focus of the depression is the death of his eldest daughter in the previous year. Mixed in his turmoil are questions about why God could allow this to happen to him.

Discussion

1. Where is Henry in terms of his faith development?
2. How does his faith reflect other developmental issues?
3. How has his quest to answer the question of "why bad things happen to good people" reflected his coping mechanisms?
4. How does his confusion as to his relationship with God enter into his depression?

REFERENCES

Bharati, A. 1973. Hinduism, psychotherapy, and the human predicament. In R. H. Cox, *Religious systems and psychotherapy*. Springfield, Ill.: Charles C. Thomas. 167–79.
Erikson, E. H. 1950. *Childhood and society*. New York: W. W. Norton.
———. 1968. *Identity, youth, and crisis*. New York: W. W. Norton.
———. 1982. *The life cycle completed*. New York: W. W. Norton.
Erikson, E. H., J. M. Erikson, and H. Q. Kivnick. 1986. *Vital involvement in old age*. New York: W. W. Norton.
Fowler, J. 1986. Faith and the structure of meaning. In C. Dykstra and S. Parks, *Faith development and Fowler*. Birmingham, Ala.: Religious Education Press.

————. 1987. *Faith development and pastoral care*. Minneapolis: Fortress Press.

————. 1981. *Stages of faith: The psychology of human development and the quest for meaning*. San Francisco: Harper.

Fowler, J. W., K. E. Nipkow, and F. Schweitzer, eds. 1991. *Stages of faith and religious development: Implications of church, education, and society*. New York: Crossroad.

Galloway, G. 1909. *The principles of religious development*. London: Macmillan.

Hellwig, M. K. 1990. A history of the concept of faith. In *Handbook of faith*, ed. J. M. Lee, 3–23. Birmingham, Ala.: Religious Education Press.

James, W. 1902. *The varieties of religious experience*. Reprint 1958, New York: New American Library.

Mosely, R. 1993. Education and human development in the likeness of Christ. In J. L. Seymour and D. E. Miller, eds., *Theological approaches to Christian education*. Nashville: Abingdon Press.

Wright, J. E. 1982. *Identity and religion*. New York: Seabury Press.

Chapter 5

SPIRITUAL AND RELIGIOUS CONCERNS IN HUMAN SERVICE PRACTICE

Spiritual development, like other aspects of our lives, is part of the human experience. We experience the world around us. We also have to a greater or lesser degree, a sense of the sublime.

THE INCLUSION OF SPIRITUAL VARIABLES IN ASSESSING AND TREATING CLIENTS

In his article entitled "The Repression of the Sublime," clinical psychologist Frank Haronian discusses the seemingly innate human urge to strive for meaning and reality beyond the every day self and its mundane experiences. He states that ". . . it is out of a sense of boredom and dissatisfaction with the gratification of the senses that we begin to look for higher meanings in our life" (Haronian 1974, 52).

Haronian's definition of activity toward the "sublime" includes the following categories:

1. all of the human being's impulses, urges, and drives to be something greater than he or she is;
2. orientation toward the true, good and beautiful in life;
3. tendency toward community, brotherliness, and caring, based on the belief that, ultimately, we all share the same destiny;
4. the finding of our deepest satisfaction in some form of service to others;
5. the urge to trust life, give freely of oneself and to go beyond mere interest in one's own concerns;
6. the need to ask and answer for oneself the basic, existential question—Who am I? Where am I going?

7. the desire to dedicate the self to a purpose that one considers more significant than one's transient existence and powers

Haronian further states: "When we sense the sublime as the feeling of communion with and dedicate to something that is greater than ourselves, then we are experiencing this basic spiritual impulse. It may be religious, agnostic, or atheistic; it does not require a belief in God, but it is consonant with such a belief" (1974, 52–53). Haronian asserts that it is the role of the direct practitioner to aid the client in becoming more in tune with what are normal spiritual impulses and to free one's mind from ill-conceived theology acquired in childhood. Equally challenging for the clinician is to assist the client in converting spiritual energy into reflection and mindfulness that results in political or social action.

Haronian claims that the experience of this urge for the sublime is common to all, but that it is often repressed or denied. Evasion of opportunities for personal growth due to fear of abandoning the familiar for the unknown, excessive fear of death, loss of a sense of community with others through emphasis on independence and personal autonomy, overvaluing of the material goods of life and excessive demands for security are all symptoms of this repression of the sublime in one's life. But the question of meaning, or what is beyond the self, remains and for some people, becomes an intense need to know, to experience that reality.

The most common (but not the only) answer to the question "How do you know God?" or the ultimate reality of life is "Through the environment and people around me." Listening to this experience of spirituality can be accomplished by exploring three areas: modeling of the ideal, transcendent relationship with a higher reality, and social support.

1. *Modeling of the ideal.* The literature suggests that spirituality, whether involving a traditional religion or a personal philosophy, offers at least four modeling variables to the individual: (1) coping, (2) meaning, (3) forgiveness or grace, and (4) values.

   Work by Koenig, Smiley, and Gonzales (1988) and Pargament (1990) suggests that both religion and personal spirituality are used as primary and secondary *coping* mechanisms. Either can help the individual to reframe catastrophic situations. Pargament illustrates this when he says, "Religious beliefs can contribute to the sense of integrity and continuity between what has been and what is. While other aspects of the self (e.g., physical and social) are often disrupted by disease processes and social events such as widowhood, religious beliefs offer a more stable contextual framework that lends steadiness to the life of the elderly person." (1990, 195) Personal philosophies have been understood for many years to offer ideals and beliefs that impact the way a person copes.

Religion and spirituality also offer *meaning* for the individual. The concept of meaning as an important construct for the individual is an essential tenet of existential philosophy. As discussed by such authors as Alfred Adler, Viktor Frankl, and Rollo May, meaning is central to the individual's sense of well being. In Frankl's work, meaning emanates from the "nöetic," or spiritual, dimension of the person, which in turn reflects his or her self-transcendent aspect.

A third way spirituality models the ideal reflects the methods of *forgiveness* (or *grace*). One's personal philosophy or religion often dictates when to forgive and when to condemn. Basic to forgiveness is the fourth ramification, *values*. Religion, one's spirituality, and personal philosophy will offer personal values that will often match with other persons of like mind. In contrast they may collide with persons who hold different values.

The modeling aspects of religion and personal spirituality are rooted in some type of cognitive input. One sees others cope, hears how one is supposed to cope via public presentations of philosophy or theology and one is offered opportunities to display for external reward the behaviors held as important to the peer group or religious organization. In this way, these aspects start as cognitive but quickly moves to the affective and behavioral dimensions of the person.

2. *Transcendent relationship with a higher power.* As stated earlier, human beings have a need to comprehend that which is veiled in mystery. Through various human intermediaries, people have offered philosophies, religions, and spiritualities which claim to offer mediation with this mystery. This common human need offers to the person and social group three things: (1) hope, (2) relational power, and (3) faith.

As noted by Frankl and others, *hope* (or the lack of it) affects both physical and emotional well being. Many people find hope in religion or spirituality. One reason is that most religious and spiritual systems offer some explanation of what happens after death. Group relationships in a community of believers, such as a church congregation, may also instill hope in individual members.

In the same way, religion and spirituality offer a relationship with the sources of energy or power and love in the universe. By being related to sources of power, many people feel that they receive some type of energy. This power may be used to enable people to live through terrifying events, even as catastrophic as the Holocaust as experienced by Frankl. This sense of power can also be used destructively in interpersonally manipulative situations such as when Jim Jones and David Koresh led their cultic groups to mass death. This power can be meaningful to people for very different reasons, just as it may not be meaningful to others.

Faith is the cognitive context for the relationship with the mystery of the divine. In other words, by faith, one can hope to connect to the divine and thus be closer to that source of life and power. Frequently, practitioners have found that as they listen to and encourage clients to discuss the elements of their faith the various elements of their spirituality that affect other aspects of the person (physical, emotional, social) are revealed. Such variables as the belief in God as present in and working in the world, the techniques necessary to be close to the divine, and the symbols used by one's faith group to communicate with one another about this relationship, are all bound up in the concept of faith and will impact the well being of the client.

This second way that religion affects behavior generally starts less rationally than the first. Anecdotal evidence suggests that it is spawned by feelings and only moves to the cognitive when it needs to be communicated and shared with others. This second area offers little evidence of logical thought and intellectualization. Rather it reflects deeply held feelings which then become cognitive with behavioral ramifications.

3. *Social support.* Religious groups often translate shared beliefs and values into group action on behalf of others. The work of Tobin, Ellor, Fahey, Moberg, and others have offered numerous examples of ways religious congregations offer support for individuals. Among the lists of activities offered are spiritual and emotional support, as well as physical services. In the United States, religious congregations are among the oldest sources of physical support in the event of illness. Tobin et al. (1986) suggest that the role of religious congregations in the network of services for older adults in the United States is as a gap filling service. The clergy are also a part of the helping network

of professionals. Clergy generally participate as "role related helpers" (Froland et al. 1981, 49).

The area of social support is the most tangible and objective of the three areas. It is evident in the acts, thoughts, and feelings of many of the people that are served by the helping professions. Often without the knowledge of the counselor, psychiatrist, or other human service worker, a religious congregation is providing emotional and spiritual comfort to a client. These services can parallel and enhance the work of the helping professional or they can work in opposition to their efforts. The practitioner can only be sure of the impact of the work of the religious group if they are knowledgeable about it and interact with it at least in a marginal way.

IMAGES OF GOD AND THEIR INFLUENCE ON THE CLIENT

A significant number of people who seek clinical services will assert a belief in God (or an ultimate reality) or will have had a belief in God in the past. In some cases the client's current issue is influenced by the image of God to which the person subscribes. This image can be either functional or dysfunctional for the client.

M. Vincentia Joseph states that "Despite the centrality of this belief (in God), there has been little systematic study on its formation or on how we formulate our understanding of God" (1987, 15). She cites the work of Rizzuto, whose research has conceptualized the issue of one's personal image of God as "the God representation." According to Rizzuto, the person develops his or her image of God by combining visual images, internal conscious and unconscious feelings, early memory tracings, and subsequent relationships with significant others. These variables are in constant flux, subject to change with each new experience and each new interpretation as they are incorporated into the changes that take place across the lifespan. When the representation or internal image of God has been formed, it assumes "all of the psychic potential of a living person who is nonetheless experienced in the privacy of conscious and unconscious processes" (Rizzuto 1979, 87). Joseph asserts that this process is intertwined with overall development. "Thus, the meaning of God and religion evolve in the life long development of the self in interaction with others. Each new phase of life brings with it specific religious crises and growth potential" (Joseph 1987, 15).

Rizzuto asserts that even those who have no belief in God harbor an internal God representation, which may be either suppressed or repressed. Gaining an understanding of the overt or suppressed God representation may help the practitioner understand the developmental variables that have influenced other relationships—for example, the client's image of God could affect their expectations of a spouse or employer.

CLINICAL ISSUES RELATED TO SPIRITUALITY AND RELIGION

The following guidelines can be useful to human service providers who wish to integrate religious and spiritual factors into their work.

Need for Provider Self-Assessment

When a human service provider decides to include spiritual and religious dimensions in direct practice with clients individually and in groups, several unique factors must be taken into account and a number of questions asked. The first relates to self-assessment. The provider must ask him/herself, When it is appropriate to deal with the spiritual domain? How it is to be accomplished? The practitioner should also assess the nature of his or her own spiritual experience or the absence of it. A detailed method of self-assessment is discussed in chapter 7.

Need to Develop a Working Paradigm

A number of approaches to working with clients' needs for transcendence have been cited in the literature. Among the most promising is the approach of transpersonal psychology, primarily because it is inclusive of both Eastern and Western religious beliefs and philosophies. Thus, it may be the most general as well as most useful. In addition, it is concerned with developing the highest levels of human consciousness, as well as taking into account the wide spectrum of psychopathology. A broad knowledge of the work and techniques of such major proponents of this approach as Maslow, Frankl, Assagioli, Grof, Wilber is helpful.

ASSESSING THE SPIRITUAL

Bullis (1996, 11) defines *assessment* in clinical social work as "the process of identifying the nature of internal and external stresses disrupting the group's or individual's steady state." Just as other domains—the physical, psychological, interpersonal, environmental, occupational, etc.—must be taken into formal consideration when assessing the status and needs of the client, a formal assessment of spiritual status should also be undertaken. Until recently, very few assessment instruments have been available for the practitioner. The basic components of such an assessment, with or without the use of a standardized instrument, include:

1. taking a spiritual life history, with particular emphasis on lifelong patterns of religious or spiritual belief and practice and their influence on bio-psycho-social-spiritual development;
2. determining how important religion and spirituality are to the client;
3. determining how spiritually autonomous or institutionally or community-connected the client is;
4. determining whether the client's spiritual and religious beliefs and practices are positively transformative, adaptive, or maladaptive;
5. determining whether spiritual or religious pathology exists, such as extreme fear of punishment for sins, fear of God, addiction to liturgy or other religious practices, or spiritual abuse of the client by parents or religious authorities;
6. determining if and why the client's spirituality is in conflict with the spirituality of his or her significant others;
7. determining how spiritual and religious beliefs are translated into or influence the physical, psychological, interpersonal, societal, and environmental activities of daily life;
8. determining how spirituality helps or hinders the client when thinking about or experiencing suffering and dying;
9. determining what the client's spiritual goals are;
10. determining what part spirituality plays in the overall therapeutic process; and
11. determining whether the provider is the most appropriate source of intervention or if the client should be referred to a professional whose specialty is in the religious or spiritual domain.

Although a wide variety of formal instruments have been developed to enable researchers to assess spiritual and religious variables, only a few are of practical use to the clinician. Clifford Kuhn, a psychiatrist and faculty member of the University of Louisville School of Medicine who has long been interested in the spiritual domain of his patients, has developed a "Spiritual Inventory of the Medically Ill Patient" (Kuhn 1988, 87–100). Kuhn's inventory assesses the spirituality of the medical patient in the following domains: attachment of meaning or purpose to the illness; the roles of belief, faith, love, forgiveness, and prayer; capacity for quietness and meditation; and involvement in worship. Although designed for the medically ill, it can also be used in a psychotherapeutic setting. According to Kuhn, it "elicits data that lead to a diagnosis of a patient's spiritual condition, which can enhance and augment the biological, psychological, and sociological diagnoses currently valued by contemporary medicine. It enables the physician to address health and illness along all four parameters of a bio-psycho-social-spiritual model. In our experience its use not only broadens understanding of the illness experience, but very often stimulates our patients to pursue, independently and spontaneously, personally meaningful initiatives that improve their capacity for recovery" (Kuhn 1988, 98).

Ellor, Bracki, Thibault, and Netting have developed an instrument to assess the spiritual strengths and needs specific to older adults. Called the SPINAT (Spiritual Needs Assessment Tool), this instrument was developed in response to the need for a concept that would not dictate either the theoretical paradigm or personal theology of the practitioner while offering an approach to understanding the spirituality of the client. The theory behind the instrument offers a window for psychology to view spirituality and for spirituality to interface with psychology. The SPINAT consists of forty-seven closed ended variables, using a five-point Likert-type scale. The questions are divided into six groups:

1. those that gather demographic data;
2. those that address the cognitive domain of spirituality, such as "I enjoy talking about and thinking through the various ideas and concepts of my faith";
3. those that assess the domain of affect, such as "It is important in my life to feel the spirit of my faith (spirit of God, or a power beyond myself) in my life";
4. those that evaluate behavior, such as "How important to you is your engagement in reading scripture, prayer, liturgy, attending religious services, and listening to religious music?"
5. those that elicit the person's style of coping;
6. those that relate to the desire to engage in spiritual or religious activities.

In late life, perhaps more than at any other time, religion and spirituality can become extremely significant to the concepts of wholeness, coping, meaning, purpose in life and a sense of well being for some people. Religion/spirituality may be even more significant than physical health when well being is assessed (Levin 1994, 6). Thus, providers of human services to the elderly have a professional responsibility to think seriously about the importance of their knowledge and practice expertise in this area. Pargament states that, "Religious beliefs can contribute to the sense of integrity and continuity between what has been and what is. While other aspects of the self (e.g., physical and social) are often disrupted by disease processes and social events such as widowhood, religious beliefs offer a more stable contextual framework that lends steadiness to the life of the elderly person" (1990, 195–224).

NEED TO IDENTIFY SPIRITUAL HEALTH AND SPIRITUAL ILLNESS

In *The Varieties of Religious Experience,* William James introduced the concepts of "healthy-mindedness" (James 1902, 76–139). James equated healthy mindedness with the power of positive thinking; Kuhn gives a more modern definition of what he calls the "healthy spirit." He indicates that the healthy spirit can be seen in persons who have the capacity to infuse life with meaning and purpose, with relatively little guilt attached. He goes on to say that these persons have the ability to forgive themselves and others, and to celebrate and engage in life with humor. "To be healthy is to be whole, involving the optimal function of body, mind, and spirit in whatever the social context" (Kuhn 1988, 98).

Optimal spiritual health is often accompanied by mystical experiences, consider the "higher" stages of spiritual development. These areas are of increasing interest to the lay person and pose special concerns for the provider. Hindu, Buddhist, Jewish and Christian mystics from earliest times through the Middle Ages to the present have often described detailed developmental stages of psycho-spiritual growth when prayer, mediation, and other techniques are used as the primary mode of introspection and therapeutic self-analysis. Among the greatest of these mystics, the Carmelite nun Teresa of Avila (1515–1582), was called by William James "the expert of experts in describing such conditions." Explaining her own psycho-spiritual development from "sinfulness" to identification with the image of God, which she termed "spiritual marriage," Teresa provides a detailed description of the psychological stages of spiritual growth in her work *The Interior Castle.* She was a genius in introspection and presents herself in an almost Freudian stream of consciousness in narrating her spiritual autobiography. Her teachings, because they describe a human experience, are still relevant today.

A consummate therapist, the founder of the Jesuit order and mystic, Ignatius of Loyola (1491–1556), developed an intricate method for analysis of the self and a 30 day "treatment" program to enhance the person's growing relationship with God. Of his *Spiritual Exercises,* which are carried out by the person with the help of a spiritual counselor over an intense period of four weeks, Ignatius claimed: (1) that "one can actually seek and find God's specific will for oneself"; and (2) that God will "communicate Himself to the devout soul" and "deal directly with the creature, and the creature directly with the Creator and Lord" (Egan 1993, 523). As increasing numbers of people are learning about mysticism and practicing various spiritual techniques, the provider needs to know about the mystical teachings of the various religious, as well as the more "mundane" theology.

CONCLUSION

The study of religious development combines the rich resources of theology and psychology. It offers the human service professional insight into the dynamic nature of the spiritual aspect of the person. The various world traditions in religious beliefs offer one criterion for diversity between people. However, individual growth and development also offer a basis for diversity, even among persons of the same religious tradition. The task of the human service worker is to listen to individuals as they reflect on their experience, their beliefs, and their faith traditions.

CASES FOR REFLECTION

John and Judy Robbins live in Home Town and have come to a local family and children's agency for counseling. They have been married for twelve years. They agree that "nothing's the same. We can't find one thing that we agree on anymore. We're constantly arguing about something."

Judy: I have enjoyed the last twelve years—have no complaints about that. But I did leave college after one year to marry John and take a job to help him finish school. We both agreed at that time that I would someday go back to school to complete my degree. Now I believe that John thought kids would come along and I would just forget about school. But they didn't. And a couple of years ago we were in a financial position that allowed me to quit my job and enroll in college on a full time basis. Last June, I graduated with a straight-A average, and now I want to go to graduate school in clinical psychology. But John says I have had enough schooling for now and he wants us to adopt a special need's child. He says my background in psychology would make us perfect parents for such a child. I feel selfish, but I just don't want to. I believe I grieved about our not being able to have our own children and put up with all the snide remarks from his family and mine, but now I'm ready to create another type of life. He says it's important for us to hand down our tradition to the next generation, but I feel I can help children just as well as a child psychologist as I could as a mother.

John: I just don't know how she can say that! We're Jewish. We belong to the Reform synagogue Judy was brought up in. I was brought up in Conservative Judaism and switched when we were married, much to my parents' dismay. But they've gotten used to it. It's very important to us as Jews to have a child—particularly a son—to carry on the family name, traditions, values, etc. When we were married, I thought this was important to Judy as well. When she didn't become pregnant after three years, I suggested that we go for all the tests. We did and found that I have a low sperm count and Judy doesn't ovulate regularly. The doctor offered us the full treatment process—hormone therapy and artificial insemination with my sperm, but Judy wouldn't have anything to do with the idea. She said it was too "unnatural" and that if God wanted us to have children, we would have been able to conceive "naturally." I was very disappointed but figured she'd change her mind. When she didn't, I started talking about adopting. She kept putting me off but never said no.

All this time we've been getting comments from both our parents like "So when are we going to be grandparents?" All four of them are OK with the idea of adoption—they just want a grandchild to love and to carry on the family heritage. This is really tearing me up. It goes against all my religious and cultural values not to have at least one child to pass on my tradition to. Judy just doesn't seem to care about our traditions anymore. And I'm finding that my feelings toward Judy just aren't the same—did I just think I knew what her religious values were?

Discussion

1. What is the primary problem?
2. How much do religious differences contribute to this couple's problem?
3. Are John and Judy at the same stage of faith development?
4. What are the couple's predominant coping skills?
5. What are the abnormal and normal responses in this situation?
6. What kind of treatment is needed?
7. What is the role of the professional in this situation?

REFERENCES

Assagioli, R. 1965. *Psychosynthesis*. New York: Viking.

Bullis, R. K. 1996. *Spirituality in social work practice*. Bristol: Taylor and Francis.

Egan, H. D. 1993. Ignatian spirituality. In *The new dictionary of Catholic spirituality*, ed. Michael Downey, 521–29. Collegeville, Minn.: Liturgical Press.

Furnish, D. J. 1990. *Experiencing the Bible with children*. Nashville: Abingdon Press.

Haronian, Frank. 1974. "The Repression of the Sublime," in *Synthesis*, 1 (1): 51–62.

James, W. 1902. *The varieties of religious experience*. Reprint 1958, New York: New American Library.

Joseph, M. V. 1987. The religious and spiritual aspects of clinical practice: A neglected dimension of social work. *Social Thought* (Winter 1987): 12–23.

Koenig, H. G., M. Smiley, and J. P. Gonzales. 1988. *Religion, health and aging*. Vol. 10. Contributions to the Study of Aging. New York: Greenwood.

Kuhn, C. 1988. A spiritual inventory of the medically ill patient. *Psychiatric Medicine* 6 (2): 87–100.

Levin, J. S. 1994 *Religion in aging and health*. San Francisco: Sage Publications.

Nipkow, K. E. 1991. Stage theories of faith development as a challenge to religious education and practical theology. In Fowler, J. W., K. Nipkow, and F. Schweitzer, eds. *Stages of faith and religious development: Implications for church, education, and society*, 82–98. New York: Crossroad.

Pargament, K. 1990. God help me: Toward a theoretical framework of coping for the psychology of religion. *Research in the Social Scientific Study of Religion*, 2: 195–224.

Philipchalk, R. P. 1990. *Psychology and Christianity: Introduction to counseling*. Lanham, Md.: University Press of America.

Rizzuto, A. M. 1982. The father and the child's representation of God: A developmental approach. In S. Cath, A. Gurwitt, and J. Ross, *Father and child*, 371–81. Boston: Little, Brown.

Thibault, J., J. Ellor, and E. Netting. 1991. A conceptual framework for assessing the spiritual functioning and fulfillment of older adults in long-term care settings. *Journal of Religious Gerontology*, 7 (4): 29–46.

Tobin, S. S., J. W. Ellor, and S. Anderson-Ray. 1986. *Enabling the elderly: Religious institutions within the community service system*. Albany: State University of New York Press.

Chapter 6

PSYCHOPATHOLOGY OF RELIGION AND SPIRITUALITY

Throughout human history, religious symbols, concepts, and behavior to convey perceptions of unknowable or mysterious forces are evident. Early ancestors employed art, mythic stories, music, and ritual to express their understanding of the world they perceived and the events they experienced. In contemporary cultures, these same activities continue to be the vehicle through which human beings create meaning in their lives and participate as social beings in communities.

Religious symbols, concepts and behaviors also accompany other human behaviors which may, in a particular culture, be understood as maladaptive. The earliest psychological theorists in Western society, striving to employ the scientific method to explain human behavior and alleviate human suffering, often found themselves opposed to religious authorities in the Judeo-Christian traditions. As discussed in previous chapters, until the nineteenth century little differentiation had been made between psychological and spiritual disorders. Many forms of dysfunctional human behavior were understood as spiritual problems resulting from demonic possession or moral deficiency. Freud's denigration of the concept of soul may partly explain the recurrent thread through many of the earliest theories of human personality and behavior which equate religious ideation and behavior with arrested personality development or with pathology. In more recent years other theorists have focused attention on describing the development of healthy, functional adult personalities. Both transpersonal psychology and depth psychology have emphasized that the healthiest personalities are autonomous and capable of making choices in a way that benefits both the individual and society. Religious behavior and ideation are viewed from the perspective of their ability to help individuals achieve these goals; distinctions are made on the basis not of differences in creed, but of the universal human experience of connectedness to self and others and to the making or finding of meaning. In these theories, human desire for an experience of the universal unity of all creation is viewed not as pathological, but as an indicator of full human potential.

RESEARCH ON RELIGION AND MENTAL HEALTH

Clinicians and researchers have studied the question of whether religion is more likely to have positive or negative effects on mental health. The results have been inconsistent. Some studies have demonstrated a positive association between some aspects of religious experience and psychological health or wellness (Bergin 1983; Bergin et al. 1987). Those aspects of religion which enhance individual well being are religion's capacities to promote (1) a perception of belonging and social connection, (2) a perception of worth independent of the secular culture's measure of success, (3) a sense of personal efficacy during periods of loss and transition, and (4) an ability to sustain meaningful interpersonal relationships by developing the capacity to forgive oneself and others.

Other studies associate certain religious behaviors with mental illness (Larson et al. 1986), and still others reveal no clear relationship between mental illness and religious themes (Spilka, Hood, and Gorsuch 1985). A significant body of research explores the frequency with which religious ideas, symbols, and rituals occur in the presentation of some of the more severe forms of mental illness, such as obsessive compulsive disorders, schizophrenia, and the dissociative disorders, including multiple personality disorder and post traumatic stress disorder. Although these studies, too, have produced inconsistent results, there is agreement among the findings which suggests that the degree to which religious symbols, rituals, and ideation are used to explain or justify physical, sexual or emotional abuse correlates with the expression of religious material as a feature of later psychopathology.

The particular denominational or affiliational identity of persons who experience dissociative disorders appears to be less important than the underlying structure of the religious symbol system and the social network that sustains it. Higdon (1986) suggests that one particular type of religious conceptualization (frequently labeled as fundamentalist or Pentecostal) occurs frequently in the etiology of dissociative or compulsive disorders. This conceptualization equates "bad" actions with being a "bad" person, and further defines "bad" thoughts as literally equivalent to "bad" actions. When thoughts and feelings are equated with behavior, negative feelings are banned from consciousness or engender guilt. If expressed, these feelings merit severe punishment, which fosters an extremely negative self-concept and enables parents or religious authorities to justify abusive behavior "for the good of the child."

Bowman (1989) describes religious ideation systems that are less than psychologically healthy, focusing in particular on systems which equate emotional difficulties with sin and spiritual weakness. Constant exposure to the message that one's very being is unlovable, unworthy of kindness, and deserving of repeated emotional, physical, sexual, or spiritual boundary violations from authority figures engenders intense feelings of shame. In such families or religious communities the victim is taught that the primary rules in social relationships are: (1) don't talk, (2) don't trust, and (3) don't feel. In relationships that operate under such rules, emotions lose their capacity to "alert" the person to violations of body, mind, or spirit, thus diminishing the person's capacity to protect the self from further trauma. Such religious systems literally "kill the spirit" and can promote or sustain psychopathology.

RESEARCH ON CHILDHOOD TRAUMA: IMPLICATIONS FOR RELIGION

Many large scale studies have noted a strong correlation between childhood abuse and the dissociative disorders, and the similarity of symptoms between the dissociative and the post traumatic stress disorders. The mechanisms used to cope with the emotional and cognitive overloads associated with abuse or severe trauma may appear very similar to psychotic symptoms. The effects of childhood trauma may include psychotic-like experiences and behaviors, such as visual hallucinations, hypervigilance, visual avoidance, paranoia, and "frozen watchfulness." Terr (1985) identified five post traumatic cognitive states that overlap with "supernatural" experiences: (1) intensely vivid and repeated memories of perceptions and sensory impressions of a traumatic event, leading to a sense of being "haunted"; (2) subsequently elaborated and distorted remembrances of perceptions that account for "seeing what one had never actually seen" and/or a sense of being hounded by aggressors; (3) post traumatic hallucinations that are conceptualized as "ghosts," "spirits," or "demons"; (4) intrusion, after traumatic events, of images that appear as "possessions"; and (5) the contagious nature of post traumatic symptoms and their accompanying anxiety, which disseminates these supernatural phenomena into the group at large.

Green (1985) suggests that other forms of mystical and mainstream religious expression may serve as outer manifestations of a victim's inner turmoil. Rigid morality, strict codes of behavior, and punitive authority in the name of God, imposed on one's self and others, may also express an unconscious identification with the abuser. The post traumatic stress disorder symptoms of vigilance, visual hallucinations, and visual avoidance, if chronic, may evolve into long standing cognitive, personality, and interpersonal deficits. These psychological and social deficiencies may in turn discourage reality testing, positive interpersonal relationships, and mature religious experience. James Leehan, who has written extensively about the interaction between family violence and spirituality, describes the effects of negative experiences in the home: "As a survivor you do not need an emphasis on evil and sin—you have had more than enough of that. As a victim, you were constantly told how wicked and bad you were. As a survivor you are struggling to overcome that image. You do not need to be told to suppress your pride. You have so little self-confidence that pride is not a deadly sin: it is an impossibility. Your self-esteem is too damaged for you to suffer from arrogance. You do not need lectures on asceticism and mortification. You have been sufficiently humiliated and mortified by members of your family" (1993, 18).

ADDICTIVE DISORDERS

The relationship between traumatic or abusive experiences of lesser severity has increasingly come to be recognized as a precursor of many of the addictive disorders, which often share clinical features with other forms of compulsion. In addition, the extreme need to control the chaos that arises from a dysfunctional early life experience or that exists in the present can contribute to engagement in addictive behavior. Fr. Leo Booth, who has written widely about religious and spiritual addictions, quotes Craig Nakken, a chemical dependency therapist, on how addicts attempt to control the cycles of their addiction: "When addicts engage in a particular object or event to preclude a desired mood change, they believe they can control these cycles. And at first they can. Addiction, on its most basic level, is an attempt to control and fulfill this desire" (Booth 1991, 28).

It is in the area of addiction theory and treatment that we find the closest interdependence between psychological treatment and spiritual practices. The phenomenal growth of 12 step recovery programs, first developed by Alcoholics Anonymous, in addressing a variety of psychological disorders—encompassing dependence on substances (alcohol, drugs, food), emotions (depression, rage, martyrdom), and processes (sex, religion, caretaking, or work)—is attributable in part to the spiritual and social components of this method of treatment. Although some critics warn against the tendency to view such a wide range of human behavior as rooted in "addiction," these programs have nonetheless demonstrated at least as much ability as traditional psychotherapy to enhance the growth of individuals through elimination of the self-destructive, addictive patterns of behavior.

At the core of the groups that use the 12-Step model is an explicitly spiritual component. Addiction is seen as resulting from failure to acknowledge one's ultimate dependence upon a "higher power." What distinguishes these groups from traditional religious communities and from cults is the insistence that each individual must relate to his or her unique images of this higher power. Unlike traditional religious institutions, 12-Step groups have no creed that ascribes a particular set of characteristics to the higher power; part of the work of recovery is seen as opening oneself to the beneficial effects of a personal experience of the divine, the image of which will be unique to each person. The other feature of these groups which distinguishes them from more traditional psychotherapeutic approaches is the fact that all members are seen as equally capable and accountable for others' healing through simple acceptance and listening to one another. The work of healing from addiction is seen as the work of the higher power, not of the individual or the helping professional.

The founders of Alcoholics Anonymous, who formulated the 12 Steps as a description of the behavior that leads to "sobriety," were strongly influenced by principles developed earlier by the Oxford Group, composed of English men and women whose religious training had taken place in the Anglican tradition and who met regularly with the explicit purpose of mutual spiritual growth and direction. This group's members were also influenced heavily by the psychological writings of Carl Jung, a Swiss psychoanalyst. Jung described alcoholism as a spiritual disease and was one of the first to suggest the connection between its development and psychic numbing or dissociation.

Later theorists have described the "addictive personality" in which the individual's self-concept is so unrelentingly negative that he or she is forced to create a "false self" in order to continue to function. Arterburn and Felton offer this definition of addiction: "When a person is excessively devoted to something or surrenders compulsively and habitually to something, that pathological devotion becomes an addiction." (1992, 104) Addictions vary; some persons are attached to a substance, others to work, still others to destructive relationships. "Addictions develop when people seek relief from pain, a quick fix, or an immediate altered mood. When a person develops a pathological relationship to this mood altering experience or substance that has life damaging consequences, addiction exists. The addict becomes devoted to the source of mood alteration and, by giving up everything for that change in feelings, comes to worship the addictive act with body, mind and spirit" (Arterburn and Felton 1992, 104–5).

The concept of addiction as a distorted form of worship has led to increased attention to the importance of values, image of self, and image of God (however understood) in designing holistic interventions for addictive behavior. As an example, Kirk Schneider has described the "religious existential approach" to addiction to food. He suggests that those who exhibit compulsive eating can benefit from identifying and altering dysfunctional habits first, then identifying and transforming the values underlying those habits (Schneider 1990, 95).

Recognition and description of the similarity in personality dynamics underlying addictive behaviors regardless of the object of the addiction has also been noted by writers from a number of different religious traditions who have sought to apply family systems theories, depth psychology, and addiction theory to religious institutions or systems of religious thinking. Edwin H. Friedman, a rabbi and family therapist has noted that: "The emotional processes in a family always have the power to subvert or override its religious values. The emotional system of any family, parishioner or congregational [sic], can always 'jam' the spiritual messages it is receiving" (Friedman 1985, 6–7). Addiction is one such emotional system that interferes with spiritual messages. Indeed, to the extent that the beliefs of a particular religious community demand or reinforce the key injunctions "don't trust; don't feel; don't talk," mentioned earlier as characteristic of addictive systems, the religious community will itself function as an object of addiction. Religious addiction, called by some authors "toxic faith," can be manifested as compulsive religious activity; unwillingness to take responsibility for personal change and growth, waiting instead for God to "rescue" the addict; habitually giving to the religious institution or authority with the expectation of material or spiritual rewards; self-obsession; extreme intolerance; and/or an addiction to a religious high (Arterburn and Felton 1992, 37; Arterburn and Felton 1991).

CULTS

Other authors have turned their attention to the processes through which particular religious traditions or groups actually participate in the development of addictive or pathological behavior. Much media attention focused on cults during the period of the late 1960s and 1970s. The violent deaths of large numbers of cult members in Jonestown, Guyana in the 1980s and again in Waco, Texas in the 1990s have brought the issue of cults to the forefront of concern. Current social and political debates about values and morality in public life, and the use of the media as a vehicle for numerous "charismatic" religious personalities who have subsequently been shown to be abusive, fraudulent or dishonest have again raised questions about the potential of religious symbols and experiences to harm people. Although there is no common agreement among the social sciences about what differentiates a cult from other small, unconventional religious groups, it is generally agreed that a cult is usually characterized by three related tendencies: (1) an authoritarian organization in which the leader has ultimate power; (2) dissimulation about the true nature and beliefs of the group; and (3) the practice of techniques that facilitate and maintain altered states of consciousness (Sirkin 1990, 116). During the last decade, the anticult movement has enjoyed increase professionalization, "a process in which research and the roles of psychiatrists, psychologists, and social workers have become more salient" (Robbins 1988, 6). Expanded credibility has been given to the "brainwashing" or "coercive-persuasion" model by mental health professionals who argue that involvement in nontraditional religions stems from manipulative psychological practices inducing ego destruction and overstimulation of the nervous system, resulting in a loss of rational decision making capabilities and even a loss of free will. Popular media portrayals and public conceptualizations have been shaped largely by the brainwashing thesis. According to Snow and Malchelek (1984, 167), this explanation has become popular among the public because it provides a convenient account for those who are at a loss to explain why individuals are attracted to bizarre groups. Contributing further to this victimization approach is the alleged spread of Satanic cults among youth, an allegation fostered by law enforcement agents, mental health professionals, and the media, though little empirical evidence can be shown to support these claims (Bromley 1989, 221). While the public has reduced conversion to brainwashing or mind control, it has commonly characterized disaffiliation as a clandestine escape analogous to the perilous flight of inmates from concentration camps or prisons. Departures aided by deprogrammers, therapists or exit counselors have been commonly characterized as rescues in which individuals are benevolently extricated from debilitating environments endangering their mental health. The coercive persuasion model is the most popular explanation of conversion to new religions outside of sociological circles (Snow and Malchelek 1984, 170).

The brainwashing or coercive persuasion model is built upon the studies of indoctrination practices by Chinese communists on American P.O.W.s. It rests on critical assumptions that participants are passive, unwilling or unsuspecting victims of devious but specifiable forces that manufacture conversion. Induced psychological dysfunctions of the brain are achieved by systematically controlled environments engendering heightened receptivity to new ideas through such techniques as guilt manipulation, forced confessions, food deprivation, self-denigration, and information control. This model has found some clinical support (Singer 1979, 16) though most clinical evidence is in conflict with this model (Levine 1985, 37). Other researchers and clinicians have questioned the popular model, noting that the more sensational cases which are popularized represent only a very small fraction of those who are involved with cults and raising ethical questions about "deprogramming," a process one author likens to "familial kidnapping" (Gordon 1983, 605).

The helping professional is most likely to become involved with the families of those individuals who have (voluntarily or otherwise) left the religious group, whether a traditional religious institution, a sect or a cult. Clinicians are almost unanimous in reporting that these disaffiliations are extremely stressful, even if voluntarily chosen. Former adherents face the formidable task of completely restructuring their social, vocational and belief systems, a process not unlike that faced by alcoholics in giving up their dependence on alcohol. Family systems theorists have proposed a model which posits that affiliation with cultic religious groups represents a failure of the individual to successfully negotiate the transition from the family into independence. Seeking to negotiate this transition, the individual is often vulnerable to the acceptance and welcome with which most cults, sects or religious groups first approach potential converts because these emotional qualities may be missing from the family environment. Cults are frequently terrifying to parents, particularly those whose own religious beliefs have become part of the process of the family struggle, and so affiliation with a cult may function as a way for the member to repudiate family authority while still maintaining dependence. This model, then, leads clinicians to see the task of "deprogramming" not as an effort to break through coercive conditioning, but as a therapeutic opportunity to assist a family system in successfully negotiating a normal life transition.

Human service workers and religious professionals are often called to evaluate or intervene when issues involving the treatment of children and their involvement in cults arise. Reports of bizarre and drastic discipline or the withholding of commonly accepted medical care from young children are not infrequent in the United States. Mistreatment of children within a cult may also involve neglect, when the group leader actively discourages parents from involvement with their children because it detracts from their spiritual practice or support of the group. Parents may project onto their children the ideas and desires which are unacceptable to them as cult members, subjecting the children to criticism or harsh and unrelenting punishment as the parents attempt to exorcize their own unacceptable fantasies from the child. It is often a difficult task for the human services professional to assess the presence or extent of such abuse given the closed nature of cultic groups and the unswerving loyalty to the group leader which adherents almost always exhibit.

ALTERNATIVE GROUPS

Timothy Bakken looked at the similarities between reported religious conversion to traditional and what he calls "alternative" groups in an effort to determine whether religious conversion "is simply a timely psychosocial intervention by religious intermediaries, a deviant experience, or a true reinterpretation of one's fundamental beliefs that leads ultimately to behavioral changes" (1985, 158). Bakken cites Abraham Maslow (1954), who theorized that in order to develop, every human being must satisfy certain psychological and physiological needs—love and a sense of belonging being crucial to achieving the individual's full potential, Bakken points out that both traditional and alternative religious groups attempt to convert people to believe that a particular spiritual philosophy will help the individual to achieve the satisfaction of these foundational needs. For many individuals, these conversion processes have been tolerated and result in healing and a higher level of functioning. For others, though, affiliation with a doctrine or lifestyle labeled "deviant," "cultic," or "radical" may in fact be an attempt to seek escape from temporal existence rather than aiming for mastery over it. Bakken states that those "who convert for *psychosocial* rather than doctrinal reasons can be characterized as one-dimensional persons who become static in their thinking and relating to the world. The groups dogmatically foster intraorganizational unity but advocate separation and escape from the rest of society" (Bakken 1985, 159).

The constellation of beliefs characteristic of the addictive thought system can predispose the individual to the type of rigid thinking and denial Bakken describes. Lee Jampolsky (1991, 39) describes some of the core beliefs of the addictive thought system:

1. "I am alone in a cruel, harsh and unforgiving world. I am separate from everybody else."
2. "If I want safety and peace of mind, I must judge others and be quick to defend myself."
3. "My way is the right way. My perceptions are always factually cor-

rect. In order to feel good about myself, I need to be perfect all of the time."
4. "Attack and defense are my only safety."
5. "The past and the future are real and need to be constantly evaluated and worried about."
6. "Guilt is inescapable because the past is real."
7. "Mistakes call for judgment and punishment, not correction and learning."
8. "Fear is real. Do not question it."
9. "Other people are responsible for how I feel. The situation is the determiner of my experience."
10. "If I am going to make it in this world, I must pit myself against others. Another's loss is my gain."
11. "My self-esteem is based on pleasing you."
12. "I can control other people's behavior."

Such a belief system leads to chronic fear and shame, an obsessive focus on the past or future while denying the possibility of change in the present, a harshly judgmental stance toward self and others, coupled with a belief in scarcity which precludes the experience of love and intimacy with self, others, or a higher power.

Assessment of these situations requires careful listening for the beliefs Jampolsky outlines. Healing in most cases will require the skills of physical, psychological, and spiritual healers. Mention has been made elsewhere in this work of the importance of including a spiritual assessment when psychopathology or physical disease is suspected. It is also important to the practitioner to obtain information on the individual's experience of religious ritual, participation in religious groups, and experience with religious authorities as a child.

CONCLUSION

It cannot be overstated that religious phenomena are complex, multicausal, and—because they deal with the human spirit—perhaps impossible to understand from a solely scientific perspective. The same could be said of human cognitive and emotional processes. Research in the biological and physical sciences is converging with the arts and philosophy as the artificial divisions between body, mind, and spirit are recognized as inadequate to account for much of human experience and behavior. Concepts of psychological functioning and spiritual development are increasingly sounding similar themes regarding the importance of the human capacity to tell stories, engage in ritualized behavior, and maintain productive social relationships. As the human service professional seeks to understand the significance of religious themes, behaviors, and rituals in the lives of individuals, it is critical to maintain the awareness that the specific content or form of religious experience is only an incomplete expression of the human encounter with the mysteries of life. Nevertheless, there can be power in religious expression to foster healing, to "rebind" through shared beliefs, ritual, and the experience of community. Religious expression can also be distorted and result in horrifying and seemingly inexplicable events such as mass suicide, religious warfare, ritualistic physical, emotional, or sexual abuse in the guise of religion, or murder claimed to be at the command of God. Attempting to understand the religious context of individuals' life stories is so complex that human service providers will need to work closely with clergy in understanding these expressions of spirituality and religiosity.

CASE FOR REFLECTION

Mary and Joe Clements live in Home Town. They are meeting with a human service worker at the local shelter for teenagers. Their son, Bill, recently ran away from home and was found wandering downtown late at night in the cold by the workers from the shelter. The workers called them down to the shelter after obtaining Bill's reluctant permission. Bill is seventeen years old. He claims that his parents are trying to keep him away from God and that God no longer wants him to live under their "nonreligious" and "evil" influence.

Joe and Mary: Bill was a normal, reasonably well adjusted teenager until about nine months ago. He was never very outgoing and all of his life had just a few friends, but he had been close to two neighborhood boys since grade school. About a year ago one of the boys moved out of state with his parents and the other became involved with a girlfriend and never had time for Bill. Bill seemed to go through a few months of depression. He stayed around the house and his grades—usually solid B's—dropped to C's and D's. His parents were worried. Then he appeared to find a new set of friends, a group of his schoolmates who all belonged to the same church. These boys were very active in the church; it occupied all their spare time. They went on trips, did volunteer work, and prayed a great deal. They openly encouraged Bill to join the church.

109

"We're not regular churchgoers," says Mary, "so we were somewhat surprised that Bill became interested in actually joining the church. But we decided he was involved in good, healthy activity that was a great alternative to drugs, so we told him to go ahead and join." Soon afterward, Bill became very critical of his parents' lifestyle. He wanted them to stop smoking (they had tried), drinking (they were very moderate social drinkers), playing cards with their friends, and buying state lottery tickets. "That was the last straw," says Joe. "I told him he could be as straitlaced as he wanted to be, but he was not allowed to interfere with our lives."

After that, Bill seemed to withdraw from his parents and spent increasing amounts of time at church and in his room praying. He carried a Bible wherever he went, even to school. A friend of Mary's who teaches at Bill's school told her that some of the other students had been making fun of his new behavior. The teacher said that she was worried about Bill and suggested that Mary take him to a mental health center. However, Mary and Joe believed that as long as Bill was not involved in drugs or illegal activities he was doing just fine. The night before Bill left home, he became angry with his parents because they were planning an outing with some of their friends to the riverboat casino that had just opened in Home Town. He told them that God would punish them for gambling. Joe could no longer take his son's righteous attitude and told him to "shut up or get out." Bill interpreted Joe's outburst as a sign that God wanted him to leave.

Bill: Bill was very reluctant to talk. Asked about his parents, he finally stated that he believed the devil had taken over his parents and they were beyond God's help. He said that God had been talking to him, telling him that he must leave home or the devil would take over his soul as well. He did not want to see a counselor. When asked if he wanted to see a minister from the church to which he belonged, he refused, saying that the members of the church had also fallen into the hands of the devil. Only he had been spared because he was willing to do anything God told him to do.

Discussion

1. Is Bill's behavior symptomatic of religious addiction or of a more serious psychopathology? On what do you base your diagnosis?
2. What are the emotional and spiritual developmental issues presented by both Bill and his parents?
3. What should the human service workers at the shelter do at this point, in the middle of the night?
4. What kind of treatment is needed? Who should be treated?

5. How could this situation have been avoided—what were the very first symptoms that should have been heeded?
6. Would you involve a clergyperson in this situation?

REFERENCES

Arterburn, S., and J. Felton. 1991. *Toxic faith: Understanding and overcoming religious addiction.* Nashville: Thomas Nelson.

———. 1993. *Faith that hurts, faith that heals.* Nashville: Thomas Nelson.

Bakken, T. 1985. Religious conversion and social evolution clarified: Similarities between traditional and alternative groups. *Small Group Behavior,* 16 (2): 157–66.

Bergin, A. 1983. Religiosity and mental health: A critical reevaluation of meta-analysis. *Professional Psychology: Research and Practice,* 14: 170–84.

———. 1987. Religiousness and mental health reconsidered: A study of an intrinsically religious sample. *Journal of Counseling Psychology.* 34: 197–204.

Booth, L. 1991. When God becomes a drug. *Common Boundary,* September/October: 27.

Bowman, E. 1989. Understanding and utilizing religious material in the therapy of multiple personality disorder. *Proceedings of the Fourth Regional Conference on Multiple Personality and Dissociative States.* Akron: Akron General Medical Center, 115–27.

Bromley, D. G. 1987. The future of the anticult movement. In *The future of new religious movements,* ed. D. G. Bromley and P. E. Hammond, 221–34. Macon, Ga.: Mercer University Press.

Friedman, E. H. 1985. *Generation to generation: Understanding family process in church and synagogue.* New York: Guilford Press.

Gordon, James S. 1991. The cult phenomenon and the psychotherapeutic response. *Journal of the American Academy of Psychoanalysis,* 11 (4): 603–15.

Green, A. 1985. Children traumatized by physical abuse. In *Post traumatic stress disorder in children.* Washington, D.C.: American Psychiatric Press.

Higdon, J. F. 1986. Association of fundamentalism with multiple personality disorder. *Proceedings of the Third International Conference on Multiple Personality/Dissociative States.* Chicago: Rush-Presbyterian St. Luke Hospital, 161.

Jampolsky, L. 1991. *Healing the addictive mind.* Berkeley: Celestial Arts.

Larson, D. B., E. M. Pattison, D. G. Blazer, A. R. Omran, and B. H. Kaplan. 1986. Systematic analysis of research on religious variables in four major psychiatric journals, 1979–1982. *American Journal of Psychiatry,* 143: 329–34.

Leehan, J. 1993. *Defiant hope: Spirituality for survivors of family abuse.* Louisville: Westminster/John Knox.

Levine, S. 1985. *Radical departures: Desperate detours to growing up.* New York: Harcourt Brace Jovanovich.

May, G. 1992. *Care of mind, care of spirit.* New York: HarperCollins.

Robbins, T. 1988. *Cults, converts, and charisma*. New York: Sage.

Schneider, K. J. 1992. The worship of food: An existential perspective. *Psychotherapy,* 27 (1): 95–97.

Singer, M. 1978. Therapy with excult members. *Journal of the National Association of Private Psychiatric Hospitals,* 9: 15–19.

Sirkin, M. 1994. Cult involvement: A systems approach to assessment and treatment. *Psychotherapy,* 27 (1): 116–23.

Snow, D., and R. Malchelek. 1984. The sociology of conversion, *Annual Review of Sociology,* 10: 167–90.

Terr, M. 1985. Remembered images and trauma: A psychology of the supernatural. *Psychoanalytic Study of the Child,* 40: 493–533.

Chapter 7

RELIGION AND SPIRITUALITY OF HUMAN SERVICE WORKERS

The focus of previous chapters has been on providing practitioners with an understanding of how religion and spirituality influence their clients' lives. In this chapter, we emphasize the importance of being in touch with one's own beliefs. It should hardly be necessary to add that every provider brings his or her own values to the profession.

Over the past ten years, increasing interest has been shown in the clinical significance of the beliefs, practices, and attitudes of human services providers regarding religion and spirituality. Some of the ground breaking researchers in this area include Joseph (1988), Canda (1988), Dudley and Helfgott (1990), and Sheridan and Bullis (1992). Sheridan et al. (1992) report having investigated such attitudes and behaviors of 328 licensed mental health clinicians in Virginia. They conclude that very little attention is paid to the need for education in the area of spirituality. The authors specifically discuss the implications for social work education.

May (1982, 297) observes: "It is a maxim in contemplative traditions that one needs help from others in the course of one's spiritual pilgrimage. But this maxim is not complete without its corollary: Helping others is part of being a pilgrim. . . . Spiritual pilgrimage involves solitary searching, receiving help, and offering help to others." This statement is revealing because May points out that human beings decide to offer help along their journeys through life. The human service worker is a helping professional who has made the choice to help others, for whatever reasons. Some reasons may be grounded in a rich spiritual life, participation in a religious community, or based on providing new opportunities (both religious and secular) for clients to search for meaning in whatever form that emerges.

The previous chapter makes very clear that, in addition to being a positive means of coping with the trials of life and reaching one's full potential, religion and spirituality can also, when abused, be very destructive to the human personality. Thus, this variable should be approached with great caution in the counseling or human service encounter. Perhaps just because it is so potent— to the point of influencing vast arenas of history—that practitioners have often shied away from taking religious/spiritual values into consideration. The cliché "Never talk about religion or politics" seems to be the rule even in the intimacy of the counseling situation.

Yet as we have noted, religion and spirituality are increasingly evident as topics in the media—and the media reports current social concerns. Two-thirds of the respondents to a randomized recent survey stated that religion was "very" important in their lives. It is also an important factor in shaping the collective values and behavior of society—not just in this country, but globally. Wars are fought in the name of religion, and political coalitions often frame their causes in religious terms. In the United States and throughout the world, religious symbolism and language permeate the secular environment (Faver 1987, 210).

Faver points out that social work educators and students often react to religious discussions with strong emotion because these dialogues touch upon basic human beliefs. For many people, including both (social work) educators and students, discussions of religion arouse anxiety and elicit strong reactions. "There is no 'value-free' education. Ignoring or lightly dismissing religion is as much a bias as 'pushing' a particular religious perspective. . . . Social workers should acquire a basic understanding of the meaning and effects of religion in their own and others' lives" (Faver 1987, 213).

PARADIGM FOR CONCEPTUALIZING SPIRITUALITY/RELIGION

Religion and spirituality have the potential to act as coping mechanisms, sources of growth and self-transcendence, or sources of pathology for clients and practitioners alike. Is there a general paradigm or model for understanding of the spiritual aspect of life and its relationship to the biological, psychological, and social domains that the human service provider could use to discern the role that both religion and spirituality play in the life of the client as well as in his or her own life? What is greatly needed is a model or paradigm that would be user friendly for the human service worker who is a nonspecialist in spirituality. Does such a model exist?

The SPINAT

The literature suggests a need for a model which is both multidimensional and multidirectional. The SPINAT, or Spiritual Needs Assessment Tool, was

114

developed in response to the call for a tool that would not dictate either the theoretical paradigm or personal theology of the practitioner while offering an approach to understanding the spirituality of the client. The theory grounding the instrument offers a window for psychology to view spirituality and for spirituality to interface with psychology. To clarify this process, we refer to the work of the theologian Paul Tillich and the call for a holistic approach.

One of the important contributions of Paul Tillich (1967) is found in his approach to theory. Tillich understood that he was articulating theology from the perspective of human beings, not from the perspective of a higher being or God. For many years the idea of including any kind of metaphysical concept into a social science or clinical instrument defied methodology when the metaphysical aspects of the relationship were emphasized. By *what is meaningful to the client,* can apply more of the methodology found in the social sciences. The SPINAT instrument employs a holistic approach to understanding the spiritual dimension, especially that of elderly clients. The concept of holism on which it is based provides a model or paradigm which can apply equally to the development of instruments or informal interview formats for any age group.

The concept of holism is not new, although its meaning has changed somewhat over time. In current usage *holism* refers to the existential concept of the person as a unique and unified self. Thus, the parts or dimensions of the person cannot be separated. As early as the 1920s, such psychologists as Alfred Adler spoke of a holistic view applied to the needs of clients. More recently, Granger Westberg (1995) emphasized the concept of the "wholistic" approach to meeting health needs. (Westberg included the *w* in order to emphasize the addition of the spiritual.) Although theorists have conceptualized holism in different ways, they have one thing in common: All discuss the individual as having several aspects, or dimensions. These include the physical self, the emotional self, the social self, and the "fourth dimension," the spiritual self.

Each of the four dimensions can be conceptualized as a separate entity or domain. Physicians, for example, generally consider the physical self to be their domain; psychologists address the emotional dimension; group or recreation therapists and social workers deal with the social self; and clergy and spiritual advisers attend to the fourth dimension. However, what Adler and others pointed out that it is difficult to address each of these dimensions *as if the others did not exist.* The central principle of holism is that all four dimensions must be included in any attempt to understand the person in his or her totality and uniqueness. In fact, holistic (and wholistic) theorists agree that the various dimensions cannot really be separated.

However, if conceptualized as parts, then they can be treated separately. In

Spiritual Domains

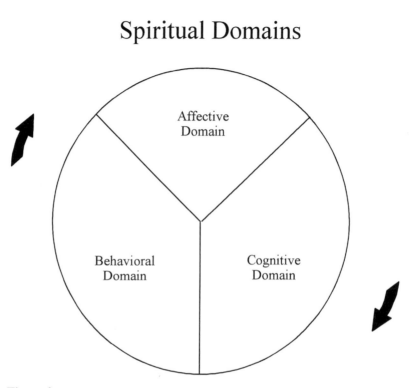

Figure 3

medicine, specialists treat specific parts of the body; in this same way the concept of wholism would view a single dimension and see it in the context of the others. Here the concept of spiritual health or well being asserts that the role of the spiritual is to be an *integrative* element in the life of the individual. Thus, the spiritual is not just one more dimension among others; it also has an integrative function or force, connecting and interacting with all the other dimensions in forming the whole individual (see Figure 3).

The developers of the SPINAT see the potential for any one of the dimensions to contribute to the integrative function. The same is true of the various subdimensions of spirituality. The SPINAT encompasses three such subdimensions—the cognitive, affective, and behavioral:

1. *Cognitive.* This subdimension includes knowledge and belief. It involves primarily an intellectual exploration and assent to the specific

ascription of meaning and value given to historical, current, and personal events by a religion or philosophy.

2. *Affective*. This subdimension includes all aspects of the inner life of the person—that is, the experience of the self as it exists apart from others' "selves" and from the external world. It also includes the sense of "connectedness"—the feeling that one exists within and in relation to a larger reality of meaning that is simultaneously within the self and external to it. The interior life is activated by the interaction of acquired knowledge, belief, and emotional and physical experiences. This interaction allows for and leads to the personal attribution of meaning to experiences and events.

3. *Behavioral*. This subdimension involves the individual's overt activities relating to religion or spirituality, whether those activities are performed by the individual alone or with others. It can include the relationship of the individual to an organized religion or spiritual system. The behavioral subdimension is the vehicle through which the individual publicly affirms his or her beliefs. In exchange, the person receives validation, affirmation, and social and emotional support (Thibault et al. 1991, 34–35).

In "real life" the various domains and subdomains overlap and interact in a dynamic interplay which results in the person's unique religious or spiritual identity. In the SPINAT, the integrative dimension is seen as the life force of the individual, which is a product of the total spiritual dimension as it impacts the whole person. From this perspective, the various elements or subdimensions of spirituality may well perform integrative functions in this model, but they do not have to do so. The individual can exercise free will in determining who he or she will be. Thus, each individual is unique in the way the various elements are used and brought together. Instruments that assess only religiosity or involvement in religion focus only on the behavioral subdimension of spirituality. Thus, a simple correlation between religious behavior and the other domains of the person neglects the other elements of spirituality. It is the dynamic relationship between all three subdimensions that offers the energy for the integrative potential of the individual (see Figure 4).

Another instrument, the precursor of the SPINAT, was developed based on a theoretical model by Thibault, Ellor, and Netting (1991). In this model—proposed as a paradigm for understanding the dynamics of spirituality—the three-part (cognitive, affective, and behavioral) spiritual domain is conceptualized as a potentially integrative structure that can be visualized as an overlay to the (holistic) physical, emotional, and social domains of the individual. The

The Whole Person: A Model

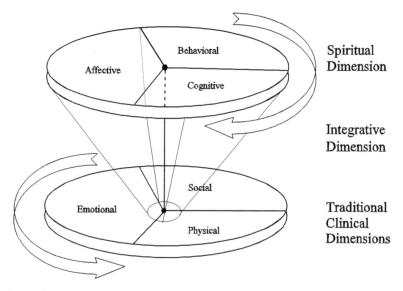

Spiritual
Dimension

Integrative
Dimension

Traditional
Clinical
Dimensions

Figure 4

essentially spiritual domain overlies the physical, emotional, and social domains and can interact with any aspect of them. For example, the cognitive and
emotional domain or inner life of the person can interact with the physical aspect in the following way: A person in great pain with a terminal illness can
choose to offer the energy of suffering invested in their unrelievable pain to be
used for the well being of a particular person or the rest of the universe. In this
way an individual's pain, which is primarily a meaningless, life diminishing
physical experience, can become meaningful to the individual (as well as to the
rest of those who are in sympathy with his or her belief system) by being connected with the cognitive and affective spiritual domains.

This model is a highly dynamic one. The correlation between the various
subdimensions of spirituality will be different from one person to the next and
within the same individual over time. Like a top spinning on a platter, the spiritual domain can touch other single domains, but most frequently it moves, encompassing some or even all of the several domains in the holistic view of the
person (Ellor et al. 1993). This model has been employed as a vehicle for de-

veloping dialogue on spiritual matters in the analysis of spiritual material, but most importantly, as an approach to interpreting the spiritual dimensions as a part of the emotional and psychological dimensions of client assessment. The model can also offer clinical insight. The following case provides an example.

Mr. Smith is an eighty-two year old Caucasian male, a member of the Roman Catholic Church. He recently sought help from a clinician for depression brought on by an overwhelming feeling of guilt from actions that he had taken earlier in his life. Mr. Smith and the worker discussed his guilt, utilizing cognitive behavioral techniques. During this time, he was able to see the intellectual thought patterns that brought on the feeling of guilt, as well as the behaviors that he participated in when he felt the guilt. Unfortunately, he came to a standstill at the point where he felt that he now knew the source of his problem, but could not *feel* that he was forgiven, particularly since the other parties involved were deceased. One day he happened to be talking to the priest of his church, who responded to their brief discussion about Mr. Smith's guilt by offering him absolution. Mr. Smith returned to the clinic, now *feeling* forgiven. Subsequently he was able to successfully terminate treatment.

In this case, the practitioner was able to support Mr. Smith's efforts to resolve his depression in the cognitive and behavioral aspects, but was unable to fully impact the emotional domain. By receiving absolution from his priest, he was able to feel fully forgiven and thus experienced resolution of the guilt and subsequently the depression ended. Diagnostically, it could be seen that the plateau in the treatment process was caused by the absence of his ability to feel forgiven, but was resolved by the use of the symbols of his faith, within the affective domain of spirituality.

This case offers one example of the potential use of the model. Had the helping professional been able to utilize the spiritual variables upon initial assessment, he/she would have been able the see the client's need for holistic insight into his feelings related to spiritual affect and the need for support of the whole self. When this model is used in the initial assessment the practitioner is offered both insight into the specific aspects of spirituality, as well as the rest of the person's bio-psycho-social and even environmental (nature plus organizational structures) life.

SPIRITUAL SELF-ASSESSMENT OF THE DIRECT PRACTITIONER

Nearly every introspective person, at some time in life, is faced with having to make a decision about the part that religion and spirituality will play in his or her life. For most, this is an intensely personal decision making process. However, when persons function as helping professionals, when even nonverbal behavior can convey values and influence clients via the dynamics of transference and counter transference, they have a professional obligation to examine and ultimately understand the role religion and spirituality play in their own public and private lives. This can be accomplished formally or informally, according to Strean (1978) who suggests that everything from peer supervision, ongoing self-scrutiny, case conferencing, on going therapy, and continuing education are all possible avenues for personal and professional growth.

The spiritual journey, or spiritual self-examination by the human service worker, is as important as the personal therapy or psychological examination the prospective therapist is encouraged to undertake before embarking on a mental health related career.

Helping professionals in the United States are faced with many opportunities for religious expression. Within the "mainstream" religions there are a plethora of subgroups representing differing ideas about the transcendent dimension, and also, as Kelsey states, "We live in an age of spiritual fads" (Kelsey 1978, 3). For this reason it is very important for human service providers to understand at least the basics of the theoretical foundations not only of their own, but of the prevalent spiritualities in their geographical area of practice.

Performing an inventory of the human service provider's own knowledge, beliefs, attitudes, feelings, and practices regarding spirituality and religion is the first step in the incorporation of these areas into professional practice. Using and building on the definitions and descriptions of religion and spirituality provided in the introduction to this book, the following are basic questions the human service provider can use as a guide in the process of self-assessment in the areas of religion and spirituality:

1. Do I experience a personal need for the spiritual, the "sublime"? Have I recognized an urge or desire for self-transcendence, ultimate meaning, or a relationship with a "higher power"?

    To the extent that one identifies this need as a significant variable in one's own bio-psycho-social-spiritual development one will be able to recognize and respect the same tendency in the client, even if the urge is not expressed in the same way. It is more likely to become an acceptable area for exploration. To the extent that this is not an important variable, the practitioner may downplay its importance to the client in the areas of coping, transcending, and pathology and thus miss a significant factor relating to either health or dysfunction.

2. How intense is my urge toward the spiritual or transcendent dimension of my life?

If this is an area of intense interest and active personal pursuit, the human service provider will have to be cognizant of the dynamics of transference and counter transference. Religion and spirituality should never be imposed on the client; some say it should not even be suggested as a therapeutic modality. In addition, the discussion of religion and spirituality, especially the more experiential aspects, can arouse intense emotional reactions in both clinician and client—not unlike discussions of sexuality. Scott Peck, in considering the relationship of sexuality and spirituality, expresses the situation pithily: "As a friend of mine once put it, 'The sexual and the spiritual parts of our personality lie so close together that it is hardly possible to arouse one without arousing the other'. . . So it is that you hear stories about ministers who become involved with female parishioners. Ministers and other people in similar positions tend to be sitting ducks when such passions are aroused." (1993, 226).

On the other hand, if this is a domain which the provider has avoided or has not experienced as a value to personal life, it may become a therapeutic "taboo." The client may ascertain this attitude, feel uncomfortable about discussing spiritual urges for the sublime for fear of being thought "unsophisticated," and never mention an aspect of life which enables coping, growing, or which impedes growth.

3. How have I expressed this spiritual urge? How have I repressed it? Has the provider found an outlet, in thought and/or behavior, for the urge for self-transcendence? Chandler et al. state that "any experience of transcendence of one's former frame of reference that results in greater knowledge and love is a spiritual experience" (1992, 170). In what areas of life has the provider grown in the past five years? What are their spiritual desires or goals?

Haronian describes the state in which the person denies a recognized urge toward transcendence as the "repression of the sublime," and claims that this condition can result in either hypoactivity or hyperactivity. He asserts: "To feel the pull of the sublime is an essential part of being fully human . . . However, we often do repress it. There are many ways in which we evade the call of the sublime. Why do we evade, for example, the challenge of personal growth? We fear growth

121

because it means abandoning the familiar for the unknown. And that involves risks" (1974, 55). Maslow's term for such repression is "desacralization," which occurs at all points along the lifespan continuum. He claims that often younger people deny their urges toward self-transcendence because they are trying to protect themselves from disillusionment. They have not had adequate role models to show them how the striving for self-transcendence actually "plays out" in reality.

4. To what degree do I express my spirituality through formal religious activity? If the practitioner is a member of a particular religion, was it chosen freely as an adult as part of the expression of the urge toward transcendence, or is it a relatively meaningless habit left over from childhood? Related questions include: Why have I chosen this religion, this particular community, through which to express my spiritual aspirations or needs? How well does it meet those needs? How much of my time do I spend in activities related to formal religion? How does my religious or faith community view bio-psycho-socio-spiritual growth? Do my religious values and my professional values ever clash?

For many helping professionals, social workers for example, there are built in paradoxes such as client self-determination that lead to clashes between religious and professional values. Acknowledging that one lives with paradoxes is an important developmental task.

5. To what extent do I feel that my way of expressing my spirituality is the "best" or "better" or "preferred" way?

It is imperative that human service professionals be aware of preferences and prejudices regarding religion/spirituality. As stated previously, religious or spiritual orientations must not be imposed on clients. Keep in mind that clients are very sensitive to nonverbal cues. An attitude of superiority on the part of the professional interferes with the helping process because it devalues the client's views. If a practitioner believes their own spiritual "way" is superior to that of their client's, inevitably this condescension will become known to the client in any discussion of religion or spirituality and negatively interfere with the need for unconditional positive regard. The client's growth in this area may then be impeded.

6. How do I feel about serving a client whose spiritual and/or religious views are diametrically opposed to my own? What happens when basic values of spirituality and religion—basic world views—are not

just different, but in conflict with one another? Can the service provider give honest service to the client? Should the client be sent to a worker whose ideas are more closely allied with their own? Can the helping professional offer unconditional positive regard or even respect to the client whose world view is in conflict with her own?

This is not merely an issue of diversity but of potential hostility. Some human service providers will not have the luxury of sending their clients to a more like minded worker, particularly in this era of managed care. Can the service provider transcend his or her animosity—or the client's?

7. To what extent am I willing to learn about the basic spiritual/religious views of my client if they are different from my own? How important is it to the practitioner to be able to incorporate yet another client variable into the therapeutic process? If one truly offers unconditional positive regard and desires to be empathic, is it not necessary to become at least cursorily acquainted with those variables that influence the client for better or worse? How can helping professionals deal with religious and spiritual issues if they know nothing about the historical, philosophical, and behavioral foundations of the religious system the client has chosen or has been taught?

8. To what extent am I willing to include other professionals with expertise in religion and spirituality as my supervisors or consultants? Also, to what extent am I willing to recognize when a particular spiritual issue is beyond the domain of my expertise and, in such a case, to consult with a religious practitioner (minister, priest, rabbi, etc.)?

It is unrealistic to imagine that the human service provider would, in all cases, be professionally equipped to handle all religious and spiritual issues, particularly in times of "spiritual emergency." When the issues are predominantly spiritual or religious, the client should be referred to a more appropriately trained professional who is known and respected by the practitioner. When the issues include spirituality/religion as part of the broader bio-psycho-social aspects of coping, growth, and self-transcendence, the service provider can feel free to attend to them. Situations may occur, however, in which a religious or spiritual issue is beyond the expertise of the service provider, but to change workers would be detrimental to the client. In this case, two alternatives present themselves. First, the client could be seen by the spiritual professional in addition to the primary practitioner. Second (and more practical), the clinician can seek the advice or supervision of a trusted religious professional with expertise in the problem area which has emerged in the course of service provision. The second alternative is actually the better one, because the supervision itself becomes a source of new knowledge for the practitioner.

In addition, there may be a situation in direct social service, when the involvement of the client's spiritual leader or pastor would be of help. For example, if a disabled person without family is to be discharged from the hospital in an area where there are few home care or other services, the pastor/rabbi may be called in as a team member or colleague in a case conference. He or she may assume responsibility for mobilizing the members of the congregation to help with some of the care on a volunteer basis. In the case where there are no family members, the religious leader may be the only person who can give accurate information about the client.

9. To what extent do I feel a need to share my spiritual or religious insights with clients?

This question falls under the general category of professional self-disclosure. A variety of views on the issue of self-disclosure are held by the different schools of psychotherapy. In analytic psychotherapy, therapist self-disclosure is definitely taboo. In the existential, humanistic, and transpersonal modes the issue is not as clear cut and allows for self-disclosure when appropriate. Research on the incorporation of spirituality into human service provision indicates that most clinicians would allow the worker to inform the client of his or her spiritual/religious orientation but would caution the professional to refrain from engaging in spiritual activities such as prayer and meditation with the client. Suggesting that clients explore locally available religious or spiritual offerings in which he or she may be interested in the community is appropriate. Proselytizing or suggesting that the client join a particular religion or a specific spiritual group should *never* be done.

10. If I do not believe in self-transcendence, can I provide service to a client whose need is to find transcendent meaning in life?

If the primary goal of the intervention is religious or spiritual, the service provider would be advised to refer the client to a professional with an interest and belief in this area. Helping professionals are people, with their own values, beliefs, and interests. It may be possible to overcome denominational prejudices, but if the provider does not believe in the reality or existence of the goal of the client, it may be very difficult to develop an alliance. If, on the other hand, religious or spiritual issues emerge as only part of the overall problem, the provider should consider the client's belief system as a variable related to diversity and attempt to deal with it in the same way other diversity issues are approached—with respect and with empathic attempts to understand the client's real needs.

CONCLUSION

The integration of the spiritual domain with human service provision is not a matter of simply asking a few questions related to religious preferences or spiritual activities. Rather, spirituality and religion are complex, dynamic forces that interact with all the other domains of life. The provider must keep this in mind in deciding when and if he or she is going to deal with such issues in her own life and in the lives of her clients.

CASE FOR REFLECTION

Marilyn lives in Home Town. She is a therapist who grew up in a very fundamentalist Christian church. As she progressed in her education and life experience, she went through much soul searching to determine the stance she wanted to take regarding religion in her life. In her early twenties, after two years of therapy, she decided that she was basically a very "spiritual" person but that she did not want to express her spirituality via any formal religious practice. She believed that she would honor others' decisions to belong to formal religious denominations and faiths, but that she had no reason to include such practice in her own life.

When Marilyn had been a counselor in private practice for fifteen years, Louise came to her for career counseling. In the course of discussion Louise revealed that she did not want to make any move away from her home town community because she was so attached to the church to which she belonged and of which she had been a member since childhood.

Marilyn found herself becoming upset. She wanted to free her client from the "fetters" of the church. She began to see Louise as a personal challenge and believed that she was fighting for Louise's future.

Discussion

1. What is happening to Marilyn—why are such strong emotions being evoked by Louise, who did not consider her church membership a problem?
2. Is Marilyn's response normal? abnormal? justified?

3. How should Marilyn deal with these feelings?
4. How should Marilyn proceed in her relationship with Louise?

REFERENCES

Canda, E. R. 1988. Spirituality, religious diversity, and social work practice. *Social Casework,* 69 (40): 238–47.

Chandler, C., J. Holden, and C. Kolander. 1992. Counseling for spiritual wellness: theory and practice. *Journal of Counseling and Development,* 71 (November–December): 168–75.

Dudley, J. R., and C. Helfgott. 1990. Exploring a place for spirituality in the social work curriculum. *Journal of Social Work Education,* 36 (3): 287–94.

Ellor, J., M. Bracki, and J. Thibault. 1993. Assessing the spiritual aspect as a part of clinical assessment with older adults. Presented at Sixth Congress of the International Psychogeriatric Association, Berlin, Germany, September 7, 1993.

Faver, C. 1987. Religious beliefs, professional values, and social work. *Journal of Applied Social Sciences,* 2 (Spring/Summer): 206–19.

Garfield, S., and A. Bergin. 1978. *Handbook of psychotherapy and behavior change: An empirical analysis.* New York: John Wiley and Sons.

Haronian, F. 1974. The repression of the sublime. *Synthesis,* 1 (1): 51–61.

Joseph, M. V. 1988. Religion and social work practice. *Social Casework,* 69: 443–52.

Kelsey, M. 1978. *Discernment.* New York: Paulist Press.

Malony, H. 1995. *The psychology of religion for ministry.* New York: Paulist Press.

May, G. 1982. *Will and spirit: A contemplative psychology.* San Francisco: Harper and Row.

Oates, W. 1961. *The minister's own mental health.* New York: Channel Press.

Peck, S. 1993. *Further along the road less traveled.* New York: Simon and Schuster.

Sheridan, M. J., and R. K. Bullis. 1992. Practitioners' views on religion and spirituality: A qualitative study. *Spirituality and Social Work Journal,* 2 (Summer): 2–10.

Sheridan, M. J., R. K. Bullis, C. R. Adcock, S. D. Berlin, and P. C. Miller. 1992. Practitioners' personal and professional attitudes and behaviors toward religion and spirituality: Issues for education and practice. *Journal of Social Work Education,* 28 (Spring–Summer): 190–203.

Sinetar, M. 1992. *A way without words.* New York: Paulist Press.

Strean, H. 1978. *Clinical social work: Theory and practice.* New York: Free Press.

Thibault, J., J. Ellor, and F. Netting. 1991. A conceptual framework for assessing the spiritual functioning and fulfillment of older adults in long-term care settings. *Journal of Religious Gerontology,* 7 (4): 29–46.

PART *III*

ORGANIZATION, COMMUNITY, AND POLICY APPLICATIONS

Chapter 8

COMMUNITY AND RELIGION IN THE UNITED STATES

Rothman, Erlich and Tropman identify three arenas in which the process of community relationships is built: (1) the community, (2) both formal and informal organizations, and (3) groups (1995, 3). In this chapter we will focus on the ways in which groups seek to establish a sense of community, as well as the functions served by community building. Chapter 9 will examine a particular type of group called the faith-based community or religious congregation, and chapter 10 will focus on a specific organization called the religious affiliate. These last chapters will take the reader from what has been a more microfocused perspective to how religion and spirituality are operationalized in macro arenas (for a full discussion of macro practice, see Netting, Kettner, and McMurtry 1998).

The ability to understand the power of religion and spirituality is intimately tied to understanding why people search for group identity and ultimately for a sense of community. Although many modern day forms of transpersonal spirituality can be viewed as highly individualistic, historically organized religion by its very nature has been a community building endeavor in which groups of people come together for one or more common purposes. Such groups have developed different "styles." On one end of the continuum, members of some religious groups adhere closely to strict doctrine, and the resulting community is highly structured and controlled. On the other end, many groups and communities built around faith traditions primarily provide emotional nurturance and support for persons who have been oppressed in the larger society.

Regardless of how community is perceived, religion, group development, and community are highly interrelated. In this chapter we focus on the reasons why people seek community, followed by an historical perspective on how religious groups have developed. Second, we examine the urgent push to locate groups of people who have similar issues, concerns, and values in contemporary society. Third, community functions are examined, followed by several religiously based models of community building designed to perform these functions.

DEVELOPMENT OF THE SMALL GROUP MOVEMENT

The small group can be viewed as "the most intimate social unit that is an arena for community intervention" (Rothman, Erlich, and Tropman 1995, 12). Groups in general have often been categorized as task oriented and socioemotional. Religious and spiritual groups that have developed through the years often combine both characteristics.

Use of the small group context to counter forces of personal anonymity, societal fragmentation and the need to band together for protection from inimical outside forces has a long history. The development of religion and spirituality have been fostered through small group involvement which extended beyond the natural family and the tribe. From the tribal units of the ancient Israelites to the itinerant discipleship groups of Jesus, the act of intentionally bonding together in groups larger and more diverse than the family has been reflected in the development of the connectedness of the people to self, one another, and to a transcendent source. Judaism, for example, has always been a communal, never a privatized, religion. The basic group from which a synagogue could be formed was made up of ten men, called a minyan. If ten men could not be gathered, communal reading of the scriptures and worship could not take place. In the days of Jesus there were two diverse groups of followers, the itinerant and the resident. The itinerants were transient and followed Jesus into the countryside, whereas the residents were local sympathizers who remained at home to spread the message there (Lee 1993, 186).

In the early days of Christianity house churches were the basic Christian communities. Members of various house churches gathered occasionally, but the basic groups did not lose their identity when these gatherings took place. During the first thousand years of Christianity, membership in "intentional" communities became a significant way of life. Certain Christians, because of their feeling, understanding or even desire for intense connectedness with ultimate meaning, chose to go apart from their families and the conventions of the local society to live more radically the teachings of Jesus. The age of monasticism developed first: the mendicant and apostolic religious orders and their lay associates emerged later. These religious communities not only spread

Christianity, but also served the surrounding community with material goods, education, and acts of charity. In reality, not all people entered monasteries to grow more connected to God; some, including "landless sons and unmarriageable daughters" (Rausch 1990, 59) were deposited there for life care purposes by their families. However, through their membership in these communities they found a more respectable place for themselves than if they had to remain as second class citizens in their family homes.

In the Christian tradition, women have been especially cognizant of the value to themselves and to others of living together in community. There have been far more communities of religious women than those of men. "From the nineteenth century until the great changes in religious life which followed the Second Vatican Council, religious sisters provided a whole infrastructure of social and educational services for Catholics throughout the world. As Christian communities of dedicated women, they did missionary work; ran and staffed hospitals, schools, and colleges; and cared for sick, orphaned, elderly, and disadvantaged persons. Their contribution to the life of the church has been enormous" (Rausch 1990, 95).

Even though the Reformation emerged from the model of small group meetings in homes, Protestants often looked askance at "Catholic" community life. However, several strongly community oriented Protestant groups, such as the Quakers, the Moravian Brethren, and the Mennonites, soon arose. Many Protestant denominations made use of small groups for purposes of growth. Methodists gathered people together in classes that became the traditional Sunday schools; Baptists made use of the Wednesday evening prayer meeting and Bible study. In the early years of the twentieth century, Sunday worship services in most Protestant churches could accommodate all congregants, but there also reemerged the home based prayer and Bible groups. In the church itself, "the most common group offerings were the prayer meetings, ladies' missionary society meetings, youth organizations, and an occasional task oriented gathering, such as choir practices or meetings of elders and deacons" (Wuthnow 1994, 43).

In the 1950s, 60s, and 70s there emerged a new kind of small group movement—one based heavily on the desire to share personal feelings and inner experiences. This new kind of group sharing had its roots in the 1950s, with the conviction of certain psychotherapists that group sharing could be as healing to emotionally disturbed patients as individual psychotherapy. The 1960s saw the emergence of both "T" or training groups and encounter groups. T-groups were primarily designed to develop more efficient teams in business settings by facilitating a higher quality of interpersonal relationships. The objective was not to heal, but to enhance skills. The encounter group's main focus was to deal with intra-and inter-personal difficulties through confrontation; its purpose was primarily therapeutic.

To date, the two most significant supporters of small self-help groups have been mental health professionals and religious leaders. A sense of spirituality, even if it is very vague, seems to pervade most small group meetings, so that even in the secular self-help groups such as AA there is reference to the value of connectedness to ultimate meaning (the "higher power"). Because of the small group's ability to ameliorate feelings of alienation and isolation, it has become a major force in American religion. Religious congregations are highly intentional in their use of small groups. For example, the RENEW movement has created small sharing groups in Catholic parishes, whereas Jewish congregations have experimented with small, informal *havurot* gatherings in the home. Groups have essentially permeated the American lifestyle.

COMMUNITY BUILDING THROUGH GROUP DEVELOPMENT

The small group movement is a highly significant trend in American society, that is altering our culture in two distinct ways—"both by changing our understandings of community and by redefining spirituality" (Wuthnow 1994, 3). Not only are its effects felt at the level of the individual person, but at a societal level, and it is occurring at an unprecedented rate of growth. These communities are places in which relationships develop, people testify about how their lives have been enriched, and addictions have been overcome. Wuthnow asserts, "these groups are also affecting the ways in which we relate to each other and how we conceive of the sacred. Community is what people say they are seeking when they join small groups" (1994, 3–4). In essence, Wuthnow believes that small groups are "both providing community and changing our understanding of what community is" (Wuthnow 1994, 11).

Just what is it about small group membership that is so attractive and life enhancing to so many? The Reverend Art Baranowski, in charge of small Christian communities in the Chicago Roman Catholic Archdiocese, asserts that today's society is basically unreflective—people are so pressured to accomplish myriad tasks at home and on the job that they have little time to notice "what happens from day to day and how they are affected." He states that "small communities recapture this missing ingredient of reflection on one's own experience. In the small community, people slow down, use quiet time, recall the day and the week, and learn to listen to themselves and others. The small community values the life experience of each person and people begin to know that their life is sacred. This process is gradual, but the regular meeting offers reinforcement in a alternative way of life" (Baranowski 1995, 1).

WHY PEOPLE SEEK GROUP AND COMMUNITY EXPERIENCES

Up to this point, our focus has been somewhat micro based. However, the practice of religion is intricately connected with macro issues because, by definition, religion ties large groups of people together. As people grow and develop psychologically, morally, and spiritually, there emerges the realization of being an integral part of a great, interconnected system which is made up of other unique and integral parts. There may develop a feeling of kinship with people of diverse characteristics. Concurrent with the sense of "we-ness" may be the need to nurture some aspect of the person's sphere of influence. One of the many possible outcomes of this feeling of responsibility toward others is the development of community based attempts to gather people into groups so that diverse needs can be met efficiently, justly, and with compassion. The groups themselves become communities, and it is through the vehicle of community building that healing or growth takes place. It is important to note, however, that the human being has also demonstrated the capacity to bond with others "against" something or some group. The building of community in our postmodern society can be uplifting and caring, just as it can be designed to organize hate. Religious groups have the potential to do tremendous good, as well as incredible harm, depending on their ideologies and motivations.

The mere act of organizing people with similar needs and interests into a group does not create community, for in the United States there is still a deep rooted push toward individualism, amid talk of interdependence. The word "community" is applied indiscriminately to everything from an apartment complex to a support group. "If we are going to use the word meaningfully, we must restrict it to a group of individuals who have learned how to communicate honestly with each other, whose relationships go deeper than their masks of composure, and who have developed some significant commitment to rejoice together, mourn together, and to delight in each other, (making) others' conditions our own" (Peck 1987, 59–61).

What is described here is not just based on a connection—a state of "being joined together" as defined by Webster—but a connectedness based on intimacy, on sharing the self at levels beyond the superficial realities of everyday life. Bellingham et al. (1989, 18) enumerate three kinds of connectedness—"connectedness to oneself, connectedness to others, and connectedness to a larger meaning or purpose." Unfortunately, psychological developmental theory has taught that autonomy and independence are the goals and markers of growth in adulthood; the significance of relationship is downplayed or relegated to earlier life stages. As a result, society, particularly American society, puts great emphasis on and rewards individualism above and at the expense of community. This trait was observed even in the early years of the country when Alexis de Tocqueville called it one of America's "habits of the heart." Bellah and his colleagues, in their book of the same name, discuss Tocqueville's vision in this way: "He singled out family life, our religious traditions, and our participation in local politics as helping to create the kind of person who could sustain a connection to a wider political community and thus ultimately support the maintenance of free institutions. He also warned that some aspects of our character—what he was one of the first to call 'individualism'—might eventually isolate Americans one from another and thereby undermine the conditions of freedom" (Bellah et al. 1985, vii).

Why is individualism so potentially dangerous? Why do Bellah et al.—not to mention Tocqueville—see it as a possible threat to freedom? Sullivan states that "a personality can [should] never be isolated from the complex of interpersonal relations in which the person lives and has [one's] being" (Bellingham 1989, 19). If people do become isolated in this way—disconnected from self, others, and meaning—a disintegration of their personalities (and ultimately, of society) may follow.

When we lose connection with others, loneliness results. Besides being unpleasant, loneliness can have other adverse effects at any stage of life. Infants who are well tended but not nourished emotionally may die of marasmus; neglect may often cause failure to thrive and develop properly. In adults, loneliness can have negative consequences on health, including depression and high blood pressure. "Medical statistics on the loss of human companionship, the lack of love, and human loneliness reveal that the expression *broken heart* is not just a poetic image for loneliness and despair." (Bellingham et al. 1989, 19).

In addition to the ability to lose connection with ourselves and others, we can lose connection with our sense of meaning or purpose. This kind of loss occurs when people become alienated from the values and principles—often religiously or spiritually based—that previously guided them. The individual may become listless, depressed, and "ungrounded" and engage in either self-destructive attempts to distract the self from the pain of this loss or in frenetic, hyperactive attempts to engage in meaningful activities.

Connectedness, community, a sense of belonging—whatever one calls it, is essential not just for happiness, but also for physical and emotional development, and even maintenance of health. If one lives in a culture of extreme individualism, how can the sense of connectedness that promotes health, growth, meaning, and wholeness be developed and nurtured? The following sections examine some of the ways in which communities address these diverse human needs for belonging and meaning.

COMMUNITY FUNCTIONS AND ORGANIZED RELIGIOUS GROUPS

Definitions of *community* are as plentiful as the authors attempting to define the concept. In 1955 Hillery reported over ninety discrete definitions of community in the scholarly literature. Classic works examined community as a physical location, as interaction, as shared values and institutions, and as a system of subsystems (Warren 1978). More recent definitions have explored the complexity of the concept itself, given the many cultural differences among communities (Rivera and Erlich 1992).

Building on Warren's functional approach to communities, Pantoja and Perry (1992) identified a model that is helpful in understanding how various institutions within the community address human needs. The model includes the following functions:

- production; distribution and consumption;
- socialization;
- social control;
- social placement;
- mutual support;
- defense;
- communication.

The community's survival depends first upon an adequate system of production, distribution, and consumption—in other words, goods and services must be exchanged in a viable economy so that people can obtain what is necessary to live. Once such an economy exists, the remaining functions are developed by human beings to address other needs and to undergird this first function. *Socialization* implies that members of the community learn customs and norms (what is expected in the community). *Social control* serves to keep people within acceptable boundaries and usually requires the creation of rules and laws, as well as rewards and punishments. *Social placement* is participation in the associations and ceremonies of the community so that members find ways to be accepted and recognized by others. *Mutual support* implies a social welfare function that addresses community needs in times of stress or emergency. *Defense* includes protection from harm. Communication requires shared language, symbols, and other forms of expression.

Given this model, one can easily see how pervasive religious groups are in the support functions defined above. Socialization to norms and customs can occur within secular as well as religious parameters. Because it is often difficult to separate religious influences from secular purposes, this socialization is often intermixed and all pervasive. For example, one may not realize how socialized he or she is to religious norms until someone challenges whether a Nativity scene should be placed on public grounds. Social control is often the purview of the legal system, manifested in everything from traffic citations to acts of Congress. It also takes place on a less official but all encompassing level whenever social norms and customs are not observed or are violated. For example, more subtle means of social control may be exercised when ecclesiastical norms are violated such as participating in a prochoice rally when one is a member of the Roman Catholic community.

If there is a function that is most frequently performed by religious groups within the community it is most likely that of social placement, sometimes called social participation. Because faith communities are formed for the express purpose of providing corporate worship opportunities and offering membership in a voluntary association of believers, many religious groups provide chances for social placement and participation.

Mutual support is a function that was originally performed in communities by multiple voluntary groups, both religious and secular. With the development of the welfare system in the United States has come a more formalized version of mutual support that is often characterized by red tape and bureaucracy. Simultaneously, however, have been the continuous growth and development of those agencies sponsored and supported by religious groups, as well as the many volunteer efforts performed by persons representing churches, synagogues, temples, and other houses of worship in the local community.

Defense has been predominately a function through which the community is protected. In the local community, defense means that people feel safe from persons or forces that might do them harm. One could argue that religious groups provide psychosocial defense in that they knit close networks whose members look out for one another. Theologically, one could argue that the church provides a place where persons can defend their faith and the lifestyles they have chosen. This is a positive element of feeling protected. Jim Corbett, an Arizona Quaker, is recognized as the person who started the Sanctuary Movement which defended the right of illegal immigrants to seek refuge in this country from persecution (see, for example, Kent and Spickard 1994). Corbett's efforts were not always met with accolades in local communities that feared the intrusion of those who were different. Conversely, those religious groups that supported the Sanctuary Movement and, even to the point of civil disobedience, harbored refugees extended their protective arms to persons who were in desperate need of help. Clearly, they provided those persons with defense from harm.

Communication, the last of the community functions, focuses on language, symbols and expression as the ways in which people learn to relate to one another. Because so much of human communication and exchange is established in the roots of tradition and culture, it is virtually impossible to identify all the ways in which religion influences this function in communities. In the southern United States, for example, the concept of "being saved" is a prevalent way of expressing one's conversion to a religious group. This concept of "being saved" may not translate as easily in communities located in other regions of the country.

Different communities exhibit the functions in the Pantoja-Perry model to different degrees. If certain functions cannot be performed in the local community, then members may go beyond local boundaries and seek services elsewhere. For example, if a person has recently moved to a new environment and finds that the way people there express themselves is very different and alienating from previous locations, then he or she may maintain tight communication with family and friends beyond the local community. For persons who have been engaged in a faith tradition, there may be a desire to seek a local "church home" or "parish community" in order to affiliate with others who have common beliefs and values. There will be familiarity in doctrine, ritual and ceremony that transcend geographic location. Finding such a place can make the difference in whether some persons feel they are being accepted into the community or whether they feel alienated.

The ways in which religious groups influence and participate in the functions of community will tell many stories of how people view their environment. Human service practitioners must understand that their practice is set in this community context—a context that encompasses diverse faith traditions, all of which participate (sometimes in agreement and sometimes not) in the dance of community building.

SELECTED MODELS OF RELIGIOUS COMMUNITY BUILDING

In attempts to meet the needs of community members to perform many of the functions just discussed, a variety of models have emerged. In this section, we will highlight three models that have particular relevance for helping professionals who want to access, understand, and/or develop community groups that have religious and spiritual dimensions: (1) mutual help/self-help groups, (2) ecumenically based community ministry movements, and (3) intentional communities.

Mutual Help/Self-Help Groups

A self-help group is essentially a member run lay organization of people with mutual problems, needs, or goals. Although it may be organized or even facilitated by a professional leader or mental health or religious organization, the group remains "owned and operated" by its members. Levy (1973) lists four kinds of mutual help organizations:

1. Those whose purpose is to change undesirable conduct or improve self-control. Prime examples are Alcoholics, Narcotics, Overeaters, and Gamblers Anonymous.
2. Those whose members share a particular type of life predicament or stress with which they need help. Examples are the Alzheimer's Disease support groups, Parents Without Partners, Widow to Widow, and Recovery, Inc.
3. Those whose members are somehow marginal to society and desire to gain social power through group bonding. Gay and lesbian support groups, the Gray Panthers, and black pride groups are examples.
4. Groups dedicated to experiencing more abundant or self-actualized life. "The objectives of these groups tend in one way or another to focus on personal growth, self-improvement, character development, and greater joy and effectiveness in living. . . . Few of these groups have any degree of national representation" (Levy 1973).

According to Caplan and Killilea (1976, 39), characteristics common to self-help groups include:

1. similar experience of their members;
2. intent to give and receive mutual support;
3. realization that members receive benefits from the process of helping other members;
4. assurance of normality rather than marginality;
5. validation of feelings;
6. emphasis on education and up-to-date information;
7. constructive action toward shared goals.

138

Self-help groups differ from orthodox psychotherapy groups in that there is not always a professional leader, no fees, no records, and no therapeutic milieu. Peers themselves are the teachers and role models; peer style is active, judgmental, supportive, and intimate in mutual sharing. Power struggles are between members rather than professional-client. Commitment to the well being of the group as an entity is primary. Members cherish the idea that responsibility for self-growth leads to the growth of the entire group.

Self-help groups may or may not be religiously oriented. However, the human service practitioner will find that many may meet in local churches or synagogues, where space is freely provided, and were begun by persons who felt a spiritual calling to establish a community that addressed common needs. Unless they are highly politicized, chances are that it will perform the mutual support, social placement, and communication functions already described.

Ecumenically Based Community Ministry Movements

As we use it here, the phrase ecumenically based community ministry means "a particular way of ministering to society in which congregations of more than one denomination and of a particular locality (neighborhood, small town, rural county) agree to pool their resources" (Bos 1993, 1). Such a ministry "is congregation based and very local, covering as small an area as practicable. It is a social ministry that sees the issues through the prism of its own community. It is ecumenical, interfaith, or both" (Bos 1993, 2).

Bos states that the concept of community ministries emerged historically from the East Harlem Protestant Parish. The term *parish* is more common to Catholics than to Protestants and is broader than *congregation*. A church congregation assumes the responsibility for serving those who are formal members; a parish theoretically includes all the people and organizations within the catchment area of the church, whether or not they belong to that particular congregation. The use of the term *parish* "allows Protestant congregations in particular to view the claims of the surrounding community as legitimate" (Bos 1993, 3). Bos elaborates on the responsibilities of a congregation which becomes a member of a community ministry organization in the following way: "Your membership in the community ministry stands for a new level of commitment by your congregation to the immediate community. Through this ministry you say that you are taking the community's needs seriously and that you will invest leadership, facilities, and funds on a cooperative basis in order to define and respond to those needs, that your support of missions in other places will not excuse you from the one in your own front yard, and that you have a social and ecumenical/interfaith ministry that is local" (Bos 1993, 3).

As discussed earlier, communities are not always able to meet all or even most of their social service needs. These needs cannot always be met by state or local social service agencies, nor can they be met by the individual church. A local consortium of churches and synagogues serves to help fill in the gap and provide necessary services. It can also define areas where advocacy for a client population is needed and can confront the local agencies and government in support of those whose needs are not being met. Perhaps one of the most significant aspects of the community ministry movement is the way it impels individual congregations to go beyond their familiar horizons. Because of the local nature of such ministries, they tend to be perceived as value based and more personal in their service style. In summary, community ministry "gives several congregations a joint territorial parish in which to carry out social ministries. It reintroduces the congregation to its neighboring peoples and institutions" (Bos 1993, 75).

Community ministry can become highly politicized because it calls group members to include persons who may not be part of organized religion. Given its broad based nature, this model serves community functions such as socialization, social control, social placement, and mutual support. Persons are socialized as they participate in activities, and social control may emanate from the principles that drive the initiatives taken. It would be naive to think that the persons served will not be influenced by the values of those who provide service. The practitioner who works with local networks of religious groups needs to recognize the value issues that can arise in this type of intervention.

Intentional Communities

Intentional communities provide another model for becoming connected to self, others, and a transcendent source. Indeed, such communities are deliberately organized to enable people to feel these connections and to operationalize those feelings in terms of mutual action. One of the most outstanding models of intentional community is the L'Arche Community for mentally handicapped people, founded by Jean Vanier. Vanier defines a community as an entity in which there is "interpersonal relationship, a sense of belonging, and an orientation of life to a common goal and common witness" (1989, 13–35). He states that an intentional community is a grouping "of people who have left their own milieu to live with others under the same roof, and work from a new vision of human beings and their relationships with each other and with God" (Vanier 1989, 10).

Vanier founded the first L'Arche community in 1964 at Trosly-Breuil, a village approximately seventy miles north of Paris. At the time he was a philosophy professor in Toronto. Vanier had come to France to visit a priest friend who was serving as a chaplain at a home for mentally handicapped men in Trosly-Breuil. Vanier visited the facility and was profoundly moved by the conditions in which these men lived. He developed relationships with two of the residents who had no families, and ultimately invited them to live with him at Trosly.

Today there are more than one hundred L'Arche communities in the world, with more than ten in the United States. Most are Roman Catholic, but the more recent communities have been ecumenical. Regardless of denomination, the life of the community is based on spiritual values of service, prayer, simple lifestyle, solidarity with the poor and these words of Jesus: "Whoever welcomes one of these little ones in my name, welcomes me; and whoever welcomes me, welcomes the one who sent me" (Luke 9:48). The community itself is composed of the mentally impaired and their assistants, who live and work with them. The assistants are mostly young people, male and female, married or single, and ordained or not ordained, from a variety of backgrounds. Some have made a lifelong covenant with the community while others dedicate a certain number of months or years. The emphasis is on a shared life between mentally able and mentally impaired, with each having gifts to give the other.

There are many intentional communities of many different kinds and sizes operating in Alabama, Pennsylvania, Ohio, Iowa, Washington, D.C., New York, Massachusetts, Montana, and Washington. In general they involve both task oriented and socio-emotional aspects of group experience. The task is obviously targeted on a cause or social problem, whereas the socio-emotional benefits derive from the intense interaction that occurs in the process. Although we have elaborated on one example of this model, there are many such examples operating in local communities throughout the United States. Human service practitioners will quickly recognize that this model is one that serves multiple community functions.

CONCLUSION

Communities are composed of multiple groups that interact. Groups are the smallest social units of communities and, depending on their purposes, can be highly influential in performing various community functions.

The search for community is one in which helping professionals will encounter diverse groups of people coming together for religious and social causes, support, friendship, healing, and the performance of other functions. It is apparent that the small group movement is becoming a major force in the transformation of American society. Groups of all kinds are reshaping both psychological and religious thought and practice and will continue to do so in the future. The human service practitioner needs to recognize the importance of diverse religiously and spiritually motivated groups in influencing and delivering community based services.

REFERENCES

Baranowski, A. 1995. Creating small faith communities. *Community Connections,* 6 (Summer): 1–4.

Bellah, R., R. Madsen, W. Sullivan, A. Swidler, and S. Tipton. 1985. *Habits of the heart.* New York: Harper and Row.

Bellingham, R., B. Cohen, T. Jones, and L. Spaniol. 1989. Connectedness: some skills for spiritual health. *American Journal of Health Promotion,* 4 (1): 18–24.

Bos, D. 1993. *A practical guide to community ministry.* Louisville: Westminster/John Knox Press.

Caplan, G., and M. Killilea. 1976. *Support systems and mutual help.* New York: Grune and Stratton.

Hillery, G. 1955. Definitions of community: arenas of agreement. *Rural Sociology,* 20: 779–91.

Kent, S. A., and J. V. Spickard. 1994. The "other" civil religion and the tradition of radical Quaker polities. *Journal of Church and State,* 36 (2): 373–87.

Lee, B. 1993. Community. In *The new dictionary of Catholic spirituality,* ed. M. Downey, 183–92. Collegeville, Minn.: Liturgical Press.

Levy, L. 1973. Self-help groups as mental health resources. In Caplan, G., and M. Killilea, *Support systems and mutual help,* 78. New York: Grune and Stratton.

Netting, F. E., P. M. Kettner, and S. L. McMurtry. 1993. *Social work macro practice.* White Plains, N.Y.: Longman.

Peck, S. 1987. *The different drum.* New York: Simon and Schuster.

Rausch, T. 1990. *Radical Christian communities.* Collegeville, Minn.: Liturgical Press.

Rivera, F. G., and J. L. Erlich. 1992. *Community organizing in a diverse society.* Boston: Allyn and Bacon.

Rothman, J. 1995. Approaches to community intervention. In Rothman, J., J. L. Erlich, and J. E. Tropman, *Strategies of community intervention,* 26–63. 5th ed. Itasca, Ill.: Peacock.

Rothman, J., J. L. Erlich, and J. E. Tropman. 1995. *Strategies of community intervention.* 5th ed. Itasca, Ill.: Peacock.

Rothman, J., and J. Tropman. 1987. Models of community organization and macro practice. In *Strategies of community organization,* ed. F. Cox, 3–26. 4th ed. Itasca, Ill.: Peacock.

Vanier, J. 1989. *Community and growth.* New York: Paulist Press.
Warren, R. 1978. *The community in America.* 3d ed. Chicago: Rand McNally.
Wuthnow, R. 1994. *Sharing the journey.* New York: Free Press.

Chapter 9

RELIGIOUS CONGREGATIONS AND
HUMAN SERVICES

No two communities are identical when it comes to how religious groups develop and interact. Given the proliferation of both religious and secular groups discussed earlier, this chapter focuses on those established groups that are known as religious congregations. We begin by examining religious congregations as community resources with which helping professionals often work. Congregations are seen as informal providers that are beginning to be the subject of systematic research efforts. Finally, we will focus on the importance of connecting human service agencies with congregations and the contemporary challenges facing human service professionals who interface with religious congregations in the United States.

Given the separation of church and state, there are few established boundaries on how religious groups participate in community activities. Faith traditions may expand and develop at the will of interested community members, leaving each community with a unique constellation of faith traditions and community based institutions.

WHAT ARE RELIGIOUS CONGREGATIONS?

Religious congregations are those groupings in which people come together for religious purposes. There is no set form for a congregation, in that religious groups meet in large and small buildings, call their facilities by different names, and may or may not connect or affiliate with a parent religious body. "Members of congregations are defined by social identification as those people who regard themselves as participants in a congregation and are regarded by others as such" (Harris 1995, 262).

There is some debate in the literature over whether or not congregations should be understood according to established organizational theories or whether a specialist theory is needed that focuses on the unique features of these type organizations. Much like human service organizations, those theorists who have analyzed congregations have drawn heavily from classical orientations such as bureaucratic theory, building on Weber's typology of churches, denominations, sects, and authority in general. Change within congregations has been examined by Harris (1995) using Tonnies' *Gemeinschaft* (community) and *Gesellschaft* (association) distinctions. Other analysts have used open or natural systems to understand the religious congregation. Most recently, Harris (1995) suggests that understanding nonprofit organizations has direct application to religious congregations. In applying nonprofit theory, however, Harris cautions that one does not neglect the features of congregations that distinguish them from other nonprofit organizations. For example, the obvious fact that congregations are closely tied to religious values must be carefully considered.

For the purposes of this book, we acknowledge that there are unlimited ways to analyze religious congregations. Human service practitioners must be careful to recognize that these voluntary associations have unique features and that congregations will vary within and across faith communities. Persons who have participated in or visited various religious congregations can confirm that each has its own culture. Approaching congregations to become part of the human service network will require great respect for their diversity.

RESEARCH ON RELIGIOUS CONGREGATIONS

Until the 1980s, there had been only limited research on religious groups within local communities. No one knew how much money these groups contributed to human services or how involved they were in volunteering time to charitable activities. Neither did anyone know much about how helping professionals used clergy and churches as resources. Empirical research in social work, psychology, and psychiatry had lagged behind in considering the impact of religion on the practice of helping professionals (Joseph, 1988).

A number of trends appear to have facilitated the study of religion and human services during the 1980s. First, it was a time of political conservatism. The Reagan administration's push to return the function of mutual support to local communities and to encourage churches to take care of their own preceded the Bush administration's "thousand points of light" campaign, which drew on the initiatives of local community volunteers to reprivatize mutual support efforts. Attention turned to the religious sector as a resource for fulfilling what had become a public community function. The 1980s led to what has now been described as "a clear change in who does what in service development in the United States. In essence, the federal government will use resources and influence to cajole states, localities, and the private sector to take charge in service design, implementation, and evaluation. An increasing local emphasis will challenge communities to use their resources efficiently, effectively, and creatively" (Wineburg 1992, 108).

A second trend was the budding research effort on the role of nonprofit and voluntary sector agencies which have come to fruition over the last decade. Researchers from many disciplines began collaborating and communicating through organizations such as the Association for Research on Nonprofit Organizations and Voluntary Action (ARNOVA). As this organization reached maturity, publishers like Jossey-Bass began their voluntary sector series which highlighted scholarship in this area. Research specific to religious congregations in local communities emerged during this time. Salamon and Teitelbaum (1984) conducted the first national study of expanded religious involvement in providing community services and assisting local service providers. Case studies of congregational involvement with various target populations were reported, paving the way for a more intensive national effort to examine just what the local congregations in various communities were doing (Wineburg 1992).

Third, and pivotal to our understanding of religious groups within local communities, was a series of studies by the independent sector to begin to quantify what was known about community service activities and finances of religious congregations in the United States. For the first time there was information on what community based congregations did and a national profile was begun (Hodgkinson and Weitzman 1993). Until the Independent Sector took on the task of surveying congregations, every helping professional could relate anecdotal information on how local clergy sat on boards of directors for service providers in their community or how local congregations contributed to community based services. But until the independent sector surveys, there was no systematic way of knowing just how pervasive these situations were.

For the purposes of their study, religious congregations were defined as "a community of people who meet together for worship, for fellowship, and for service to their members and the larger communities in which they live" (Hodgkinson and Weitzman 1993, xi). They noted that because of the separation of church and state, there were no available statistics to document the expenditures of congregations, the volunteer activities or charitable contributions made by members of religious groups, so the Independent Sector began its task. "Because there is no government census of congregations as there are censuses of most other major institutional groupings in our society, developing a national sample in both the 1987 and 1992 surveys was the first major challenge" (Hodgkinson and Weitzman 1993, xii). A National Advisory Committee representing Catholics, Protestants, Jews, Mormons, Muslims, and Buddhists was formed to assist in the effort.

Findings indicated that in 1991 there were approximately 258,000 religious congregations listed in telephone directories in the United States. On average, they depended on individual contributions for 81 percent of their revenues. Total expenditures of religious congregations approximated $48.4 billion, of which $6.6 billion (14 percent) was directly contributed by congregations to other organizations and individuals. "Of the $6.6 billion donated by congregations, $4.7 billion (70 percent) went to denominational organizations and charities, such as Catholic charities, $1.3 billion (20 percent) was donated to other charitable organizations in the community, and $0.7 billion (10 percent) was given in direct assistance to individuals" (Hodgkinson and Weitzman 1993, 1).

Congregations participated in many programs and services that went beyond their religious activities. About 92 percent of congregations had one or more human service activities, focusing heavily upon programming for youth. Ninety percent reported health related programs, including visitation and shut in programs. Programs varied considerably in their structure, some being run within the congregation itself, others being separately incorporated, and still others being part of denominational programs to which the congregation contributed. Nine out of ten congregations had programs in human services and health, and six out of ten reported that other groups in the community used their facilities (Hodgkinson and Weitzman 1993, 2–3).

Among the many implications of the independent sector studies was that, "Congregations not only engage in religious ministry and education but are deeply involved in serving their members and communities across a broad range of activities. The natural affinity between religious belief and improving the human condition is probably much stronger than most people think. Almost as many congregations offered programs in human services as offered religious services and religious education. In 1991 92 percent of congregations reported such activities compared with 87 percent in 1986" (Hodgkinson and Weitzman 1993, 105).

The 1990s have witnessed an increased interest in understanding the roles played by religious congregations in local communities, particularly in the realm of human service activities. Wineburg (1992) reported a study of 128 congregations in the Greensboro, North Carolina area. Congregations embraced the opportunities to take an active role in human service provision, either by developing their own solutions or by working in coalitions with human service providers. Wineburg provides guidelines for those human service planners who want to work with local congregations, indicating that it is important to recognize the nature of the religious congregation. For example, when congregations address needs such as the respite needs of persons caring for someone with Alzheimer's disease, they rarely conduct extensive evaluation of service outcomes. This is very different from the human service agency's culture in which outcome measurement is required. Recognizing that Wineburg's study focuses on only one community, Wineburg calls for additional research to determine the roles played by congregations and their members in local service delivery.

Religious congregations are often viewed by local service providers as resources for both revenues and volunteers. Although much is still to be learned about financial resources, there are even more questions about volunteers. In an attempt to examine the link between religious motivation and volunteering, Cnaan, Kasternakis, and Wineburg (1993) uncover many uncertainties in our knowledge of who volunteers for what reasons. Although they find no statistically significant link between religious motivation and volunteering in human service activities, they readily admit the complexity of examining these factors. They confirm the difficulty in how one defines religious motivation, given the fact that attending church services is not always indicative of being religious; just as not attending does not necessarily mean that a person is not religious. In short, there is a great need for further study in understanding the complex interplay of forces that drive religious congregants to engage in human service activities in local communities.

RELIGIOUS CONGREGATIONS AS COMMUNITY RESOURCES

Early in his administration, President Reagan stated that if every church or synagogue would adopt two poor persons, there would no longer need to be a public social welfare system. While it is true that religious congregations are active in supporting the needs of people, this statement reflects a lack of understanding about the nature of both religious congregations and the social welfare delivery system. One outcome of this statement, however, was a reexamination of the availability of local congregations to support the human services offered by local agencies. In part the product of cuts in federal funding and in part a reflection of renewed interest in the religious congregation as a

148

provider of human services, many human service agencies attempted to work more closely with religious congregations.

It is likely that some agencies and congregations met with more success than others, as they connected with one another. "Churches try to incorporate members who bring widely different denominational and cultural backgrounds, life-long residents and newcomers who are only passing through, old timers who may want more stability and younger members just beginning their families" (Dudley and Johnson 1993, 1). Dudley and Johnson (1993) go on to note that the average clergy person changes congregations every five years. This is not the picture of an organization whose primary purpose is to provide social services. Rather it is a group of persons who often expend many of their energies just being a group and maintaining their group identity.

Possibly, one way to think about a religious congregation is more like a family unit. Families provide a lot of services to their members, from shopping to personal care to financial aid, families help out one another. However, much like religious congregations, families do not keep case files, they generally have a very informal needs assessment process, and their evaluation procedures for quality of aid often amount to little more than a smile or thank you from the recipient.

Religious congregations provide services via a range of models. At times they are formal services with traditional elements of service provision. At other times they are as simple as "Mrs. Smith calls Pastor Jones about getting a ride to the doctor. Pastor Jones then calls Mrs. Brown, who picks up Mrs. Smith and takes her to the doctor." These brokerage services do not include needs assessments or case files, only a verbal presentation of need and the known resource to facilitate an appropriate response. When a resource is not known to the clergyperson, they may be able to make a referral or they may simply not be able to respond.

CONNECTING HUMAN SERVICES AND RELIGIOUS CONGREGATIONS

Given that communities are the arenas in which human service providers address client needs, it is the rare helping professional who does not encounter the influences of local religious congregations on their practice. This is as true for the clinician who sees clients on a one to one basis as it is for the macro practitioner who practices the art of linking various organizations and groups within the local community.

The direct practitioner treats clients from all walks of life and many of

149

those clients will be persons who are members of religious congregations. But even those who do not actively participate in religious activities may be influenced by, socialized to, even socially controlled (motivated or oppressed) by the multitude of religious influences that permeate the local community. Some clients will have left religious groups in which they felt uncomfortable or about which they harbor great anger, whereas others may be recruited to religious sects that are unfamiliar to the practitioner. It is incumbent upon the human service worker to know the community context in which these clients live their lives. The practitioner must learn to work with various groups; sometimes those groups with which he or she has little previous familiarity and with which his or her beliefs may not always blend well.

As discussed earlier, connecting with religious groups within the local community requires a sensitivity toward diversity as well as knowledge and understanding of how various faith communities developed. Each religious group will have its own culture, complete with language, traditions, rituals, ceremonies, and artifacts. Although different faith groups comprise the same geographic community, it does not mean that these groups can be treated homogeneously. The community practitioner must approach each tradition without preconceived notions.

HUMAN SERVICE ROLES OF RELIGIOUS CONGREGATIONS

Based on their work with religious congregations in the early 1980s, Tobin, Ellor, and Anderson-Ray (1986) identify four human service roles played by religious congregations:

1. *Providing religious services.* This function is viewed as basic to most religious groups. It extends beyond weekend worship to include Bible study, meditation groups, Rosary societies, and many other activities.
2. *Providing pastoral services.* This function is traditionally associated with the clergy, but many lay individuals and groups also offer informal support to congregants.
3. *Hosting outside service providers.* Many churches rent out space in their buildings for day care centers, meal sites for seniors, and similar enterprises. Sometimes entire social service agencies rent space from religious groups. In the case of the church as host, however, the critical factor is that there is little or no interaction between the worshiping congregation and the service being provided. The agency simply rents space.

4. *Congregational human service provision.* This category includes services provided by the congregation and clearly identified as part of its ministry. In such cases space is generally made available at no charge and many members of the congregation may volunteer.

These four roles reflect some of the differences between the informal and the formal provision of service. Religious congregations represent more than a single role on this continuum. They actually play a more fluid role, moving between the two extremes, depending on factors that are not generally based upon the religious congregation's desire necessarily to be a formal service provider. These factors may include items such as sensitivity to human service needs, desires to serve certain population groups, changing conditions in the community in which the congregation is located, the influx of new members as other members leave the congregation for various reasons.

INFORMAL PROVIDERS

Froland et al. (1981) describe a continuum of helping services, again ranging from informal to formal. Informal helpers are categorized as follows:

Family and friends. Although its exact role varies from culture to culture, the family is a key help provider in all cultures. In the gerontological literature it is often said that 70 to 80 percent of all the needs of the elderly are provided by immediate family members. Clearly the family unit is a principle caregiver for the needs of any person who is physically or emotionally disabled. For many persons, friends are also among the first persons to whom one would go for help.

Neighbors. Particularly in communities where the geographic community is strongly bonded, neighbors are another critical source of support. These neighbors may or not be members of the same faith communities.

Natural helpers. Some people seem to gravitate naturally to helping others, whether on a city block, in a suburban neighborhood, or in a rural area. Natural helpers are often well known to other residents, but they may not be as easily identified by helping professionals.

Role related helpers. This group includes individuals whose jobs bring them into contact with people in need, but whose primary job description does not include the helping process. Mail carriers, hairdressers, grocers, pharmacists, repair people, and others can often

151

provide help in small ways to those with whom they come into contact. For example, in many communities, human service agencies have informed mail carriers that if they notice something that seems out of the ordinary, such as an older person not picking up their mail for several days, they can call someone who will stop in and check on that person. Clergy often fit the concept of role related helpers. Even though their primary job descriptions may not focus on human service provision, they are often in a position where they are asked to engage in such service. However, Steinitz (1981) suggests that more than 80 percent of the actual services provided by churches and synagogues to older adults are provided by lay persons rather than clergy, which may indicate that clergy often delegate these tasks to others within their congregations.

People with similar problems. People who share ailments, conditions, or experiences often bond with one another. For example, Alzheimer's disease support groups are available to the families of people with this illness. Similar self-help groups, devoted to various problems, have proliferated all over the United States. Many of these groups meet in local churches, temples, or synagogues.

Volunteers. Volunteers are persons who provide help in some formal, organized manner but are not usually paid for their work. Volunteers are often recruited from and even organized by local congregations. In a recent study of food pantries conducted by one of the authors, it was found that the average congregational volunteer had a thirteen-year tenure, even though few concrete rewards such as recognition dinners and pins had been given. In contrast, persons volunteering for human service agencies in the same community averaged only six years' tenure, even though they received all manner of concrete rewards. Obviously, more research needs to be done, but it is possible that the fellowship, sense of continuity, and ability to serve one's faith community may be critical factors in retaining volunteers in congregations, even in the absence of a more formalized reward system.

DESIGNING PARTNERSHIPS WITH LOCAL CONGREGATIONS

Wineburg (1994) states that "literally hundreds of examples cite congregational involvement throughout the 1980s and 1990s" in what would be partnerships between local congregations and local human service systems. Yet, he goes on to say that these accounts "are not yet found in the scholarly literature but are in the local news stories" (160). These projects focus on everything from homelessness to AIDS, and address the needs of many population groups targeted by human service professionals.

Working together requires mutual respect. Human service agencies and religious congregations alike are motivated by the desire to serve people. However, their approaches and often their languages are different. Where the helping professional refers to a client, the clergyperson refers to a parishioner. He or she may be the same person, but these words imply different perspectives and types of relationships. If either party sees themselves as superior to the other, there can be nothing less than a strained relationship. Mutual respect between clergy and other helping professionals requires a desire to work as partners, not with one in a dominant role. For example, if education is needed the human service staff need to call upon clergy for staff development, just as the local congregation should feel comfortable inviting helping professionals into its space. Cooperation may also mean treating clergy as part of the treatment team, rather than as external agents.

Designing a partnership between human service providers and local religious congregations begins by assessing and understanding both groups involved. This will mean meeting with one another and discussing mutual concerns and interests. Traditional human service agencies fear that clergy and lay members of congregations will try to proselytize their clients. Clergy and congregations often fear that other helping professionals will fail to support the religious practice of their members and, in some cases, convince congregation members that they do not need to continue to be members. These fears need to be articulated and addressed in a way that is meaningful to all concerned.

Many successful programs have begun with in-service and simple gatherings in which respect can develop. In one program involving a mental health agency, the clergy were invited to a brown bag lunch. Agency staff alternated with clergy as discussion leaders. Topics included depression, spiritual development, and working together after discharge from treatment. After several months of this type of person to person contact, a member of one of the congregations entered the in-patient unit at the mental health center, the congregant's minister, with permission from the family, was treated as a consultant to the in-patient staff. The clergyperson also counseled the family regarding the member's return home. The situation then became a case study for the group's next meeting on how to work with local clergy.

THE CHALLENGES IN CONNECTING CONGREGATIONS AND HUMAN SERVICES

In the 1990s probably one of the most difficult tasks for practitioners to do is to approach fundamentalist religious groups with an open mind. Yet fundamentalism itself is not easy to define: "Many of the religious movements often described as fundamentalist disagree on the term's meaning and whether it applies to them at all. Over the years fundamentalism has evolved as a concept from describing Protestant factions that rejected the more liberal theology of the mainline churches in favor of living by literal translations of biblical text. Since then, the word has crossed both religious and national borders to apply to a growing number of conservative movements" (Ladestro 1993, 18).

Health and human service workers may protest that there would be little reason for them to work with fundamentalist groups. After all, the value systems of many helping professionals are bent on changing hierarchical and patriarchal structures in order to be more sensitive to persons who have been oppressed (i.e., women, people of color, gays and lesbians, etc.). Although avoidance is certainly one approach to dealing with these value conflicts, it is unlikely that this will be possible for the community practitioner in the immediate future. At this point the United States is experiencing a revival of fundamentalism and these congregations are growing. The very issues that community practitioners are most concerned about are likely to be the target for change by these fundamentalist groups.

Prior to the 1992 Presidential election, there was much discussion about the Moral Majority and the Religious Right. But it was not until the 1992 election that the visibility of the Christian Coalition was most evident. The Religious Right has become more visible and the influence of these committed people is being felt in political circles around the country. This is as true for local as it is for state and national politics. Within the Republican Party the rise of the Christian Coalition is creating incredible waves and has been described as "unlike the religious right groups of the 1980s, [this] is not devoted mainly to spreading its message through television and radio shows. Instead, it runs training seminars for political cadres, at which participants are taught the rudiments of taking control of local Republican organizations from the bottom up" (Blumenthal 1994, 36). And bottom up means that these efforts are happening at the local community level.

Again, one might ask why this is of concern. After all, religious groups are separate entities that have every right to be involved politically, in fact are often the consciousness of a secular society. The reason the fundamentalist movement is particularly relevant to human service professionals is that the issues embraced by the Religious Right are relevant issues to health and human services. For example, labeling of homosexuality as a sin, anti-abortion campaigns, movements to censor children's books, and support of patriarchal systems are the very kinds of concerns that community practitioners encounter when they seek community change. These issues are at the heart of a secular health and human service delivery system.

Certainly knowing the history and background of various religious groups within the community is mandatory. However, there are many other tasks for the community practitioner. Knowing how to approach local congregations is extremely important. Religious groups vary in their structure, referred to as church polity. For example, the local Catholic parish is very hierarchical and conforms to mandates from the Pope in Rome, but the local American Baptist Church may be structured from the ground up and makes decisions in the local congregation. Recognizing these structural differences is imperative to knowing how to target change and in recognizing how much power the local congregation may or may not have.

Congregations impact human services in at least three major ways. First, they are often part of the local service delivery system, whether they serve only "their own" or open their doors to the broader community. By the nature of what we know about congregational membership, at least some human services (i.e., counseling, transportation, meals, day care, etc.) are provided to persons who affiliate. Second, local congregations often reflect the social norms of the community. This means that they contribute to the functions of socialization and social control mentioned earlier. In this regard they will have spokespersons who address causes consistent with the beliefs of their membership and these persons may be very powerful people because they are backed by the institutional church. Third, congregations typically have buildings in which they worship and these buildings may be empty several days a week. Therefore, they own property that could be used for human service activities by local providers.

Religious congregations are in a unique position within the local community. They are not beholden to the multitude of government regulations that often tie the hands of local service providers. They are part of what is often considered the "informal" system, yet they are organized enough to have newsletters, bulletins, and meetings that can be turned toward a social cause. Religious groups can mobilize to picket abortion clinics or to support a public housing development in the community. Local congregations often participate in larger social movements that range from civil rights demonstrations to gay rights marches. The community practitioner must have an understanding of what issues and concerns are being considered by local congregations for these informally organized groupings are potential sources of great support or incredible resistance to human service change efforts. "Understanding local congregations and their enmeshment within the social service delivery system is important to any social work practitioner who hopes to effect community change" (Netting, Thibault, and Ellor 1990, 22). There is a growing literature on how religious congregations provide informal support as well as formal services (see for example: Delgado and Humm-Delgado 1982; Haber 1984; Tobin, Ellor, and Anderson-Ray 1986; Wineburg forthcoming).

Getting to know community clergy is particularly important as well. Depending on the religious group, clergy will have different types of training. It is equally helpful to know how much authority is vested in clergy by their denominations because this will vary greatly. A study of African American congregations and clergy revealed great variety in how referrals were made to mental health agencies in the community. Clergy were important linchpins in determining when referrals should be made, and the need for understanding between clergy and helping professionals was emphasized (Chang, Williams, Griffith, and Young 1994). In a local Mormon congregation, the "minister" is actually a lay Bishop. In a local United Methodist Church the "minister" is a professionally trained seminary graduate. In a local Buddhist temple, the monks are highly educated professionals who have "undergone stringent training and discipline. The ethnocentric view of many Euro-American social workers that monks are merely folk healers or paraprofessionals needs to be corrected" (Canda and Phaobtong 1992, 65). Human service professionals need to be sensitive to these colleagues who provide leadership for community based faith groups.

Being sensitive to the internal politics that occur within faith communities is extremely important too. Just as the Republican Party is struggling with the meaning of the Christian Coalition, the Southern Baptist Convention is struggling with its new fundamentalism and the role of women. Just as Protestant denominations are struggling with the Sophia Movement, which came out of a national Presbyterian women's conference and is causing a reexamination of models of authority and raising issues of what constitutes heresy, so are faith communities divided on issues of abortion and homosexuality. In short, religious groups are as subject to politics as any other institution within society and because they deal with highly emotional, moral, controversial concerns their issues are not easy to resolve. The community practitioner who is sensitive to these divisions and struggles will be better able to interpret the responses received from various religious leaders and to know if there are possible alliances that can be built.

It is necessary to realize the incredible potential for religious groups to join forces in making community change happen. For example, on December 15, 1970 the Taos Pueblo located in New Mexico finally had its Sacred Blue Lake returned to it. Because the U.S. Forest Service and recreational visitors were allowed to enter the Blue Lake area, the Native Americans argued that their religious privacy was violated because the sacred rituals performed on this ceremonial ground were not possible if not done in isolation. It was the backing of the National Council of Churches (NCC) that made the difference in whether the religious claims of these people were heard. The NCC was a powerful body that represented numerous mainline churches. "The senators were suffering from an 'edifice complex'—believing that a place of worship is an artificially constructed building of a determined size with exact boundaries. They could not grasp the idea of an entire watershed as a sanctuary" (Gordon-McCutchan 1991, 790). A community practitioner who wanted to see this sacred land returned to the native people would have to understand the religious and cultural nature of the issue, and would have to recognize the value in forming a coalition with a powerful organization in order to begin to organize for change.

The local congregation, denominational bodies, and interdenominational federations are all resources for the community practitioner. Developing alliances and coalitions with these groups requires skills in community building, an understanding of power dynamics and a theoretical understanding of how alliances and coalitions work. Recent literature on community organizing provides a fresh approach to analyzing the dynamics of coalitions and the complexities of these relationships (Mizrahi and Morrison 1993).

CONCLUSION

The role of a faith community may be priestly or prophetic. Priestly roles imply attention to how the members of the religious group conform to prescribed norms and values. Prophetic roles imply an eye toward changing the status quo, to go beyond what is, and to challenge the existing structure. It is most likely the prophetic role that human service practitioners will seek in tapping the resources of a local church or synagogue. Much of the change initiated by these professionals is designed to alter existing structures and to improve the lives of those who are oppressed.

In actuality, religious groups perform both roles simultaneously, for it is important to attend to the established system of beliefs (priestly) while moving toward changes consistent with what is valued (prophetic). In a diverse society there are many faith traditions, some of which seek to maintain conformity with a status quo that other faith traditions seek to change. It is the task of the helping practitioner to recognize these complexities and to negotiate relationships that enhance the health and human service needs of community members.

REFERENCES

Blumenthal, S. 1994. Christian soldiers. *New Yorker* (July 18).

Canda, E. R., and T. Phaobtong. 1992. Buddhism as a support system for southeast Asian refugees. *Social Work,* 37 (1): 51–67.

Chang, P. M. Y., D. R. Williams, E. H. Griffith, and J. Young. 1994. Church agency relationships in the black community. *Nonprofit and Voluntary Sector Quarterly,* 23 (2): 91–105.

Cnaan, R. A., A. Kasternakis, and R. J. Wineburg. 1993. Religious people, religious congregations, and volunteerism in human services: Is there a link? *Nonprofit and Voluntary Sector Quarterly,* 22 (1): 33–51.

Delgado, M., and D. Humm-Delgado. 1982. Natural support systems: Source of strength in Hispanic communities. *Social Work,* 27: 83–89.

Froland, C., D. Pancoast, N. Chapman, and P. Kimboko. 1981. *Helping networks and human services.* Beverly Hills, Calif.: Sage.

Gordon-McCutchan, R. C. 1991. The battle for Blue Lake: A struggle for Indian religious rights. *Journal of Church and State,* 33 (Autumn): 785–97.

Harris, M. 1995. The organization of religious congregations: Tackling the issues. *Nonprofit Management and Leadership,* 5 (3): 261–74.

Hodgkinson, V. A., and M. S. Weitzman. 1993. *From belief to commitment: The community service activities and finances of religious congregations in the United States.* Washington, D.C.: Independent Sector.

Joseph, M. V. 1988. Religion and social work practice. *Social Casework: The Journal of Contemporary Social Work,* 69 (September): 443–52.

Ladestro, D. 1993. Is fundamentalism fundamentally changing society? *University of Chicago Magazine,* 84 (April): 16–21.

Mizrahi, T., and J. Morrison, eds. 1993. *Community organization and social administration: Advances, trends and emerging principles.* New York: Haworth Press.

Netting, F. E., J. M. Thibault, and J. W. Ellor. 1990. Integrating content on organized religion into macropractice courses. *Journal of Social Work Education,* 26 (1): 15–24.

Salamon, L. and F. Teitelbaum. 1984. Religious congregations in social service agencies: How extensive are they? *Foundation News,* 5: B2–G4.

Steinitz, L. Y. 1981. The local church as support for the elderly. *Journal of Gerontological Social Work,* 4 (1): 43–53.

Tobin, S. S., J. W. Ellor, and S. Anderson-Ray. 1986. *Enabling the elderly: Religious institutions within the service system.* Albany: State University of New York Press.

Wineburg, R. J. 1994. A longitudinal case study of religious congregations in local human services. *Nonprofit and Voluntary Sector Quarterly.* 23 (2): 159–69.

———. 1992. Local human services provision by religious congregations: A community analysis. *Nonprofit and Voluntary Sector Quarterly* 21 (2): 107–18.

———. 1996. An investigation of religious support of public and private agencies in one community in an era of retrenchment. *Journal of Community Practice.* 3 (2): 35–36.

Chapter 10

RELIGIOUSLY AFFILIATED
HUMAN SERVICE AGENCIES

In the preceding chapter we discussed how community practitioners must understand the nature of local congregations in order to maximize potential coalitions and alliances for social change. We indicated that local congregations have multiple ways of structuring their human service efforts: providing direct service on an ad hoc basis, offering their facilities to outside agencies, contributing to local charities, and sponsoring their own religious affiliates. It is the sponsorship of these religious affiliates to which we now turn.

In this chapter we use religious affiliates synonymously with church agency, church related agency, church affiliate, and sectarian agency. A religious affiliate is defined as "a social service organization that publicly acknowledges a connection to a church organization. Church is used in its generic sense to indicate any organized religious group, and refers to church, corps, synagogues, [and temples] alike" (Netting 1986, 52). The religious affiliate is typically a nonprofit agency that is separately incorporated from the faith community. Its formation predates the development of the human service professions, in that this type of agency formed the backbone of the voluntary social welfare system prior to the formation of the public welfare state. Names like Lutheran Social Ministries, Jewish Family and Community Services, Catholic Charities, and a multitude of others are familiar sounding. Their historical roots run deep and their community reputations are well known. Human service professionals have referred clients to these agencies for decades and have partnered with them in forming coalitions and alliances to seek social change (Netting 1986). Ortiz explains that these agencies "are an integral part of the fabric used to weave together social welfare institutions in the United States." (1995, 2109)

HISTORICAL DEVELOPMENT OF RELIGIOUS AFFILIATES

As early as the 1700s, a parallel development of church related and secular private charities occurred in the United States. These providers were likely to offer both material assistance as well a moral instruction to the poor (Bremmer 1964). Before the turn of the twentieth century there were few Catholic and Jewish charitable organizations in the United States. Protestantism dominated the early church related charities, and because its denominations were so diverse and autonomous, each developed its own agencies (Reid and Stimpson 1987).

In the early 1880s the evangelical New York City Tract Society formed the New York Association for Improving the Condition of the Poor, a pioneer welfare program in the United States. In similar fashion, Chicago's Protestant and Catholic communities seized the opportunity to lead the development of human services in the midwestern United States. Created by faith communities in the 1800s, a constellation of agencies emerged targeted to meet human needs (Loewenberg 1988).

These organizations were heavily Protestant dominated in the United States. For tremendous numbers of Catholic immigrants who came to this country in the 1800s, there was a great fear of being proselytized. Religious human service agencies were often viewed as a means to convert the masses. These concerns led to the proliferation of sectarian agencies that were designed to target one's own faith group and to preserve the integrity of a particular religious community (Loewenberg 1988).

In chapter 1 we briefly discussed the Charity Organization Societies that emerged in the late 1870s. The COS movement was initiated by a minister, Stephen Humphreys Gurteen, and became the forerunner of the community welfare council and family agency (Reid and Stimpson 1987). According to Leiby (1984, 536) the COS was something of an "embarrassment" because it was initiated by people who believed that government had no place in social welfare and who had definite opinions about the deserving and undeserving poor. Nevertheless, Leiby suggests that we need not discard the COS workers and its well meaning leaders. He explains that those involved in the COS "based their vision on religious dogma institutionalized in the practice of charity in their time. In bypassing the dogma, we should not overlook the vision" (1984, 536).

The first large scale foster placement program was organized by Charles Loring Brace, another nineteenth-century minister. Vagrant children in the East were sent to live with midwestern families. Evangelical Protestantism is

161

credited with the development of the YMCA which targeted youth who were new to the cities. Protestant missions were the forerunners of the settlement houses, which led to the modern neighborhood and community center concept (Reid and Stimpson 1987). The settlement movement had its religious influences as well. Many of the persons who embraced the settlement movement were prominent religious leaders (Westby 1985). As the movement spread rapidly, there emerged an ongoing debate regarding whether or not a settlement should be religiously affiliated (Berger and Neuhaus 1977). Possibly leaders like Jane Addams tempered this religious zeal.

Some of the first residential institutions for orphaned children and elders were created by Roman Catholic religious orders of sisters. The first of these was established by the Ursuline Sisters in New Orleans in 1727. These establishments were "American transplants" of efforts by Catholic orders in Europe (Reid and Stimpson 1987).

In 1930 Mary Richmond, a social work pioneer, wrote: "The Church furnishes us with motive for all our work . . . and sends us forward . . . in a campaign that involves wider issues" (Coughlin 1965, 22). These words echoed as Protestants created umbrella agencies for human services, Catholic charities emerged in diocesan and national centers, and Jewish community centers and family service agencies proliferated (Chambers 1985). The influence of this era has been profound: "To a large extent, subsequent developments in voluntary social welfare in the United States can be viewed as following either of two courses: (1) the maintenance or, in some areas, the growth of sectarian forms of organization and (2) the secularization of organizations and programs begun under religious auspices or inspired by religious motives" (Reid and Stimpson 1987).

In the nineteenth century, several themes emerged in the development of sectarian welfare services. As Protestant agencies developed services, their tendency toward individualism and autonomy meant that patterns were not easy to discern. These agencies had diverse connections to their parent religious bodies, often difficult to distinguish in terms of authority and form. Clergy, acting independently of the church, or laypersons, inspired by religious convictions, were as likely to develop an organized vehicle for service delivery as was an agency to be established by a formal organizational mandate at the denominational level. These amorphous and loose ties often led to secularization of Protestant agencies, but it also allowed the autonomy necessary to engage in social action and reform. The Social Gospel movement at the turn of the century was instrumental in supporting Protestant social welfare initiatives (Reid and Stimpson 1987).

Catholic agencies were much more tightly structured than their Protestant counterparts. Tied to established religious service orders and to a hierarchical ecclesiastical structure, Catholic organizations were much more defined. Focus was placed on the development of institutions such as homes for dependent children, orphanages, schools, and hospitals. Fears that Catholics would be subject to Protestant evangelism perpetuated the closer affiliations established by these religious agencies to their parent religious body. Reid and Stimpson (1987) point out, for example, that the homeless children who were sent to the Midwest by the Reverend Charles Brace and his colleagues were often Catholic children who were sent to Protestant homes.

This tension between Protestant and Catholic agencies and their leadership was reinforced when Catholic welfare efforts were reimbursed with public dollars for the care of their children. "Such opposition stimulated Catholic leaders to play a more active role in the politics of welfare and fostered the development of Catholic welfare organizations at both local and national levels" (Reid and Stimpson 1987, 547).

Similar to the Catholic expansion following waves of immigration, Jewish welfare agencies expanded rapidly as more Jews arrived from European countries. However, Jewish welfare efforts were distinctive from other sectarian groups. These agencies were not "religious affiliates" in that these organizations were created separately from the synagogues as expressions of Jewish cultural needs rather than as solely religiously motivated services. It is not that Jewish welfare services were completely secular, it is just important to recognize that common ethnic roots and response to anti-Semitism from the dominant Protestant culture led to a blending of religious and community human service needs (Reid and Stimpson 1987).

As community wide fundraising for welfare became more systematized, sectarian and nonsectarian agencies came into competition. Between 1900 and World War I private agencies explored federated funding. The Brooklyn Federation of Jewish Charities was created in 1909 and in 1932 the National Council of Jewish Federations was established. Although the contemporary Council does not provide direct oversight for local programs, it provides considerable guidance on financing and planning issues particularly in relation to funding sources such as United Way. The National Conference on Catholic Charities began in 1910 and continues today as a linkage for 545 diocesan agencies and 200 member agencies in the United States. However, the control in agency relationships rests primarily with local diocesan leadership rather than under national auspices (Reid and Stimpson 1987). Established in 1931 the Federation of Protestant Agencies Caring for Protestants developed a fundraising arm (Cayton and Nishi 1955).

This historical perspective leads to an inevitable question—what is the status of sectarianism today? How do human service professionals synthesize this information so that they have a better understanding of religious influences on the delivery system?

For the purposes of this chapter, sectarian means "related to a sect," and a sect in this case is a religious body. However, it is important to note that in earlier times sectarian was used to mean that an agency served only clients associated with its religious group. Technically, sectarian could be used to define any agency sponsored or affiliated with a specific group, religious or ethnic (Netting 1986).

Sectarian agencies are located in all areas of health and human services, whether they are health care institutions such as hospitals and nursing homes, or are home- and community-based services such as family counseling or home care agencies. Depending on the individual organization, the meaning of sectarianism will vary greatly. For example, some Protestant agencies may be so loosely linked with a parent religious body that no one can really explain what the affiliation means. Another agency, on the other hand, may have clear guidelines for how to maintain their ties with the parent religious body. Again, the watchword is that one should never assume anything about what church affiliation means until the appropriate questions are asked. Even then, it may be hard to distinguish the exact meaning since staff within the agency may have differing perspectives.

One of the first attempts to better understand these organizations and their structures was made in 1955 by the National Council of Churches. They found that Jewish agencies tended to carry a heavier burden of the social welfare responsibility in urban areas in serving persons of their own and other faith traditions. Catholics tended to focus on taking care of their own, and Protestants were viewed as difficult to track because their efforts were so diverse (Cayton and Nichi 1955).

Religious affiliates were changing, as seen in two 1961 studies. Not only were they beginning to branch out more to serve others than their own, but they were receiving funds from sources other than parent religious bodies. These were often united funds, the predecessors of the contemporary United Way (Morris 1961; Tropman 1961). Coughlin's study (1965) in the early 1960s revealed that of 407 sectarian agencies surveyed, 70 percent received government contracts. A 1981 study revealed that Protestant agencies in one large metropolitan city were receiving large proportions of their funding from government sources (Netting 1982).

The religious affiliate is one form of a voluntary agency within a sea of diverse nonprofit and public organizations that comprise the social welfare landscape. Prior to the 1980s the meaning of religious affiliation and sponsorship was not as evident in the voluntary sector literature. However, trends identified earlier (the Reagan/Bush Administrations, the rising interest in nonprofit issues, and the important surveys of religious congregations by the Independent Sector) combine with another trend to raise concerns about the nature of religious affiliates. The additional trend is the backlash of the Pacific Homes case that rocked Protestant denominations to their core.

During the 1980s the United Methodists experienced the Pacific Homes litigation. Several retirement homes affiliated with the United Methodist Church had severe financial difficulties. Settled out of court for $21 million, this experience caused leaders in the Health and Welfare Ministries of the United Methodist Church to publish a guide on the relationship between their jurisdictional units and their religious affiliates. Each institution was encouraged to determine what relationship they could negotiate and the implications of having denominational endorsements were analyzed legally. "The statement regarding the church's debt liability depicts a growing trend to protect churches in an era in which charitable immunity (freedom from a lawsuit) is a thing of the past" (Reid and Stimpson 1987, 548).

In a modern litigious society, religious groups have to examine the meaning of their religious sponsorship or affiliation. This has led many denominations to draft or rewrite statements that define the relationships between their affiliates and parent religious bodies. This underscores the fact that religious affiliates have both secular and religious environments with which to contend (Netting 1986).

NUMBERS OF RELIGIOUSLY AFFILIATED AGENCIES

Just as it has been tedious to determine the number of religious congregations in the United States (Hodgkinson and Weitzman 1993), it has been equally difficult to assess how many health and human service organizations are related to religious groups. Since most of these agencies are formally incorporated and therefore recognized in the eyes of state corporation commissions it would seem that a simple state by state list could be generated. It has not been so simple because some agencies that have religious sounding names are not affiliated with any religious body, whereas other agencies that have secular sounding names may just as likely be affiliated with a faith tradition. In a study of continuing care retirement communities (only one type of human service organization), Netting found that there were so many variations in the way that these communities affiliated with their parent bodies that it was virtually useless to categorize their structures. In addition, it was found that some organizations had secularized or appeared to be secularized, leading one to wonder just what constitutes affiliation anyway (Netting 1991).

Loewenberg (1988) did classify sectarian agencies into three groupings: (1) church sponsored agencies, (2) autonomous institutions, and (3) agencies sponsored by an ethnic community. Church sponsored agencies were related to local congregations, regional religious bodies or entire denominations. Examples would be The Salvation Army and Catholic Charities. The second type, autonomous institutions, was viewed as legally independent (separate corporations) but had staff who remained closely tied to religious groups. Loewenberg described Lutheran agencies as representing this arrangement. Agencies sponsored by ethnic groups were viewed as "popularly identified with a religious group [or coexist] with a religious group. Thus most Jewish social agencies are not sponsored by or related to a synagogue, but are sponsored by the secular Jewish community" (Loewenberg 1988, 139–40). Other examples would be the Korean ethnic church and the services it sponsors and provides for Asian American immigrants (Hurh and Kim 1990). For further reference, Jenkins (1980) has examined ethnic agencies in detail.

If one evaluates available statistics on voluntary organizations in general, there are tremendous gaps. Although nonprofits are required to register with the IRS, religious institutions do not have to report. Determining just how many agencies are related to religious groups is difficult and the IRS has little to gain from developing a monitoring system for these groups since they are tax exempt anyway (Hodgkinson and Weitzman 1989, 14).

The 1955 study by the National Council of Churches identified 2,783 health and welfare agencies (Cayton and Nishi 1955). Obviously, these statistics are historical at best since many religious agencies have secularized and others have been established over the last decades.

It would seem that one way to locate the number of religious affiliates would be to ask each religious group how many agencies they sponsor or endorse. In 1985 one of the authors contacted the national headquarters of religious groups in the United States and found approximately 14,000 organizations were reported to have a connection to the parent religious body. This simple logic fails when one realizes how diverse the structural relationships are. A church affiliate may be related to an order of nuns but have no formal relationship with a diocese of the Catholic Church. Affiliates may be related to religious orders, jurisdictional units such as Conferences of the United Methodist Church, to independent groupings of churches representing one or more denominations, or to a group of laypeople and/or clergy who began the operation. There is no central database that categorizes agencies by their religious affiliations. Suffice it to say that 14,000 agencies affiliated in some way with national bodies is a highly conservative estimate (Netting 1986).

WHAT HUMAN SERVICE PROFESSIONALS NEED TO KNOW ABOUT RELIGIOUS AFFILIATES

There are a number of assumptions that have dominated our thinking about religious affiliates over the years. Each of these assumptions will be examined in light of their relevance for human service workers.

Legal Relationships

A common assumption about religious affiliates is that they are financially supported by their parent religious bodies. In some cases this assumption is accurate, but in many cases there is little financial compensation. Parent religious bodies vary greatly in their legal responsibilities toward church affiliates. Some religious groups have entered the 1990s with their eyes open, ready to back their agencies even at the expense of a lawsuit. Other religious groups have assessed the situation and decided to back away from their fiscal responsibilities, indicating that affiliates may be endorsed but that this does not carry the full weight of financial liability with it. In the wake of the Pacific Homes case, religious groups began to examine their responsibilities very seriously. Some agencies were advised to remove the names of their parent body from legal documents, even from stationary where logos implied the backing of a faith community.

The human service professional who works for a religious affiliate may have to probe to find out exactly what its legal status is. There is also an ethical responsibility to understand the situation so that clients are not misled. Endorsement may mean a very different thing than sponsorship which implies financial backing. This was a critical issue when retirement homes began going bankrupt and older residents believed that the church would bail them out. Equally important are how much the religious group will influence decisions made about finances within the organization since these decisions may make the difference in whether a human service program is continued.

Some organizations know what their religious affiliations mean, others do not. Charters and bylaws may refer to parent religious groups but fail to define the relationship. Interpretation of these documents may have developed quite a tradition of its own, some people believing they understand the relationship

167

until a financial problem occurs. Human service professionals need to explore what these relationships mean. If no one knows what it means, this is a finding. If one finds that there are varying opinions, this may be an important emotional issue to pursue. For example, in a Church of Christ agency the board got into a heated discussion over whether the organization was an "agency" or a "ministry." Those who argued that it was an agency cited the fact that it possessed a charter from the state and in the eyes of the state it was a nonprofit corporation. Those who argued for "ministry" indicated that the essence of the organization was to extend the boundaries of the religious community and that to lose the focus of ministry would be to disavow its very reason for being. Both constituencies were correct, for the organization was indeed both an agency of the state and a ministry of the church. This discussion underscores the difficulty in defining what is meant by a religious affiliate.

Funding

Another assumption about religious affiliates is that their monies come from church sources. Many religious affiliates are heavily subsidized by government and United Way sources, to the point that their religious donations/contributions represent a small portion of their budget. In Catholic agencies the principle of subsidiarity has been cited as the driving force to embrace public dollars. Subsidiarity indicates that if a local organization cannot obtain all the funds needed to deliver services to the people, then they are responsible for locating funds at a higher level (the state or federal government, for example). Catholic agencies, thus, have never had difficulty accepting public monies.

On the other hand, some of the biggest arguments in Protestant voluntary boards of directors have centered around whether or not government dollars will "taint" the services provided. Protestant agencies, therefore, were often more reluctant to obtain public dollars and even looked with some disdain at Catholic agencies that did tap from public coffers. However, if any religious affiliate wanted to expand in the last decades they have usually managed to get over their concern about these dollars and get on the public bandwagon. This is why the Reagan administration's push to go back to the churches was so incredibly misguided. Those agents of the churches were as beholden to the public dollar as they were to private sources of revenue.

It is extremely important for human service practitioners to understand the basic philosophies that guide religious affiliates when it comes to funding. In the last decade, many religious affiliates have struggled with whether to charge fees for service and what that will do to their charitable purposes.

Boards of Directors

Another assumption is that religious affiliates have boards of directors from their parent religious bodies. There are some agencies that do draw heavily from their faith communities so that the leadership of the agency will maintain the basic theology of the endorsing or sponsoring body. There are others that have a certain percentage of their board that is required to come from the parent body and this is usually specified in the bylaws.

If there is a place to look for the meaning of religious affiliation it may be in the board of directors' structure. If persons are selected to be on the board because they are part of a parent religious body, they most likely will attempt to represent the norms and values espoused by that body. Sometimes to maintain these ties, clergy are recruited for these boards so that there is a closer affiliation with the faith community.

Clients Served

Following a long line of sectarian traditions, many people continue to believe that religious affiliates serve their own or at least give preference to members of their faith community. What is interesting is that this was true for some religious groups but not for others. In the late 1800s when many Episcopal agencies emerged, little attention was given to whether they served members of their faith tradition. On the other hand, Missouri Synod Lutheran sponsored agencies were so specific as to serve not only their own, but only Missouri Synod Lutherans and not members of other branches of Lutheranism. So the history of who is served becomes important to know as there may be constituents and supporters who remember when the affiliate was targeting certain clientele. Even within the same religious group there are instances where some agencies concentrated on serving only their own and others did not. Variation, then, is not only across denominations but within them as well.

This was exemplified in a southwestern community, when it was assumed that the Latter Day Saints agency of the Mormon Church served only Mormon members. They were very careful to take no government funds and to target their constituents. However, a human service worker who desperately needed counseling for a client who was not a Mormon asked if an exception might be made. It was discovered that the agency was not as rigid about membership as had been assumed, and the client was welcomed.

Similarly, there are religious agencies in the community that have never been well understood. The Salvation Army is such an example. In the United States the Army is often perceived as a social agency with a religious thrust. In reality, the Army is a religious denomination in its own right, with churches called "corps." Its philosophy is to reunite people with their own faith traditions, although many persons have assumed that the Army aimed to recruit persons to their tradition. Contrary to popular opinion, the Army does not automatically recruit people to be Salvationists (Netting 1986).

Knowing whom a religious affiliate serves and has served in the past is important for several reasons. Human service agencies experience budgetary cuts on an ongoing basis. If the agency has a tradition of serving their own, one way to suffer cuts may be to return to that tradition. On the other hand, an agency that never focused on members of their religious community may not be as likely to strategize or prioritize in the same way. Knowing the organization's past can be instructive because voluntary boards of directors often seek to return to the past (which appears safe from the vantage point of the future) and to tighten old traditions that may have fallen by the wayside in the days of less restrictive funding.

Staff

Many health and human service workers are employed by religious affiliates, coordinate with religious agencies, and/or refer clients to these agencies. Workers who monitor government contracts with private agencies will find religious affiliates among their contractees.

Among those persons employed by religious affiliates, there are not data on how many of those employees are members of the faith communities with which the agency affiliates. Given the legalities of hiring personnel and receiving public funds, most church affiliates have clear statements about equal opportunity and affirmative action. This has been a point of controversy in some agencies, however, when it has come to hiring chief executive officers and administrators. Although the days of hiring clergy to fill top positions are likely over, there is still a tendency in many religious affiliates to want leaders who belong to the parent faith. For example, we are aware of an agency whose board threatened to quit over this issue if a Catholic layperson was not hired to head a local Catholic Charities agency.

WORKING WITH RELIGIOUSLY AFFILIATED HUMAN SERVICE AGENCIES

Being sensitive to these agencies and the clients that are served by them requires human service workers to recognize their differences. They can encourage religious affiliates to clarify their religious identities so that clients are not misled. Recognizing that religious sounding names and religious symbols such as logos on stationary transmit messages to clients is central to this clarification. Depending on a client's experience with religious groups, these messages may be emotionally powerful in both positive and negative ways.

If the human service worker is planning to develop a coalition to deal with a community problem, it is important to know what religious groups oppose or support the issue. It would be problematic to team Planned Parenthood with Catholic Charities for example. But equally important is recognizing that the leadership in some religious affiliates may actually disagree with parent religious bodies. In these circumstances, religious affiliates may act in ways that one would not predict given the ecclesiastical ties that they maintain. For example, a social worker in an affiliated agency who believes in client self-determination may feel obligated to share information on birth control when the religious body sponsoring that agency opposes birth control as an option in family planning.

At the heart of religious affiliation is a commitment to basic values of the parent religious body. In some agencies these are loosely related, having undergone a gradual secularization process over time. For others, there are deeply entrenched beliefs and practices that have become integrated into the agency's culture. Historical precedents, combined with how much the organization has to lose, will influence agency responses to various changes. Smith describes a historical example of how Protestant and Catholic agencies disagreed on state legislation proposed in New York during the 1940s to integrate child welfare services. The analysis reveals that Protestant agencies had much more to lose if they supported integration of African American children into their services, yet Roman Catholic agencies supported this change because it fit with their current practices. "Whereas the ideology of the Roman Catholic sector was consistent with change, the ideology of most Protestants supported continued segregation and took no responsibility for African American children" (1995, 51). Religious affiliation can have deep cultural roots, as this historical case illustrates.

Reid and Stimpson (1987) suggest that two relatively untapped strategies exist for religious affiliates: (1) ecumenical linkage and (2) outreach into parishes. One example of ecumenical linking is the Federation of Protestant Welfare Agencies in New York City; created in 1922, it had 250 constituent agencies in 1987. Phoenix, Arizona, offers another example, the Center for Developing Older Adult Resources, which began as a Church of Christ venture and now links numerous faith communities in serving the elderly.

Parish outreach means providing services at the congregational level. Although many religious affiliates grew out of local congregational grassroots efforts, as they have professionalized they have often moved farther away from their congregations of origin. Often too, a religious agency will be endorsed by a national or regional denominational headquarters, but not be an integral part of local congregations in that same faith tradition. In a way, this is how the community practice issues discussed in previous chapters are linked to the religious affiliate. If a religious affiliate is not tightly related to local congregations, then the concept of parish outreach is a natural connection for that agency. The local parish is also a logical place to recruit volunteers and even donations. The volunteers will not have to be oriented to the basic philosophy behind the agency's operation, since they will come from the same tradition. Within the Catholic system, parish outreach has made great strides in developing parish based social ministry programs (Reid and Stimpson 1987).

CONCLUSION

Those agencies that maintain relationships to parent religious bodies are very visible within the social service delivery system. Their ties to faith traditions range from loose association to tightly controlled connection. Their histories and community reputations have made them logical candidates for receiving government grants and contracts as well as United Way dollars. Health and human service professionals interact with these agencies as employees, referral sources, monitors, and collaborators. It is important that helping professionals recognize the diversity among these agencies as well as their community legitimacy.

REFERENCES

Berger, P. L., and R. J. Neuhaus. 1977. *To empower people: The role of mediating in public policy.* Washington, D.C.: American Enterprise Institute for Public Policy Research.
Bremmer, R. H. 1964. *From the depths: The discovery of poverty in the United States.* New York: New York University Press.
Cayton, H., and S. M. Nishi. 1955. *Churches and social welfare: The changing scene.* New York: National Council of Churches of Christ in the U.S.A.
Chambers, C. A. 1985. The historical role of the voluntary sector in human service delivery in urban America. In *Social planning and human service delivery in the voluntary sector,* ed. Gary A. Tobin, 3–28. Westport, Conn.: Greenwood Press.
Coughlin, B. J. 1965. *Church and state in social welfare.* New York: Columbia University Press.
Hodgkinson, V. A., and M. S. Weitzman. 1993. *From belief to commitment: The com-*

munity service activities and finances of religious congregations in the United States. Washington, D.C.: Independent Sector.

Hurh, W. M., and K. C. Kim. 1990. Religious participation of Korean immigrants in the United States. *Journal for the Scientific Study of Religion,* 29 (2): 19–34.

Jenkins, S. 1980. The ethnic agency defined. *Social Service Review,* 54 (2): 249–61.

Leiby, J. 1984. Charity organization reconsidered. *Social Service Review,* 58 (4): 523–38.

Loewenberg, F. M. 1988. *Religion and social work practice in contemporary American society.* New York: Columbia University Press.

Morris, R. 1961. Current directions in sectarian welfare in America. *Journal of Jewish Communal Service,* 38: 5–10.

Netting, F. E. 1991. The meaning of church affiliation for continuum of care retirement communities. *Journal of Religious Gerontology,* 8 (2): 79–99.

———. 1986. The religious agency: Implications for social work administration. *Social Work and Christianity,* 13 (2): 50–63.

———. 1982. Secular and religious funding of church related agencies. *Social Service Review,* 56 (12): 586–604.

Ortiz, L. P. 1995. Sectarian agencies. *Encyclopedia of social work,* 19th edition. Washington, D.C.: National Association of Social Workers Press.

Reid, W. J., and P. Stimpson. 1987. Sectarian agencies. *Encyclopedia of social work.* Washington, D.C.: National Association of Social Workers.

Smith, E. P. 1995. Willingness and resistance to change: The case of the race discrimination amendment of 1942. *Social Service Review,* 69 (1): 31–56.

Tropman, E. J. 1961. Trends in sectarian social work and their effect on community planning. *Journal of Jewish Communal Service,* 38: 60–68.

Westby, O. 1985. Religious groups and institutions. In *Social planning and human service delivery in the voluntary sector,* ed. Gary A. Tobin, 47–73. Westport, Conn.: Greenwood Press.

Chapter 11

PUBLIC POLICY AND RELIGION IN THE
UNITED STATES

One has only to read the local newspaper to find examples of religion enmeshed in the public arena. Most newspapers assist in locating these examples
by having sections on "religion" or "religious life." It is common to characterize papers in communities around the country as being influenced by various
value perspectives, political ideologies, and religious groups. This chapter is
about public policy debates and religion that often are reported in the media
and that relate to or influence health and human service providers and their
clients. If one considers the public school to be a human service organization,
the connection is immediately obvious: controversies over school prayer, cre-
ationism, sex education, and religious symbols are ongoing. If one considers
that many social service agencies have religious affiliations and are receiving
heavy doses of federal and state monies, the relevance is clear. These organizational linkages between religious sponsors and government are continually
being reassessed.

In addition, broad community and societal forces that impinge on how decision makers view the delivery of health and human services pose incredible
challenges for human service workers. For example, in the 1950s and 1960s
the impact of the black church on the Civil Rights Movement had a decided influence on the development of laws to promote the rights of minorities and on
the motivation to create programs for "maximum citizen participation" under
the War on Poverty. Black ministers were in the forefront of the effort, and
local church buildings served as organizational centers. "The role of black religion in civil affairs has been an accepted and important element in American
social and political life" (Young 1992, 80). Today we see this same kind of influence when religious groups speak out on abortion, gay and lesbian rights,
and other controversial public issues. The mixture of religious and secular interests is often complex and intense.

In this chapter we begin by looking at the separation of church and state, which is the basic premise on which the United States Constitution protects religious freedom. Following this discussion, we will look at some of the ecclesiastical policies that bring religion, politics, and social problems to the attention of human service providers. Finally, we will examine the implications of religion and politics for health and human service organizations and the helping professions.

THE HISTORY OF THE SEPARATION OF CHURCH AND STATE

As we stated in chapter 1, many colonists who came to America to escape religious persecution in their mother countries did not arrive with the intent of honoring religious pluralism. They arrived with the intent of practicing their religion without persecution, with little toleration of religions other than their own. Consequently, religious groups were persecuted and banished on a regular basis in the New World. Hostilities were open among faith communities, causing acts of toleration to be passed in various states. For example, Maryland passed its Act of Toleration in 1649 in order to encourage friendly relationships among religious groups by punishing anyone who profaned another group.

Finke (1990) muses over what caused the colonists to shift their focus to toleration. First, colonial business people found that pressures toward religious conformity were not in their best economic interest. Market niches could be expanded if arriving immigrants with different religious beliefs were considered to be valuable consumers. Therefore, intolerance and exclusion would not be good marketing strategy. Second, vast expanses of land made it virtually impossible for any religious establishment to create one church. Thus, the growing numbers of diverse settlers who became part of the market economy combined with large amounts of space, contributed to the recognition that there was room for many religious groups. Gradually, colonists came to believe that a free and democratic society was strengthened by persons of character and integrity who adhered to various religious beliefs. This latter realization was strongly facilitated when anger toward the mother country led these varied groups to focus on a common enemy (Davis 1994).

Davis identifies three factors that brought diverse colonial religious groups together as allies during the Revolution. First, they were joined by a deep desire for independence, liberty, and justice. Second, many patriots believed that God had the interest of the emerging United States at heart and that destiny was controlled by God. Third, many religious groups shared a belief in republican government which included "government by the people, separation of powers, limited government without jurisdiction to interfere with the people's natural rights, and a dependence upon public virtue" (Davis 1994, 247). There was consensus at the Constitutional Convention that religious pluralism should be protected and government should not interfere in religious matters. These beliefs were embedded in the opening clause of the First Amendment: "Congress shall make no law respecting an establishment of religion, or prohibiting the free exercise thereof." The Constitution of the United States thus rested on the fundamental principle that religion is a private matter, not to be tampered with by the state. Gradually, state laws that recognized established religious groups were abolished. For example, Virginia rescinded its law permitting capital punishment for blasphemy, impious reference to the Trinity, or habitual cursing (Davis 1994). The last holdout of the original thirteen colonies was Massachusetts, which rescinded its Congregational establishment law in 1833. Thus ended a time when colonies (and, later, states) established religions and imposed penalties and punishments on other faith communities.

Although there was some concern that without the state's stamp of approval religion would diminish in importance or even disappear, no such thing happened. In fact, the freedom accorded religion resulted in what could be characterized as a religious market economy. The First Amendment symbolized the deregulation of religion in the United States. Hundreds of religious groups sprang up, free to compete for members without regulation (Finke 1990). "If the constitutionally mandated framework of religious freedom can make any claim whatsoever, it is that it gave official sanction to a phenomenal growth in religious diversity" (Davis 1994, 251).

COURT INTERPRETATION OF THE LAW

Even though religion was deregulated by the First Amendment, its freedom was protected because it was named in the law. A basic concern in the naming of any entity is the operationalization of what that name means. Anyone involved in the development of policy knows that even seemingly obvious terms are incredibly difficult to define, and that clarity is almost impossible. Some group will always see the definition as influenced by an alternative value or would choose other language altogether to name the concept to be regulated, protected, or deregulated.

The concept of "religion" is such a term. Tremendous amounts of time have been devoted to defining what religion means from a public policy perspective. In 1947 the Supreme Court attempted to define what was meant by the establishment clause. Although helpful, this clarification was subject to question (Ignagni 1994). In 1961 the *Torcaso* v. *Watkins* case was heard by the Supreme Court. Justice Hugo Black delivered the majority opinion of the Court, distinguishing religions founded on beliefs in God from those with different belief systems. However, a footnote explaining these different beliefs caused controversy when secular humanism was joined with Buddhism, Taoism, Ethical Culture, and others (McKenzie 1991). This spurred a controversial argument over whether secular humanism was actually another form of religion.

Definition of Religion

It is not within the scope of this book to engage the reader in an in-depth discussion of the implications of legal definitions. On the other hand, a brief examination of terminology and the complexity encountered when trying to interpret what religion means in the United States is instructive. McKenzie (1991) provides a great deal of insight into what *religion* may and may not mean. Drawing on Paul Tillich's discussion of "quasi-religions," McKenzie notes that socialism and communism would be "religions" if one believes that an intensely held belief system constitutes religion. Tillich talks about religion in the narrower and broader senses, the former meaning what we typically have discussed in light of attachment to some established group, the latter being a sense of transcendence which has often been characterized as spirituality.

As these arguments progress, each attempt to operationalize "religion" becomes more complicated. For example, if a religion acknowledges a higher power it is by definition based on traditional belief systems to the exclusion of many non-Western religious groups that do not believe in a higher power. If religion is viewed as perspectives held strongly or intensely, persons who are strongly antireligious become religious by this definition. This makes it virtually impossible to be nonreligious unless one does not feel strongly about anything. Paradoxically, such definitions mean that atheists are "religious" because they strongly believe in no religion! Definitions of religion are therefore weak and generalized, rendering them virtually meaningless. McKenzie (1991, 738) sums it up as follows: "As the Court has used the term 'religion,' every philosophy of life is a religion and it becomes, therefore, logically impossible to distinguish religion from nonreligion. The word 'religion' no longer works. It does not set off beliefs about God or the gods from other beliefs."

McKenzie goes on to point out that the very act of attempting to define

177

religion may likely violate the Establishment Clause of the United States Constitution. For if one attempts, no matter how fair minded, to define the concept the values reflected in the definition will be inclusive or exclusive of various religious groups. Obviously, this concern has not stopped the Supreme Court from hammering away at definitions of terms relevant to the First Amendment of the Constitution. These definitions continue to evolve as cases are heard. In 1970 the purpose effect entanglement test emerged under Warren Burger's tenure as chief justice, meaning that the law should not involve the government in a close entanglement with religion. Decisions during the 1970s focused heavily on whether programs under question were divided politically along religious lines. Contemporary scholars argue over whether the rulings of the Court are conflicting, confusing, and unpredictable in these cases (Ignagni 1994). For the purposes of this book, the legal machinations about factors and tests to understand the establishment clause are beyond our domain. What these discussions do point out is that the separation of church and state reflects the general tenor of a litigious society that has come of age. Although laws were enacted by the Congress, it is in the playing field of the courts where it is determined whether certain actions and events have violated the intent of that law. Thus, even though religion is separate from government, it is likely that public arms of government will be involved in the interpretation and upholding of those freedoms.

One could argue that this is a moderately interesting discussion but that it has little relevance specifically for health and human services. Yet, when one digs into the cases that have been heard by the Supreme Court, there are definite and widespread practical implications for helping professionals. Consider the Supreme Court's decision in *Employment Division, Department of Human Resources* v. *Smith*. This case focused on unemployment compensation for two drug rehabilitation counselors in Oregon who were fired for using peyote, a controlled substance. They argued that their Native American religion required the use of peyote for sacramental purposes. The Court ruled "that a state 'cannot condition the availability of unemployment insurance on an individual's unwillingness to forgo conduct required by his religion'" (Choper 1992, 367). Because this case occurred in a human service agency it raised implications for how the use of drugs for religious purposes affect the helping process of colleagues and clients who engage in behavior that is illegal but conforms with religious beliefs.

Prior to the 1940s issues on religious freedom were seldom taken to court. Since that time there have been more and more cases involving religious issues. Ironically, in an attempt to protect religious freedom it has become nec-essary to use the government system of courts to protect the rights and free-doms of various individuals and groups. For new religious groups these cases can be very costly and could be viewed as indirectly penalizing them, even in the interest of fairness (Finke 1990).

OTHER INTERPRETATIONS OF THE LAW

The courts interpret the law for society, but we would be remiss if we ne-glected to acknowledge other interpretations. Religious groups view the es-tablishment clause and the Constitution from their own perspectives, and these views have an impact on public policy making.

There are those persons and groups who are particularly concerned about the original intent of the framers of the Constitution. There are others who are more concerned with how the policy can be interpreted in the contemporary world. Still others believe that the Constitution is a document made by men and subject to human fallibility. Thus, changes in the law are a natural out-growth of a growing society. However, some believe that the American Con-stitution was divinely inspired. One such group is the Church of Jesus Christ of the Latter-day Saints or Mormons (Slack 1994). The Mormon Church be-lieves that the Constitution is a sacred document. This belief causes members of the Mormon Church to feel very strongly about their role in public policy making and service to their country in the armed services. Although they do not believe that the Constitution was a direct revelation from God, like the Ten Commandments, they do believe that the doctrine was foreordained. Foreordi-nation means that the framers were placed by God at that particular point in time and that the document reflects the influence of Christ acting upon them (Slack 1994).

Interpretations of the separation of church and state are in the forefront as we enter into the third millennium. The Christian Reconstruction Movement, for example, seeks to move the United States toward theocracy, which is the direct rule of God by divinely inspired spokespersons—and a political system based entirely on biblical law. Such a system "would require capital punishment for adulterers, homosexuals, and incorrigible children" (Davis 1994, 253). The Reconstructionist theocracy, then, leaves no room for diverse belief systems.

A milder type of theocracy is desired by those groups united under the Re-ligious Right. Although the rhetoric of the Religious Right may sound very similar to Reconstructionism, they place more constraints on the implementation of a theocracy in the United States. Barton, writing in *The Myth of Separation,* explains the position of the Religious Right. The Founding Fathers wanted this nation to be Christian because it was to be governed by Christian principles. Non-Christians would still be able to participate and would have the right to worship, but there would be Christian symbols throughout the nation (Davis 1994).

Other scholars and writers have attempted to identify common values in the nation's spiritual life. Discussions of Civil Religion have focused on a search for meaning among American people that does not necessarily rely upon any one faith tradition. In *The Good Society* (1991), Bellah and his colleagues devote a chapter to what they call "The Public Church." Their rationale for this seeming paradox is that both Christian and Jewish traditions require that religion not be a private matter. Biblical religion is viewed as highly public in two ways. First, both Jews and Christians believe in an all seeing God, which requires a holistic view of the world. Second, the meaning of public is that citizens come together to deliberate common concerns. Religious groups are definitely public in that regard because they engage in discourse over matters of public good. The public church, therefore, is viewed as very much alive and well in American society. The writers go on to say that "the free exercise clause to the Constitution guarantees the right of religious bodies to public expression, just as much as the 'no establishment' clause ensures that none will gain any favored governmental status" (Bellah et al. 1991, 179–80).

In a similar vein, Martin Marty "distinguishes between a vision of 'the nation under God' and a vision of 'national self-transcendence.' The former sees 'a transcendent deity as the pusher or puller of the social process'; the latter sees 'the nation itself as transcendent, with a vital role to play in the world'" (as cited by Kent and Spickard 1994, 374–75).

Obviously, there are many different ways to view the separation of church and state, the relationship of religion and politics, and the ways in which faith communities interpret these policies. It is our hope that in calling attention to these diverse perspectives, the human service professional will be more aware of how controversial these issues are and the how much emotion may be brought to the subject by both colleagues and clients. These are issues that get to the core system of meaning on which national integrity is based.

RELIGION, POLITICS AND SOCIAL PROBLEMS: ECCLESIASTICAL POLICY

Although we have focused heavily on the public law of the United States, it is important to recognize that each religious group will have its' own private policies. Sometimes these policies will be consistent with secular law and in other instances they may be in conflict, reflecting two faces of religion, the priestly and prophetic. The priestly face reflects the current consensus and attempts to carry out what is agreed upon. The prophetic face is one that not only disagrees with, but may forcefully criticize, that which is accepted as the status quo.

This is why religion and politics are so difficult to analyze. At times some faith traditions will be reflecting the priestly function, very much in sync with public policy while other faith communities are protesting against it. To complicate matters, there are times when there is such disagreement within a faith community that persons of the same tradition will disagree with one another, both using religious writings to support their case. A recent example occurred in a southeastern city when members of the Ku Klux Klan distributed hate mail about Jews and African Americans. Their fliers, which were placed on doorsteps in the middle of the night, stated that they were taking action in the name of Christianity. Many persons who affiliate with Christian traditions were irate. Yet both the KKK and their opponents cited biblical passages to support their positions.

Helping professionals engage in identifying and addressing social problems on an ongoing basis. Many of these problems will be highly controversial and many will be addressed in policy statements issued by faith communities. For example, the U.S. Catholic bishops routinely issue pastoral letters on social concerns, testify before Congress, file Supreme Court briefs, and lobby for various things, such as peace education in schools (Henriot 1988).

Bullis and Harrigan (1992) examined how various religious groups have very different convictions about sexuality and discuss how these differences affect human service intervention. They summarize and contrast ecclesiastical policy statements on abortion, homosexuality, premarital sex, and sexual abuse.

Abortion

Abortion is one of the most controversial issues in modern society. It is also a topic of great concern particularly to helping professionals who deal with young adults and children. There are many differences among religious groups in how abortion is viewed, ranging from claims that the unborn child (at any stage) is a human being and abortion is unjustified in any circumstance to the view that there are many morally justifiable circumstances under which an abortion is warranted (Bullis and Harrigan 1992).

When foes of abortion were organizing to protest the Supreme Court's

Roe v. *Wade* decision in 1973, members of various religious groups met in Washington. However, they were not there to organize countermeasures to the Supreme Court decision or to protest the decision in *Roe* v. *Wade*. They were there to organize the Religious Coalition for Abortion Rights (RCAR), initiated under the auspices of the United Methodist General Board of Church and Society. "Many of the religious organizations which came together to form RCAR had expressed their opposition to restrictive abortion laws even before Roe, and they were quite unwilling to sit idly as the National Conference of Catholic Bishops and other antiabortion groups worked for a return to prohibitive abortion policies" (Mills 1991, 569).

The RCAR was not arguing for extensive public policy to oversee abortion concerns. They were arguing just the opposite, that it was not the place of government to restrict what they believed to be the right of individuals to act on their religious beliefs and to make their own moral choices. Composed of twenty national Christian, Jewish, and other religious organizations, the RCAR encouraged each group to pursue its own theological and philosophical path. Obviously, there were many variations in how these groups framed their convictions. The unifying element in this coalition was a belief that every woman has a right to make a choice in line with her own conscience and belief. RCAR representatives testified before Congress that there was indeed disagreement within the religious community and among theologians over when a fetus becomes a person and whether abortion is murder. They argued that since no agreement among religious groups could be determined, that choice had to be left to the individual to avoid forcing one religious conviction on people who did not share that conviction. The RCAR coalition is more formalized today, having incorporated with a board of directors and no longer being a part of the United Methodist Board of Church and Society. This coalition continues its efforts to educate the public and Congress about the religious nature of the abortion controversy (Mills 1991).

Homosexuality, Premarital Sex, and Sexual Abuse

Views of homosexuality, like abortion, differ across and among religious faith traditions. As times have changed, so have some of the policy statements on homosexuality issued by various religious groups. For example, the Roman Catholic bishops in the United States modified their position in recent years, arguing that homosexuality is not freely chosen but is biological in nature and therefore not a sin. However, this statement does not condone homosexual behavior and is not necessarily reflective of the larger world view held by bishops outside the United States (Bullis and Harrigan 1992).

182

Protestant denominations vary in their views. The United Methodist Church is fairly accepting of homosexuality in that it opposes homophobia and indicates that there are no easy answers to this situation. There are inconsistencies within denominational groups, depending on local congregational attitudes. For example, some churches in different faith communities have knowingly ordained homosexual ministers (Bullis and Harrigan 1992).

Faith traditions vary in their views of premarital sex, although they consistently do not condone it. The tones of their statements vary in how vigorously they oppose such behavior. On the other hand, there are few policy statements on sexual abuse because it is considered a legal issue. Various religious groups have been active in polling their members and in writing position papers on sexual abuse and domestic violence (Bullis and Harrigan 1992).

Healing/Medicine

Other areas of concern to human service professionals surround quality of life, health, and issues of life and death. Central to this theme have been publicized cases in which parents have rejected medical treatment for sick children based on their religious beliefs. When children have died in these situations, defendants have argued that the First Amendment protects them from prosecution. Forty-seven states have "spiritual-healing" statutes that technically exempt parents from prosecution for not seeking medical treatment for their children on the basis of religious beliefs. However, what constitutes "spiritual healing" is often poorly defined in these statutes. The potential for child abuse to be couched in spiritual terms is discussed by Bullis (1991), who asserts that helping professionals need to know the nature of state and federal child abuse laws as well as to understand the concept of spiritual healing. Today, given the increasing concern about child abuse, more parents are being prosecuted for relying on spiritual healing, and juries are returning convictions in many cases. The child welfare worker must be aware of these issues.

Historically Christian Scientists have always faced controversy over their religious beliefs about healing. Efforts were made since the inception of this religious group in 1866 to institutionalize protections in the form of spiritual healing statutes in various states. However, the spiritual healing defense is indicative of what happens when societal attitudes shift and change. As the nation has focused its attention on child abuse and neglect, attitudes toward spiritual healing laws have altered. In 1983, new federal child abuse regulations explicitly named failure to provide appropriate medical care and treatment as child neglect. Christian Scientists have been surprised and upset by the publicity of recent cases that indicate a basic lack of understanding of their religious beliefs. "Observing the Christian Science Church reaction to the situation of cases involving deaths of some Christian Scientist children furnishes a contemporary example of the effect of such circumstances on both the policy and practice of a major religious group in our society" (Richardson and Dewitt 1992, 561).

The Death Penalty

Human service providers who work in or with the criminal justice system will appreciate the religious issues that arise in discussing the death penalty. It is impossible to explore these issues in detail here, but one recent study indicates their complexity. Young (1992) found that evangelical Christians are more likely to favor compassion and concern for criminals, whereas fundamentalists are more likely to favor the death penalty. This study points out that evangelicals are often viewed as fundamentalists and vice versa, when in actuality these concepts are quite different. The evangelical is one who actually works to convert others, whereas the fundamentalist is one who interprets scripture literally. "Although Christian fundamentalists tend to be evangelicals, many evangelicals are not fundamentalists" (Young 1992, 78). However, when race was considered in the equation, it was found that African Americans were less likely to favor the death penalty even if they were fundamentalists. It was the white fundamentalist churches that strongly favored the death penalty. This study points out the complex array of factors that influence how life and death are viewed in the interplay of politics and religion.

Cults

A last example focuses on cults and how Cults sometimes test the bounds of freedom of religion. Helping professionals who work with estranged families, runaway youth, and other clients who are seeking alternatives may have questions about how to handle issues of cult brainwashing. Although there have been successful Supreme Court cases where multimillion dollar verdicts were awarded to plaintiffs, there are other viewpoints that these types of cases may actually stamp out exotic religions that provide alternative religious experiences. In fact, there is disagreement among professionals about whether cults actually do "brainwash." Juries may be swayed by expert witnesses advocating the brainwashing theory because the general public is basically suspicious of cults which are outside the experiences of mainline religious group members. Thus, it is important for helping professionals to examine the current literature on these activities and determine their own perspectives on how to handle these delicate situations without jumping to conclusions.

HOW RELIGION AND POLITICS INFLUENCE HUMAN SERVICES

Carter, in *The Culture of Disbelief* (1993), makes an important point about the separation of church and state. He says that the First Amendment's establishment clause was designed "to protect religion from the state, not the state from religion" (105). This distinction is critical to how human service professionals view the intention of public policy. Carter makes a passionate plea for the involvement of religious groups in making their voices heard in the public arena. Yet he also notes that religious communities have made a Faustian bargain with the state because they receive tax exemptions and charitable deductions for members' contributions; those persons who are religious are given favored treatment through the tax code. In addition, those groups that sponsor human service organizations draw heavily from government sources. "Thus the welfare state has already trapped the religions, and the day will doubtless come when they, too, face pressures to behave correctly with respect to race, sex, and many other issues, or lose valuable government patronage" (Carter 1993, 150).

That day already shows signs of dawning. Zoning battles have arisen in a number of cities that have caused churches to protest their classifications. Yale University has been conducting a major research project on churches and the role of religious institutions. The Independent Sector continues to develop a database on voluntary giving and churches. As researchers turn their attention to churches and as questions of what is and is not "charitable" are coming to the forefront, there will be more and more debate in the public arena about what exactly is meant by the separation of church and state. And as religious groups become more involved in political activities, there will be those who seek to constrain their voices. Because churches are beholden to the state for tax exemption and other privileges, they will have to decide whether they can bite the hand that feeds them and just how hard that bite can be. The Faustian bargain of which Carter speaks will have to be reexamined and the question will remain—will religious groups be constrained by what they feel they could lose or will they speak their convictions?

The history of religious involvement in politics is as old as the nation. Churches were actively involved in every political issue from slavery to prohibition. Following the Civil Rights Movement, almost every major religious group in the country established permanent lobbying offices in Washington, including interdenominational organizations, most notably the National Council of Churches (Greenawalt 1994). A study of religious interest groups in Washington indicates that they may have less impact than is often attributed to them, but that they represent an important voice in public discourse (Zwier 1991). Mainline denominations have issued policy statements on almost every social issue. The new Religious Right has come to the forefront as a viable political force representing theologically conservative Christians (Greenawalt 1994). In response to what is seen as the radical Religious Right or the Christian Coalition (Birnbaum 1995), has sprung forth the Interfaith Alliance. In a brochure (TIA 1995, 2), this group describes itself as designed to "aggressively campaign to raise awareness of our nation's religious traditions by those who seek to advance a partisan, political agenda . . . people of faith do not surrender the last word of Pat Robertson, Jerry Falwell and others who share their agenda." Anyone who does not grasp the depth of emotion and fervor associated with the contemporary interplay of church and state has missed a basic element of contemporary life in the United States.

CONCLUSION

So what does this mean for human service providers? First, it means that naive assumptions about the separation of church and state must be replaced with an understanding of the complex issues surrounding the interpretation of the law. Second, there are vast resources available in local faith communities. Tapping into these resources to serve clients requires understanding and respecting the differences among religious groups. It also requires respecting the right to exercise those differences in this nation. Third, human service workers need to know which religious groups are mobilized in local, state, regional, and national arenas. One might not always agree with the belief system that drives these groups, but one may find a joint understanding around a particular set of human service issues that could impact lobbying efforts and promote causes relevant to client needs. Fourth, there must be sensitivity to the legal issues involved when one works with a client of a particular faith tradition. A Christian Scientist family might define their child's health care very differently than the established health care system does. What does it mean for client self-determination when the family refuses medical treatment? What happens when a helping professional encounters a religious group that advocates capital punishment when she or he is working with a death row inmate to appeal a sentence? Fifth, it is incumbent upon human service professionals to recognize when political actions are being couched in religious terminology for the sake of swaying decision makers. The use of religious language is so prevalent in secular speech that one can be easily seduced into collusion with oppressive rather than transcendent forces. A constant vigilance is required.

In sum, this chapter has not attempted to provide an in-depth view of politics and religion, but to raise consciousness and begin a dialogue about how influential religion is on politics and politics on religion.

REFERENCES

Bellah, Robert N., R. Madsen, W. M. Sullivan, A. Swidler, and S. M. Tipton. 1991. *The good society.* New York: Knopf.

Bullis, R. K. 1991. The spiritual healing 'defense' in criminal prosecutions for crimes against children. *Child Welfare,* 70 (5): 541–55.

Bullis, R. K.. and M. P. Harrigan. 1992. Families in society. *Journal of Contemporary Human Services,* 73 (5): 304–12.

Carter, S. L. 1993. *The culture of disbelief.* New York: Basic Books.

Choper, J. H. 1992. Separation of church and state: "New" directions by the "new" supreme court. *Journal of Church and State,* 34 (Spring): 363–75.

Davis, D. H. 1994. Religious pluralism and the quest for unity in American life. *Journal of Church and State,* 36 (Spring): 245–59.

Finke, R. 1990. Religious deregulation: Origins and consequences. *Journal of Church and State,* 32 (Summer): 609–26.

Greenawalt, K. 1994. The participation of religious groups in political advocacy. *Journal of Church and State,* 36 (Winter): 143–60.

Henriot, P. J. 1988. Pluralism: The role of the church in public policy. *Social Thought,* 14 (Spring): 37–47.

Ignagni, J. A. 1994. Explaining and predicting supreme court decision making: The Burger court's establishment clause decision. *Journal of Church and State,* 36 (Spring): 301–27.

The Interfaith Alliance. 1995. Brochure published by TIA, 1511 K. Street NW, Suite 738, Washington, DC 20005.

Kent, S. A., and J. V. Spickard. 1994. The "other" civil religion and the tradition of radical Quaker politics. *Journal of Church and State,* 36 (Spring): 373–87.

McKenzie, D. 1991. The supreme court, fundamentalist logic, and the term "religion." *Journal of Church and State,* 33 (Summer): 732–46.

Mills, S. A. 1991. Abortion and religious freedom: The religious coalition for abortion rights (RCAR) and the prochoice movement, 1073–1989. *Journal of Church and State,* 33 (Summer): 569–94.

Richardson, J. T., and J. Dewitt. 1992. Christian science spiritual healing, the law, and public opinion. *Journal of Church and State,* 34 (Summer): 549–61.

Slack, R. D. 1994. The Mormon belief of an inspired constitution. *Journal of Church and State,* 36 (Winter): 35–56.

Young, R. L. 1992. Religious orientation, race, and support of the death penalty. *Journal for the Scientific Study of Religion,* 31 (1): 76–87.

Zwier, R. 1991. The power and potential of religious interest groups. *Journal of Church and State,* 33 (Spring): 271–85.

EPILOGUE

Mr. Raymond or Mrs. Johnston has come for help. As you listen to them, you hear them talk about how important their religious beliefs are to them. The traditional practice at your agency would be to acknowledge the importance of these beliefs, but functionally, you would not include this information in either the goals for the client, or even the case analysis. Yet, this does not feel like it is adequate. Where do you go from here?

Or suppose that you are working with a human service agency that wants to reach out to religious congregations for resources. The agency staff has strong concerns about not promoting a religious agenda, but you want to be sensitive to the faith tradition with which you are collaborating. What do you do?

It is our hope that the contents of this book will change the way you address the client's religious and/or spiritual dialogue, whether the client is an individual or a group. This material is important to the basic identities of Mr. Raymond and Mrs. Johnston and therefore is relevant to all aspects of one's work. It is also important to the members of a religious congregation in the second example. The next step is to integrate this information into practice.

Direct human service practice (intervention) is reflective of the exchange between the client and the helping professional. The concept of holistic support assumes that the spiritual aspects of both the client and the practitioner are present and active in some way. Much of this book has addressed ways to examine the spiritual aspect of the client. In addition, there is also a need to address the needs of the worker. Most readers will find themselves somewhere on a continuum between having a firm religious belief system, to seeing little value in a personal religious system. This will be expressed differently from the various diverse perspectives. However, some persons will wish to integrate their faith tradition into professional practice; others will believe that religious diversity simply offers insight into the differing needs of clients.

For persons wishing to integrate their own views of religious practice into their human service work, some precautions need to be discussed. Human service practice has traditionally been based on a humanistic philosophy. Humanism reflects the centrality of the human experience. For the most part, clients who come to traditional agencies expect to discuss their "human" issues. If religious and/or spiritual issues are to be integrated into professional practice, the client needs to be informed of this when they first come into contact with the agency. This is an important ethical point which should not be overlooked. One way to express this is to suggest that the work of the agency is *wholistic*, but be aware that the word wholism or wholistic is used in many different ways. Be sure to identify that you are including the spiritual aspect of the person in your definition.

A second important point concerns the actual inclusion of religious practices in the human service context. The purpose of human service practice is to facilitate growth and support for the whole human being. Traditionally this has not included spiritual direction. Spiritual direction has long been considered the purview of the professional priest, minister, rabbi, spiritual director, or pastoral counselor and is most often dealt with in religious contexts. If agency policy and your contract with the client involves an open understanding of the inclusion of spiritual direction or counseling, then the client must be so informed. Only then can religious practices such as prayer between practitioner and client be ethically appropriate (Wimberly 1990, 15). These practices are entirely inappropriate if the practice of the agency and/or therapist is restricted to the traditional tools of human service professions.

This is also true of efforts to convert a client to the practitioner's personal religious practice or beliefs. It is the role of the priest, minister, or rabbi to "interpret the faith" to the parishioner or member. The role of the human service professional is very different. It is to listen to the client and support his or her belief system. It is always outside the domain which has traditionally been developed for human service professionals to "interpret the faith" to a client, in the same way that professionals do not try to change the political views of a client. Sometimes referred to as proselytizing the client, these practices are outside the purview of general human service practice and should never be included in the roles that are assumed as the result of this book. Possibly the greatest fear of human service administrators is that a book like this one will open the door for professionals to proselytize clients. This is not our intention. Professional human service practice is different from that of religious professionals or lay members of congregations. Human service professionals must hear the story of the client, but must avoid superimposing their own story on that of the client, whether the client is an individual, group, organization, or community. Client autonomy and self-determination is of the highest value in all matters, especially those of religion and spirituality.

INTEGRATING RELIGION INTO THE
HUMAN SERVICE PARADIGM

Along with the diversity of religious practices and beliefs will be found a diversity of approaches to understanding religious beliefs. Two different approaches are possible based on this book.

The first is found in transpersonal psychology, which seeks to integrate psychology with the world religious traditions. It focuses on the transcendent aspects of the human experience moving from the transcendent, interpersonal to the transcendent with that which is greater than the person. It is here the client's autonomy must prevail—in the definition and description of the transcendent.

A second approach is found in traditional religious perspectives. For professionals who are more traditional the spiritual is a part of every aspect—physical, social, and emotional—of an individual. It is difficult to separate the spiritual from any other aspect. Thus, the connection is based on the human experience of life, of other persons, and of the divine (however this is conceived). As a basis for human service practice, humanism by definition focuses on humanity as central to all of life. Wholistic practice acknowledges this focus but suggests that there is something beyond that which can also be a resource for individuals in their everyday lives. Although it is not the role of the human service professional to directly engage in the client's relationship with the divine, it is important that the practitioner be prepared to understand how the client perceives and is supported by his or her beliefs.

THE FUTURE

Persons from the various world traditions continue to enter the United States, joining persons from their religious traditions that are already part of the landscape. Native Americans and African Americans continue to get in touch with their historical religious traditions, as clients continue to explore a need for a relationship with that which is greater than the human experience. As these changes occur, religious and spiritual expression and beliefs become more important. For human service professionals, to ignore these phenomena is to ignore important aspects of human needs.

The pathological use of religious practice, both in groups and by individuals, also continues to increase. A distinction between the pathology of the client and the "normal religious practices" of the practitioner is important as one sorts out the client's issues from one's own. Honoring the spiritual needs and concerns of the client offers enhanced access to the fullest perspective of the client. It also allows the human service worker to utilize the fullest expression of themselves. By observing the diverse spiritual needs of the client, the unique understandings, vocabulary, and traditions can be observed and understood in the process of human services provision.

REFERENCE

Wimberly, E. P. 1990. *Prayer in pastoral counseling.* Louisville: Westminster/John Knox Press.

APPENDIX: COURSE OUTLINE

In the wake of the Council for Social Work Education's inclusion of religious and spiritual awareness in their standards for training social workers, questions have surfaced as to how to integrate this material. We suggest that, where possible, this material should be integrated into the curriculum. However, if a separate course is to be designed, the following outline may be of some assistance.

SPIRITUAL AND RELIGIOUS ISSUES IN HUMAN SERVICES

Catalog Description

This course will attempt to define spirituality and religion using historical and comparative approaches. It will explore the basic principles of the major religions of the world and the role of religion in public policy, service provision, and clinical practice.

Course Objectives

1. The student will demonstrate knowledge of the basic faith principles of the various world religions that may be encountered in human service practice.
2. The student will demonstrate knowledge of the basic issues addressed by religion and personal spirituality as they affect public policy, service provision, and clinical practice.

Approach of This Course to Religion and Spirituality

The focus of this course is on information and approaches needed to work with and be supportive of the various religious and spiritual beliefs of clients. In the United States, many religious groups and spiritual traditions coexist. In an average agency, the human service worker will encounter persons reflective of those religious traditions who live in the local community. It is an assumption of the instructor that when clients come to seek help from a human service worker, they bring their culture, their personal history, their whole person—including their religious traditions as well as their personal sense of spirituality. In one sense this spiritual self-understanding is always present in the counseling situation, even though the *language* of religion and spirituality may not always be present. In either sense, however, to ignore this aspect of the person, is to ignore something that can be very important to the growth and healing process of that individual.

In order to bring this healing power into the clinic, the therapist needs to have both insight and skills. Most counselors have never had such training. This class is intended to address this gap in training. To do this, the student will be exposed to individuals and religious traditions that are outside of their own. It is *not* the intention of this class to offer instruction to you as to what *you* ought to believe, or to in any way confront your current, personal beliefs. Rather it is the goal of this class to help you to understand various perspectives about religion and spirituality from a diversity of religious traditions, and how they impact the emotional, physical, and social aspects of a whole person. In some ways this reflects a fine line. To be exposed to a body of information is to risk being influenced by it. This is a risk that each of us takes whenever we interact with ideas that are not our own. If this is a concern for you, you may wish to reconsider, and not take this class. If you continue to take it and find yourself confused or struggling with this encounter, please talk with the instructor. She or he will try to help you deal with the material that you are concerned about or may feel that a referral to a counselor would be more helpful.

For some people, the psychology of religion can be more difficult to encounter than the information about other world traditions. Psychology often treats faith, spirituality, and religious traditions in objective, intellectual ways, devoid of emotion. Please be clear that it is not the intention of this instructor to compromise your faith with this material. Rather, as a human service student, you are learning about this science. It is the intention of this course to offer bridges between these two dimensions of the human experience. There are, however, many different ways to bring this material together. The instructor will try to present as many of these different concepts into the class room, as possible. However, if you do not see information on concepts that you feel will be useful to you in your practice, I would challenge you to search the literature to find that information.

In order for us to proceed as a group, we need to agree on certain values:

- We need to agree to respect the beliefs and understandings of religion and spirituality presented in the classroom. This does not mean that you must agree with it personally. Rather, that you can accept the fact that someone else does believe in it. Respect suggests that we will not ridicule any beliefs or knowingly marginalize anyone. If any member of the class feels that his or her own beliefs are not being treated with respect, he or she should bring this up to the class and/or instructor.

- In this class, no one will ask you to share more than you want to about your own personal religious or spiritual beliefs. Some classroom assignments will ask you to share what you believe, but in these assignments you are to share only what you are comfortable with. If you feel that this is being violated, please say something to the instructor and she or he will attempt to clarify the instructions.

Flow of Class Dialogue

Session 1. Introduction to the class and topics
Session 2. History of religious involvement in counseling
Session 3. Approaches to the psychology of religion
Session 4. Hindu Perspectives: A swami will speak to class
Session 5. Buddhist, Asian, Native American, and African Perspectives; guest speakers from traditions represented
Session 6. Jewish Perspectives
Session 7. Christian and Islamic Perspectives
Session 8. Abnormal psychological behavior in a religious context
Session 9. Intervention techniques
Session 10. Synthesis

INDEX